KING KYLE

A MOTHER'S LOVE:
HONORING THE TIMELESS LEGACY OF HER MIRACLE

DEANNA R. WILEY

"IN EVERY HEARTBEAT, KYLE'S LIGHT LIVES ON."

2025

KYLE'S LIGHT & LEGACY PRESS

ISBN: 979-8-9995911-0-4 (hardcover)
ISBN: 979-8-9995911-1-1 (paperback)
ISBN: 979-8-9995911-2-8 (e-book)

Gold foil cover graphic credited to http://graphicflip.com
Cover frame graphic designed by Freepik
Reflections separation graphic designed by macrovector / Freepik

Proceeds from sales of this book will be donated to American Foundation for Suicide Prevention.

DEDICATION

To my beloved son Kyle Alan Wiley.
You are and have always been my true and
miraculous gift from Almighty God. I dearly love
and treasure you with everything that I am.
My perseverance in authoring your story came
from you; my strength came from God. Kyle, you
are my reason for being. My reason to continue
to survive. You deserve to be honored for the love
you gave everyone and the life you gave me.
I want everyone to know the truth, and I will live
the rest of my days ensuring no one forgets you.
Your legacy will remain etched in the hearts
and minds of many, an enduring presence
that time will never erase.

ACKNOWLEDGMENT

To the beautiful souls who opened their hearts and entrusted me with stories of Kyle,

Thank you. Your words were more than memories, they were threads in a tapestry of love, devotion, and friendship that continues to wrap around everyone who was lucky enough to know him.

Through your laughter, tears, and gentle recollections, you allowed me to glimpse Kyle's light, the kind of warmth that does not dim with time. I felt your love for him in every pause, every story shared with care, and every moment you chose to relive for me. Your willingness to revisit that sacred space speaks volumes about who he was, and how deeply he mattered.

Because of you, Kyle becomes not just remembered, but felt, present in every page, every heartbeat of this story. I will carry your words with reverence, and I hope this memoir becomes a home where his spirit can live on.

With all my gratitude and love,

NOTE

Nothing in my son's life story has been fabricated or sensationalized in any way. It is authentic and unembellished.

It is told from my perspective, a mother doing her best to protect her child while making sense of difficult experiences. All dialogue and thoughts shared here are based on my own experiences and memory, emotions, and understanding of what happened. Some names and identifying details have been changed or softened to protect privacy.

I do not claim to speak for others or to present absolute facts about anyone but myself and my son. My intent is not to harm or accuse, it is to honor my son's life and memory by telling his story in an honest and authentic way and share the truth as I lived and witnessed it. This memoir is written with love, with prayer, and with a deep desire to help others who have walked through pain.

What you read here is mine. It is the heartbeat of a mother. I own it fully, and I stand by it.

CONTENTS

INTRODUCTION

THIS BOOK IS THE account of my nearly twenty-two blessed years spent with my son, raising and nurturing him. Also included are a few accounts from his friends about his friendship, pain, and sacrifice. When I approached family members, they declined to contribute. Before I lost Kyle, my whole heart, we were planning to move to Florida. We were searching for a fresh start, pushed by the weight of his dad's absence and the toxic influences and circumstances that had begun to suffocate him.

I thought it would be wonderful for us to author a book together on how God delivered Kyle from his burdens. I once asked Kyle how he would classify his story if he were to write it. But the thing is, life is not just one story but a collection of many.

When I began drafting my own story a few years back, I spent years adding or removing truthful parts to make the story more palatable. However, omitting real events not only discredits the reader but the writer as well. It is dishonest, and sometimes the ugly truth is what people need to hear. It may just be what can save us.

My son's life story includes both positive and negative experiences. It is important to tell the full story and not sugarcoat anything. His life was a mixture of joy, pain, triumphs, and challenges. My hope is that telling his story in an honest and authentic way can help others who may be going through similar experiences. I want this story to honor my son and be a tribute to his life and accomplishments.

When Kyle and I first discussed the idea of authoring this book, we dreamed of creating something meaningful, a story that not only reflected our journey but also served as a guiding light for others navigating similar struggles. Kyle had a way of seeing beyond the immediate, of understanding how sharing our experiences could resonate with people far and wide. I remember telling him, "Let's make this a book that everyone will want to read and pass on. A story that may help others who are going through the same thing. A story that will change their way of living and thinking."

He said, "Mom, that would be cool, but I do not know how to write." I laughed and told him, "Yeah you do, your mind is just clouded now, but someday God will cleanse your mind, and He will give you the words just as He has me." We agreed he would jot down things he wanted to include and wanted others to know.

I told him even if he were out to dinner or hanging out with a friend and something came to mind to just write a small note on his hand or a napkin or whatever he could grab just until he could sit down and pour out his heart in detail. You never know when inspiration will strike. He said he would try but mostly he would call me or come over when he had a thought and I would try to take notes for him. I tried to help him make sense of all that was going through his head. Kyle wanted to share his feelings with the world. He just did not know how to do it.

Although he was a proactive, outspoken person like his mom, he was somewhat introverted and closed like his dad, which sometimes made it exceedingly difficult for him to express his emotions. Authoring a book was an arduous process for Kyle, one that he sadly did not get to finish.

I want to share my son's life with everyone and finish the story he and I tried to write together. I have written this because I tried to give Kyle a beautiful life which unfortunately ended in tragedy and heartache. I wish Kyle were here to help me through such an arduous process. I know though, that he will give me most of the words to finish this. The rest will come from the help of God. They are working together to help me tell it so that others may know of this remarkable young man, my son. The rest of his story; things only he knows, is only his story to tell.

This is a joyful yet incredibly painful account of my son's life and untimely passing. While this book is not written as a self-help guide, my hope is that it will potentially help others who might be in my or Kyle's situation. I would never want anyone to experience what we went through, yet I am finding that what he endured is frighteningly common. If this book causes anyone to have an honest conversation with their child (and I pray that it does), seek the help they need, and open the eyes of many parents who choose to look the other way, then I will be immensely happy, and I feel Kyle would be too.

My son did not leave this earth without touching the hearts and souls of hundreds of people. Whether he chose to hold on or let go, I know that he will live on forever in the hearts of everyone who knew him. With this book, I hope many more will get to know him. I hope anyone who reads this will see his kind, empathetic side and learn from his struggles and demons (which we ALL have). As I said, this is not a self-help book, but simply the life story of my son from what I, as his mom, experienced raising him, supporting him, and walking along-side him.

Whatever you take from this book, positive or negative, thank you for taking the time to hear about my precious boy.

My King Kyle, I feel God telling me to not only tell others of the good times but also the troubled times. It would not be your story if it did not include both. I hope you are content with what I wrote and my apologies for anything that I may have left out, although not intentionally, as I am sure there are many. Your memories when mom was not near will have to be kept between you and whomever you shared them with. You can share them with me when we see each other again.

1

MEETING KYLE'S DAD

MY HUSBAND AND I met when I was twenty-three and he was twenty-one. I had been invited by friends to see a band play. We went to school with members of the band. I had no intention of dating or falling in love as I was working and building my travel career, but I happened to see the man that would be my husband and fell instantly in love. I could see my life with him with just a glance.

Our relationship was best described in three terms: intense, rocky, and extremely fast. Within six months of meeting, we had already started a life together in Las Vegas. We moved around a bit after that for his career, making a home where we could, but to me a home is not complete without children, so we began trying to conceive. I was ready for a family. I was determined to have a baby and be a mommy. But my dream of creating a family with my soulmate did not come without complications.

An ultrasound revealed that my past miscarriages had left uterine scar tissue. My doctor reasoned that this might be one of the reasons I was struggling to conceive and suggested surgery. Sadly, it did not help. However, I was determined and decided to try again. Despite taking fertility pills and HCG (Human Chorionic Gonadotropin) shots, nothing was effective. Our options were becoming limited, with the only possibility left being in vitro fertilization but we could not afford the fourteen-thousand-dollar expense for one chance of getting pregnant.

Almost eight years had elapsed, and I still did not have children. Another miscarriage left me wondering if God was telling me to just stop, look around, be still, and wait. In my view, I could not get pregnant as I was almost thirty years old, and I innocently thought it would be too late to have a baby. One day, I just decided to give up. I felt like a failure, unable to figure out why God had given me this desire to be a mother. I did not want to give up, but I had a feeling my husband felt pressured, and I did not want to lose my marriage. However, that did not stop me from wanting to give my husband a son so badly.

One day my husband came to me, put his arm around me, and said, "It's okay, it will be just the two of us. I will never leave you, Deanna. I love you so much. I will always be here for you." I was so naive, and little did I know my husband never intended to keep his word.

That was the first time I ever heard him say anything sweet or romantic. I cried and cried and eventually came to terms with the fact that I might never have a baby, and it would just be the two of us. I tried to be okay with this reality, but I was not. Like millions of other women, I wanted to fall in love with my dream man and have a family together. But after years of trying with no success, all I could do was accept that it was not going to be or wait.

Luckily, my patience paid off.

During this period, I worked full-time. I had been at my job for almost four years when one day I started getting sick and threw up. I went home early and was back at work the next day, but nauseated and sick to my stomach for days on end. The girls at work were joking that I was pregnant. I told them I could not get pregnant.

As the days and weeks went by, they kept telling me, "You're pregnant, go get tested."

I really did not want to go to the doctor. I knew I could not get pregnant, but even if I did, I would miscarry. I had experienced it several times before. I thought I might have a terminal illness, so I kept putting off going to the doctor. I feared both possibilities and I was not ready to face either of them. I feared being even more of a failure if I got my hopes up. So instead, I just kept getting more sick, more nauseated, and throwing up more, but I kept going to work. I had to go to work; we had a mortgage payment.

One afternoon while driving home from work I was feeling nauseous and light-headed, and caught myself right before I lost consciousness. I edged my way over to the right shoulder and stopped the car. I had put my head down on the steering wheel for a few moments when a car pulled up behind me and a man got out to see if I was okay. He gave me a bottle of water and stood for a while to make sure I was able to drive the rest of the way home. I made it home and decided to go to the doctor the next day. That was too close to a call, and clearly whatever I was experiencing was not going to go away.

The next day the doctor did a pregnancy test. She came back with the nurse, and they told me I was going to have a baby. I just started crying. Not a sad cry, but the most joyous cry ever. I was elated. Had my prayers finally been answered? Was this the baby God had told me to wait for?

Then came my fearful cry, "I can't lose another baby, I just can't." Even though I was happy for a moment, I was still worried due to my past. I had so many miscarriages in the preliminary stages.

The doctor told me by the looks of the test she could tell I was far along already. "It looks like you may have conceived around Valentine's Day."

I said, "Yeah, that sounds about right." I was far along enough that I felt a small sense of relief.

She told me the baby would be due on Halloween. I rushed home to tell my husband we were having a baby. This was great news, no, the best news! My husband was going to be so happy! We were finally going to be a complete family.

After I shared the news, he gave me a hug and asked, "Are you happy?"

I said, "Yes, I am very happy." Joy rushed out of me, yet my husband showed no emotion at all. He was not one to be overly expressive, but surely, he was happy too, right? I could not tell, and he never said a word about how he felt. Did he think that we were just going through the motions every single day expecting not to get pregnant?

He held me in his arms for a short while and I cried tears of happiness. The next day, I went to a bookstore and found a book for five dollars on how to raise a boy. I grabbed it. The next seven months or so I was the happiest person on the planet. I was in full mommy mode. Doing everything, I could prepare for our beautiful baby boy. I knew it was a baby boy before the doctor even knew. There was nothing you could say otherwise. Call it mother's intuition or wishful thinking, there was just something telling me that I was going to have a precious son. I knew God would not have allowed me to endure miscarriages and struggle for so long to not give me the son I desperately dreamed of all those years.

I had told everyone I wanted a boy to be like his dad, who I loved dearly, and to carry on the Wiley name, at the time completely unaware of who my husband really was. I was determined to be a mother, and my dream was finally coming true. I would be the best mother that I could be and would not strive for anything less than being the mother that God had meant me to be.

When I went to my parents' house to tell them, my brother showed up. I told them and of course they were so ecstatic. My brother and sister-in-law had one daughter and another on the way. Now my parents are going to have a grandson too. I could not wait for my son and my nieces to grow up together. It was all so perfect. My life, that is, and I was going to make sure my sons was as well.

My pregnancy was special. I struggled for eight years and through multiple miscarriages to finally have a baby. My parents hugged me and said they were so happy for me, and knowing my parents and how they so loved their first grandchild, I knew they would be ecstatic about the next two. The cousins were going to grow up together and be a big happy family. My son would have a family to play with that were close to him in age. The perfect picture life I dreamed of was coming together quite nicely.

Kyle's nursery was in a beautiful house overlooking the lake and golf course, the perfect setting to raise our son. The nursery itself had a charming sports theme, and my mom and dad went above and beyond to ensure baby Kyle had everything imaginable. They were determined to spoil him, as any loving and devoted grandparents would.

During my pregnancy, my family and those close to me catered to me. However, I felt as if my husband did not want to have anything to do with my pregnancy. I thought it was odd, but I assumed he was stressed out. So, I walked on eggshells. I did not want to lose my baby. Nor did I want to contribute to any stress on my marriage. So, I just focused on what it felt like to be with a child. It became more comfortable for me as the months went on. I loved every minute of it.

My husband, when asked, attributed his stress it to the pressure of becoming a new dad. He was scared, just as I was. But I could not grasp why he felt the need to start gambling excessively. Did he not realize it could jeopardize our plans for a family? I could not fathom what was going through his mind. I am sorry his own childhood had been difficult but that did not mean our sons had to be. Every parent should strive to do better for their child.

I remember when baby Kyle kicked me for the first time. WOW! What an incredible feeling to have a human being growing inside of me and moving around. I had fun just watching my tummy move up and down while he elbowed or kicked. It was like a drum beating from the inside out. Sometimes it even tickled.

I started being a mom to him early, doing what I could do to soothe him. For Kyle and me, it was our shared love of music. I would put headphones on my stomach and play soft jazz or gospel. I hoped he would grow to like the music I played (he did not). The myth that I had heard turned out to be just that, a myth. Nevertheless, I continued to just enjoy those moments with him.

When Kyle was old enough to express interests in music, he never liked jazz or gospel, but he did love to listen to new age Christian music. The closest my little Kenny G ever came to jazz was playing the saxophone in a sixth-grade band. The only gospel he listened to was in church or when I would play Elvis's gospel or Mercy Me in the kitchen as I prepared dinner.

Sadly, I was experiencing those exciting moments of pregnancy all by myself as my husband was in his own little world. He did not seem to want to be involved at all; not even accompanying me to Lamaze classes. I did not fully know where he was emotionally, but I wanted him to experience the joy with me. To enjoy this time of our life, not to be stressed out.

The last week before Kyle arrived, we would go to the mall and walk. I wanted to make sure he was born on Halloween like the doctor said. The due date was like a ticking alarm clock in my head. So, we would walk. When my husband was at work, I would walk up and down our stairs at home many times a day. I walked as much as I could until the big day came. I was determined to see my baby as soon as possible.

MOTHER'S REFLECTION:
I Walked Because I Believed

I did not walk the mall just to meet my son; I walked to remind myself that I still believed in him. In me. In something greater.

It was lonely, yes. But it was also sacred. Every quiet step was a promise. I did not know who my husband truly was, but I knew who I was about to become.

And that was enough.

2

MY LITTLE MIRACLE

HALLOWEEN FINALLY CAME AND I did my best to treat the day as normally as I could even though it was THE DAY!

I went to run errands and came home, as I would usually do. I had taken my maternity leave a week prior, to mentally prepare myself for the big day. Shawn and I sat at home and handed out candy to all the little trick-or-treaters, trying to enjoy the holiday for what it was. But the due date was still in the back of my mind. I started getting sad because nothing was happening. The doctor had said Halloween was his due date, right? I had done everything right and was just so excited to meet my son. I was getting anxious and frustrated.

I decided to distract myself and go downstairs and watch *Halloween* on TV while Shawn stayed upstairs and finished handing out candy to little kids. After about thirty minutes, he turned off the light and locked the doors. He came downstairs to join me, and we finished watching the movie together. It was about eleven when we decided to go upstairs to bed. As we lay down in bed, the tears begin to well up in my eyes. Nothing had happened; my son was not coming today as planned. My husband never asked me what the problem was. He never said a word. He just went to bed, silent as usual, asleep in seconds.

After about thirty minutes, I woke my husband up and told him my water had broken, and we headed to the hospital. It was finally happening after all. The doctor was right! I was soon going to meet my son and officially become a mom! The drive to the hospital was forty-five-minute and as my husband drove, I kept begging him to hurry! I did not want to have this baby boy in the car. That was not the birth story I wanted to tell in the future, that my son was born in our car because his dad could not get us to the hospital in time.

We finally arrived and it was all I could do not to push. The pressure was unreal. I had been thinking and feeling like he was just going to shoot right out of me. That, however, was not the case as the labor was hard and arduous. This was not what I was expecting or planning. What did go as planned, though, was the fact that I wanted to videotape the birth of our precious baby.

We borrowed a tape recorder from my dad, and for fourteen exhausting hours, my husband recorded my contractions and pain. Throughout the entirety of my labor, he remained silent, offering no words of comfort, consolation, or support. It took a family member stepping in to suggest he hold my hand, something that should have been instinctive. When he finally reached out, the emotional anguish from his lack of support overflowed into words. I loved my husband deeply, and I prayed he understood that my outburst came from a place of pain rather than anger.

I apologized for snapping but pleaded with him to stand by me, for the sake of our child, to support his mother and wife. All the while, the camcorder continued to capture everything.

His mom and sister were in and out of the hospital room. My mom and dad were there, of course. Dad came into the room that morning to see me, but he could not handle the pain I was in. I was his little girl. He was excited to have a grandson, but he could not stand to see his little girl hurt, so he stayed outside in the hallway. Occasionally, he would stand at the entrance of the room just outside the door to make sure I was okay and to tell me that he loved me. I kept thinking if I had taken Lamaze classes, I would not be going through so much agony, but I sure did not want to go to Lamaze classes by myself.

I remember having the worst contractions ever. I seriously thought I was dying. When I would hear women talk about how bad it hurt, I would think, how bad could it be? Women have babies left and right, I can do this. One of my girlfriends told me she had paper cuts that hurt worse after having her two kids. How is that possible? That seriously could not be true, and it did not feel true when the next contraction hit. As the pain grabbed me like a vice and squeezed HARD, my husband was nowhere to be seen so I reached my hand out to my dad and called out for him.

"Dad, please help me, tell the nurse to give me something please!" I kept saying, "Something's wrong with my baby Kyle, please make them call the doctor, something is wrong!" The doctor had yet to arrive at the hospital. The staff kept her updated on my dilations. My father shed a tear or two seeing me in so much pain. I honestly thought I was going to pass out from the pain. No way could a human have gone through that much pain and survived. I did not know what to think other than this was more painful than I thought it was going to be.

He said, "I love you Dee Dee, you're going to be just fine and so is my grandson."

That was all I needed to hear. This was the pain I needed to face if I wanted to see my son. This was going to be worth it in the end. Otherwise, why would some women like me be so driven to have children. "Just keep going and at the end of this you are going to see his sweet face," I kept thinking. I could do this.

After many hours of labor, it was time. It was not what or how I expected it to be. I pushed and pushed, but he would not come out. The doctor had to use vacuum-assisted delivery as well as forceps to get him out. I remember my sister-in-law getting behind me and holding my back up so that I was sitting upright and the nurse pushing my stomach trying to get the baby out, but he would not budge. I thought at that point that I might lose him. I had not come this far to lose him. He was just determined and needed a little help getting into this world.

There were what seemed like a dozen people in the room. Nurses, doctors, and family swirling in and out of the room like the snow that had started to fall outside. The only two people I really needed were my mom and my husband. However, everyone in the room now seemed more focused on the football game on TV. The Kansas City Chiefs were playing. I felt like I was a total intrusion during the football game. Yet, this was my room. I was going through the hardest physical act a woman can go through and could not understand why they could not turn the TV off. I just wanted some rest and to see the recording of Kyle's birth. I told my husband it was time to get the camcorder so he could tape the birth of our son. He had been videotaping me in excruciating pain and labor for several hours. Yet I knew that Kyle was coming soon, he had to be. I wanted everyone to be ready because I certainly was.

He looked at me and said, "The battery went dead." I was beyond upset. Those four words hurt me as deeply emotionally as labor had hurt me physically. Total strangers got to see the birth of my son, but not me. They could relive the moment as much as they wanted but I could not. What was the camcorder even for if we could not capture the moment of his birth? I could not see my beautiful son enter this world after fourteen very taxing hours. Still Kyle was coming so I prepared myself despite my extremely hurt feelings.

Whether it was taped or not did not change the facts. Finally, at 2 p.m. on Saturday, November 1st, 1997, I gave birth to the most beautiful little boy in the world. The moment Kyle arrived, and I laid eyes on him for the first time, I could not help but exclaim, "Oh, my little Poo Doo!" Tears of joy and relief streamed down my face. However, they did not let me hold Kyle right away; he was blue from being stuck and needed immediate attention. I anxiously asked the doctor if he was okay, but before responding, the nurse whisked him away to suction and clean him up.

Kyle had cephalohematoma from the vacuum-assisted delivery, a result, I felt, of the doctor's hurried approach and failure to heed my pleas for a C-section. I had sensed something was wrong and begged for a different course, but she insisted he was already stuck in the birth canal, and a C-section was no longer an option. Later that evening, in the hospital room, my husband told me "Deanna, you should have seen how many times the cord was wrapped around him." At my follow up visit, it was confirmed. He had been turning so much that the cord wrapped around his little body several times.

When they asked my husband if he wanted to cut the umbilical cord, the very one that had caused such complications by being wrapped around Kyle, he fainted instead. I could not understand why he would not take part in such an important moment. I wanted him to be an engaged part of our new journey as a family of three.

A new pain shot through me, just when I thought I would get a break. An experience I had not been prepared for. I yelled at the doctor and told her to stop, and she said she could not. She had to get the placenta out. She spread it out on the table and then asked my husband if he wanted to see it. He refused again and left the room.

When the birth ended, I felt the joy of this new reality set in. This was the start of a whole new life for all three of us. I was so excited. There was no one happier in the entire universe than me. When I saw my baby boy for the first time, the tears came uncontrollably yet they were so primal. A genuine soul-to-soul love and everything else was secondary from that moment on.

God, you did it! We did it! Kyle was what I thought of as the face of God. I had a beautiful baby boy and a husband who I thought loved me. He was going to be a great father and a great husband. I just knew it. It was the most incredible dream, and you could not wake me up even if you tried because it was all real. I decided from then on, I would follow God and raise my son to follow Him for the rest of my days. After all, He did create a true miracle that was not supposed to happen. My husband went across the street to get us some Mexican food, and the nurse delivered flowers to my room. I thought they were from my husband but later found out my parents had sent them and put his name on them knowing that was something he would never think of doing for me. In the moment, I was being pampered and enjoying the rewards of motherhood.

My heart expanded ten times the moment I held my newborn baby boy. However, this did not stop me from worrying about my son. My little baby would not nurse or even take a bottle. The nurses said it was normal, and it would take time. Eventually, they brought in a bottle he would accept. I was new at being a mother. I did not have any experience. Every time my son would cry, I would cry. My doctor said it was normal during the postpartum period. I was just recovering from the hormones in my body being tormented for nine months. It took me a while to get them back on track.

I wanted to do everything right. I was going to be the best mommy in the world, and I was. I kept a record every time we fed and changed him for months. After a few months, I got tired of it and realized that my little guy was doing great, and the doctor said there was no need to keep records any longer.

I think of those moments often. Kyle's entrance into the world. How I put myself under so much pressure to be a perfect mom and wife. Now all I really want is my son. To be a mom to him again. Would he have cared if I were perfect? He was so innocent then and all I have now is hundreds of photos and videos to remember him.

As I lay in bed, watched videos, and looked at photos of Kyle as a baby, then toddler, then small boy, I, nor anyone would have ever thought in a million years that he would resort to the world of substance. I cannot toast my king anymore because the dragon of substance slayed him.

MOTHER'S REFLECTION:
Where I First Saw Forever

I used to think the birth would be the pinnacle. The moment I would become whole. But it was not just about holding Kyle, it was the feeling that my soul had.

3

WHEN TRUST WAS NOT ENOUGH

I HAD TO GO BACK to work part-time after six weeks of giving birth. It was so hard, but I had no choice. I needed to leave my baby Kyle with his daddy, trusting my husband to take care of our son. I worked during the day, and he worked at night. On days he had to work, he would drop Kyle off to me at my work as I was getting off. My co-workers loved to see Kyle and his smiling face. He was such a beautiful baby that many people asked if he was a boy or a girl even though he was always dressed as a boy. He was perfect in every way. God truly did bless me abundantly.

I trusted my husband completely. I believed he would protect our child as fiercely as I would. But there were things happening. At the time I began to understand, the damage had already been done. I would come home on days my husband did not work and find Kyle asleep in his airplane walker. I talked to his dad and told him not to leave him in the walker for extended periods of time, especially not to let him sleep upright as this would hurt his neck and back. He did not seem to understand my concern and always responded the same way. "He's okay," he would say. When I recall instances where I had to confront my husband, looking back, I fear Kyle may have been affected in ways I could not fully understand at the time.

As the days went on, I repeatedly came home to find my baby dirty and sleeping in his walker, wearing the same clothes he had slept in. Horrible thoughts went through my mind. *Was his daddy taking care of him? When he cried, was my husband holding our son, nurturing him, and consoling him? Was he feeding him?* He was not rocking him to sleep or cleaning him. Kyle would often be in a soaked diaper. *Did his daddy ever change him?* I left clear, precise instructions on how to properly take care of our son while I earned a bit of money to help our household, they were ignored.

I depended on this man. Kyle and I both did. I had to do something different, and quickly! Speaking to my husband did no good. I returned to work trusting that his dad would care for him with the same tenderness I felt. I believed our son was safe. I began to sense that something was missing, that Kyle's needs were not being fully seen or met. I did not know then what I see more clearly now, and that truth still haunts me. I reached out to my mother-in-law, hoping she would share my concern. But when I spoke with her, she did not seem alarmed or even surprised by what I was beginning to uncover. It was as if it did not register, or worse, had been normalized long before. Over the years I came to understand from the conversations I had with my mother-in-law that my husband had not been properly cared for, and perhaps, without even realizing it, those around him treated our baby's needs with the same kind of neglect. As if they could not give what they had never received.

I talked to my parents who at once told me to quit my job. I quit that day and became a stay-at-home, full-time mommy to Kyle. I could care for him properly and give him the utmost, undivided attention and love every parent should offer their child.

Kyle was so loved beyond the moon and stars by me, his mommy, and I genuinely thought he was loved by his daddy. Kyle had everything a baby needed and everything a child could want or ask for. He was a happy and intelligent child.

One Saturday afternoon my husband's family was having an exceedingly rare get-together. I was so exhausted from working around the house and taking care of Bubber (another nickname I had for him) that I told my husband he should take Kyle so everyone could "Ooh" and "Aww" over him. He was only six months old and cute as a button. Like most new moms, I was tired, and this would be an opportunity for me to catch up on my sleep. I once again put my trust in baby daddy and hoped the grandma, aunt, and adult cousins would help.

Things went well, as far as I knew. It was a sweltering summer day when my husband came home later that afternoon. He told me all about the get together and how everyone loved seeing my Kyle. At least ten minutes went by with him talking and telling me he had planned to go hit some balls at the golf course.

I said, "So your mom decided to keep Kyle for a while?" He said, "No. Why?"

"Shawn, where's Kyle?"

No answer.

"Oh my God in Heaven, Shawn, where is he?"

With no emotion whatsoever, he pointed to the garage and said, "Oh, he's in the garage."

Without a second to lose, I ran out to the car and got my baby out of his car seat. He was asleep and I needed to wake him up to make sure he was okay.

He was warm to the touch but not hot and I took him inside to cool him down. I asked my husband what he was thinking and all he would say, without any emotion, was, "He's okay."

I gave Kyle a cool bath, dressed him in clean clothes, and got him something to eat. My son was worn out. I wondered how long he had been kept in that hot car or ignored by his dad and other in-laws that day, as well as other days that I trusted in my husband to take care of our boy, while I was waiting for his safe return. I wondered if Kyle had been fed or changed during the entire day. If Kyle cried, had anyone there consoled him?

Although the garage was not as hot as it was outside, ten minutes was ten minutes too long to leave him in the car unattended. I could not believe he had left Kyle unattended again, it felt like his needs were not being seen at all.

When Kyle was not yet a year old, I discovered my husband had been unfaithful. The pain was immediate and overwhelming. I wanted to leave, to protect myself, to protect our son, to escape the heartbreak I had not seen coming. I wanted to raise my son on my own, but my husband got on his hands and knees begging and pleading, pulling at my clothes and crying for me to not leave. After speaking with my parents and getting advice from a counselor, and my pastor, I decided to stay.

I now speak with many women all over the world by way of support groups and other avenues, who have gone through the same thing. I was not about to leave my husband alone with Kyle ever again. Not if I could help it, anyway. I did not want a divorce knowing that he would have weekend visits alone with Kyle. Looking back, at times, it felt like Kyle's needs were not fully understood or prioritized and that realization shattered me. I would have done anything to shield him, from being treated as anything less than the miracle he was.

My mother-in-law, even after learning of her son's affair, said she also thought it was a good idea for me to stay. Therefore, I remained steadfast to safeguard my son. Even though I was reluctant, I loved my husband dearly and was happy. For the better part of Kyle's upbringing, he was happy as well and I poured myself into giving him the love, care, and attention I feared he was not receiving elsewhere. It was my way of trying to fill the gaps, to make up for what his dad could not or would not give. However, I still felt apprehension in my bones as if Kyle did not have a chance in hell of a bright, long-lived future of happiness no matter how hard I tried.

MOTHER'S REFLECTION:
The Trust That Broke Me

I once believed love would be enough. That trust would hold. That promises could protect my son. I learned the hard way that love, without accountability, is not safety.

When I saw Kyle asleep in that car, something broke inside me. Not just my heart, but my illusion. From that day forward, I mothered out of instinct, fierce, relentless, and uncompromising.

Sometimes, staying was not surrender. It was survival. I did not just stay for love. I stayed to protect our world from unraveling. To remain present and to keep his joy intact as possible in a home that did not always reflect it. To every mother walking that same line, between heartbreak and hope, I see you and I believe you are doing more than anyone knows.

4

SWIM LESSONS

I KNEW KYLE WOULD BE a fast learner since he began to swim at the age of seven months. It was important to me that he learn as we lived within walking distance of Smithville Lake and beach. One of our neighbors was a former Marine who taught life-saving techniques and offered to teach Kyle how to swim. The technique she taught was simple. Blow in his face to get him to hold his breath, put him under water, then blow on his face again as he surfaced to get him to breathe again, slowly increasing the time under water. We did this for a few weeks, and Kyle became amazingly comfortable with water.

The big test came to see if he would swim on his own. The instructor stood at one end of the pool and daddy at the other. I hid behind the pool house, peeking out to make sure he was safe. My thought was to be close enough to rescue him if he got scared and began to cry.

The instructor blew in his face and launched him into the pool like a torpedo. We were all three there to make sure nothing would happen to him, and it did not. I was terrified that he might sink like a rock. But I was proven wrong when Kyle began to paddle. The plan worked as Kyle swam all the way down to his dad, safe and sound. He was my little fishy from the start and that remained true for many years to come. When he was older, he joined a swimming team, and even won the Mile Swim BSA, a one-mile nonstop, over-the-head open water swim which was one of scouting's most physically challenging obstacles. and Lifesaving Merit Badge in Scouts. He dove off rocks at the many lakes we went to, rafted through the mountains, floated bare back, and canoed down the Elk River as well as exploring other beautiful scenic spots.

One of my son's favorite places was Longview Lake in Lee's Summit, Missouri. He and his many friends had a special spot where they would hang out or jump off a cliff and have a blast enjoying the water. Sometimes he would wake up super early in the morning just to go swimming at his favorite location. He mentioned that he went out there by himself every now and then, yet I always urged him that it was not safe to go alone and to always have a buddy. After that, he would take a friend or two. For him, it was a peaceful haven, a place to escape the disarray of the world around him and get a better perspective.

Back to swim lessons, I recognize the subtle lessons I had taught Kyle about trust, and how important it was for me to nurture my son's early skills. At just seven months old, Kyle was too young to understand the significance of what he was learning, yet as his mother, I felt the weight of responsibility to guide him through this experience. When he got older, it was a journey of trust, not only in me being his teacher but also in my instincts as a conscientious mother. I learned that sometimes I had to take a leap of faith and allow Kyle to explore new experiences even when I was a bit apprehensive.

MOTHER'S REFLECTION:
The Water Knew Him First

Watching Kyle embrace the water, his resilience, his joy, filled me with quiet awe. It was not just swimming. It was surrender. It was trust. It was sanctuary.

He did not know it back then, but water would become his refuge. The place that gave him peace when the world was too loud. Watching Kyle grow more comfortable in the water reminded me that even the tiniest moments can plant seeds of peace. I did not know then just how deeply he would carry that feeling, but I am grateful the water gave him something calm to hold onto.

Teaching Kyle how to swim was more than a milestone. It was the beginning of his journey toward serenity.

5

MOMENTS OF LOVE

ONE YEAR OUR CHURCH had a Christmas program, and I sang in the choir. My little man, who was two years old, could not stand to be away from his mommy, but I was just a few feet in front of him, singing, as he sat in the front pew with his dad and his Momo. At one point in the program, he began crying uncontrollably and holding out his hands as if to crawl in my arms. He wanted his mommy and could not reach me. He often cried when his daddy held him, and it seemed he did not feel the same comfort he felt with me.

I remember seeing baby Kyle hit his dad while being held. I have witnessed Kyle resisting his dad on several occasions when he tried to hold him. Kyle often seemed uneasy with his dad, and I did not sense the same kind of nurturing or attachment between them. *But where did he learn to hit him?* This made me leery about my husband even being alone with Kyle.

It broke my heart to see Kyle cry as I sang in the choir, and I teared up because I could not stop the Christmas program to hold and comfort him. I tried to be as discreet as possible, signaling my husband to take our precious son outside in the lobby so we could finish the song. It took my husband a while to get the hint and finally, Kyle and Daddy watched through the window on the door, but Kyle continued to cry.

A short while later we were reunited, and he was happy once again. Poo Doo could not let me out of his sight and that was quite all right with me.

MOTHER'S REFLECTION:
He Knew Where the Love Lived

Kyle never cared about the program or the music, I was his comfort, his home. He did not cry because he wanted attention. He cried because love felt too far away and, in that moment, I learned something: babies know. They know where safety lives. They know where arms feel steady and hearts beat warm.

I may not have been able to hold him then, but I would hold him always.

6

THE QUIET RITUALS

KYLE WAS STILL JUST a baby when his father fell into a deep depression. There were days he could not get out of bed and though Kyle could not understand it, I could feel the silence settling around him like a shadow. Even before Kyle was old enough to really talk much, I would take him out early and drive along Smithville Lake to watch birds flying and squirrels playing. I carried Kyle along the water's edge as the sun rose in the distance, picking up rocks I thought were pretty or interesting. Once Kyle learned to walk, he joined in, and of course in his childhood eyes, they were all pretty and interesting. He would fill his pockets until his pants were falling off. I still laugh just picturing it in my head. I bought him a small duffle bag so he could collect as many as he wanted. Then we would go to the local diner and have breakfast, just the two of us.

As he got older, he continued collecting rocks. Kyle was so proud to show them to me and study them in books, and later online. He became more discerning as time went on. He seemed to pick rocks that were unique and depicted something he was familiar with and would often want to paint them. One Christmas he received a rock polisher from Santa, which he had fun with for a while, but like most kids, he eventually got bored with it and needed to move on to something else. But on occasion he would still bring home an unusual stone. Like reading the clouds, he could stare at it for a while and be able to imagine it as a car, boat, animal, or scene of some sort. Maybe that is where I decided to start painting rocks to create special scenes for him and others. I still hold most of his collection, if not all of it.

We did most things without daddy. We went to air shows, the drive-in, and many other places without daddy. There were times it felt, from where we stood, like Kyle's needs were competing with distractions, a TV screen, and even dad's frequent casino visits or whatever secrets may have been living inside his dad's phone; like we came second to everything else. He changed after Kyle was born. Every weekend he would come with us to the Chinese restaurant down the street. That was our one ritual. But beyond that, it felt like he had little interest in spending time with either of us. We were there but not really seen. As a baby, Kyle was not aware, but it was disheartening for me to not spend time with my husband.

MOTHER'S REFLECTION:
Small Stones with Lots of Love

Those early mornings at Smithville Lake, collecting rocks, watching birds, were my way of sheltering Kyle from the silence at home. He was so little yet already drawn to what was quiet and meaningful. Each rock he chose became a tiny joy, a way to make sense of a world we navigated mostly on our own.

Even as Kyle's daddy drifted further away, I kept showing up and his quiet strength shaped me just as much as I shaped him.

This memoir carries those moments forward. Because even when love is not loud, it endures.

7

TURTLES IN THE MOONLIGHT

We MET OUR GO-TO couple in Smithville when Kyle was about a year old, and they had a daughter the same age as Kyle. We soon became the best of friends. We went on trips together, enjoyed game night, and the kids had sleepovers. The kids grew up together until the day our friends decided to separate and then divorce. Everyone went their separate ways, and we did not see much of them after that. After Kyle passed away, two of the three children they had together came to offer their condolences. But the friends we once shared many years with never reached out. The silence was deafening. The kids are now growing up and getting married and I am so proud of them all.

One of our most unforgettable adventures with them was a trip to Miami. Just the eight of us; hubby, Kyle, and me, plus their lively crew of five. We rode fan boats through Alligator Alley, the wind whipping our hair as we skimmed across the water. We swam in the ocean, all of us tumbling in the waves like kids, no matter our age.

But the real magic happened one night when we decided to stay up late and walk the beach. The shoreline stretched endlessly, quiet and ours alone. Tourists were tucked away in their hotel rooms, and we wandered freely under the stars, barefoot and blissful.

Kyle was full of wonder and wide-eyed curiosity. He walked ahead with the other kids, their laughter echoing in the salt air. We noticed long stretches of yellow tape marking the sand; sea turtle nests, rare and protected then like the universe had saved this moment just for us, we saw it: tiny movements in the sand. One by one, baby sea turtles emerged, climbing up from their hidden nest, drawn instinctively to the ocean. More than a dozen, flippers flapping, determined and delicate. Siblings in a line, racing toward the salty waves like it was the only thing they had ever known.

Kyle bent down low, his eyes wide, whispering, "Mommy, are they really going in the ocean?" He did not blink. He watched every tiny turtle fight its way to the water. It was as if time paused just for them, to witness something sacred.

When Kyle asked me if the little turtles would drown in the ocean, I smiled and said, "Oh no, Poo Doo, they were meant for the water. This is where they thrive; where their little hearts know exactly what to do."

He nodded, still watching them paddle forward, as if he understood something bigger than both of us. I think in that moment, he saw that even the tiniest creatures have a purpose, a place they belong, and a journey they were born to take. Then as if the night had not already given us enough thrill, a baby hammerhead shark washed up nearby, giving the kids one more rare wonder to witness. We caught it all on video, but the real footage lives in our hearts.

Looking back, I believe God was showing us something that night. Not just the miracle of nature, but the miracle of presence, of being exactly where we were meant to be, with the people we loved most. Kyle got to see life begin, to witness creation in motion. It was not just a walk on the beach; it seemed to me, to be a glimpse into heaven's quiet choreography.

After the couple separated, Kyle would ask about them often. I did not know how to tell him that they were not going to be married anymore, and that we probably would not see the kids much again. It made him sad. I saw it in the way he stopped asking after a while, like he already knew. I hated that how so many of his happiest memories seemed to carry a shadow at the end. But I hold onto that night in Miami. The turtles, the moonlight, and the joy. Because even if the ending hurt, the miracle still happened, and Kyle got to witness it. That matters.

MOTHER'S REFLECTION:
Memories with Friends

Some memories arrive like postcards from heaven, unexpected, vivid, and impossible to forget. That night in Miami, watching baby sea turtles race toward the ocean, felt like one of those moments. Kyle's awe, his quiet reverence, reminded me that even in our world full of uncertainty, there are still sacred things worth witnessing.

Writing this chapter was harder than I expected. Not because the memories were painful, though some were, but because they were layered. Happiness and sorrow, connection and silence, beginnings and endings. I learned that grief comes in different forms. It comes from the absence of what once felt permanent. The friendships that faded, the questions Kyle never got answers to. and yet, even in that ache, I find gratitude. Because we were all there together. We saw the turtles. We laughed barefoot under the stars and Kyle carried that wonder with him.

This chapter is a love letter to those moments. To the children who grow up and carry pieces of us with them. To the friendships that shaped us, even if they did not last and to the quiet miracles that remind us, we were part of something beautiful.

8

GROWING AND LEARNING

KYLE'S FIRST BIRTHDAY CAME so quickly. I had the first huge birthday party for him and invited everyone I could think of including all the nearby relatives, some not so nearby, and my best friend and her family.

One of our local news stations did a first birthday segment every Saturday and Sunday morning, so I sent in a photo of my baby. They would draw a name from all the submissions, and the winner got a birthday cake. Kyle did not get chosen but my beautiful boy did get his picture and name announced on the news. It was the day after his first Halloween, on his first birthday.

Kyle still had his spider sticker on his cheek from his Halloween costume the night before. Momo had seen the cutest authentic leather Harley-Davidson jacket at a small gift shop at the restaurant where she worked as a server for many years and just had to buy it for him, so I dressed him up as a biker and put a Harley-Davidson dew rag on his head. He was just precious as could be. A lot of bikers have nicknames and his was appropriately "Baby Face."

My parents made sure they were up in time to watch their grandson on television. I let my in-laws know as well, hoping they would share in the moment, but they did not seem particularly moved. I even tried to wake my husband, knowing it was something special, something worth celebrating, but he stayed in bed. I watched alone, holding the joy of seeing baby Kyle's photo on TV, and the ache all at once.

Kyle was walking just before he was a year old and potty trained soon after that. I got him a little potty chair with a target that went on the bottom of the bowl. When he would pee on the target, it would reveal a star. This was fun for him. I would put the potty chair in front of the TV and pop in a video called "The Super-Duper Pooper." I would give him some crackers and his sippy cup, and he had a blast watching the video and singing along with the characters in the video and with mommy while doing what he needed to do. At times he fell over with laughter watching me sing and dance.

When he was done, we would clap and dance. He was so proud of himself. When he graduated to the big boy potty chair, there were times he would fall asleep sitting and waiting. I made sure not to let him topple over. Then he would say, "Bye-bye poopy, bye-bye pee pee."

I will say it time and time again, Kyle never had discipline problems growing up. He never threw temper tantrums, but he would fight me from time to time over brushing his teeth. At first it was fun as he had edible toothpaste and would brush his teeth when mommy brushed hers. As he got older, I would give him a bath and then wrap him up in a towel like a burrito and brush his teeth for him. We made it a game but sometimes he would just get mad and refuse and other times he would giggle trying to break free. But when we were done, I would always thank him for being a big boy and tell him how much I loved him.

I loved to sing to my boy even though I was not a good singer at all. But Kyle did not care. He loved to hear mommy sing to him from when he was a newborn to the very end.

When I got him, all tucked into bed he would say, "Mommy, will you sing me a song?" I would sing "Hush Little Baby" when he was tiny and as he got older, I would add different songs to my repertoire and Kyle would sing along with me.

Kyle loved the happy, upbeat tune from *The Courtship of Eddie's Father*, and it became one of our special songs. I would change a couple of the lyrics from man to mom when singing it to him. The playful melody and words always brought a smile to his face along with the repetitive chorus that was easy for him to sing along to. (Unfortunately, copyright laws prohibit me from writing lyrics. It is a bit ridiculous considering that I am just writing about my son's childhood.)

After singing it, we would laugh and giggle at each other, then he would say, "Sing it again, Mommy."

I would scratch his back until he fell asleep, and he always insisted on this ritual until he was on his own. There was no better feeling in the entire world than being loved completely by my boy and loving my boy unconditionally.

MOTHER'S REFLECTION:
Time Well Spent

Looking back on these precious moments with my baby, I realize how much joy and laughter filled our days. Simple acts of singing. Never disregard even the smallest amount of time you can spend with your children. The tiniest memory will last a lifetime and bring a smile to your face and maybe even a giggle or two.

9

THE LONGEST NIGHTS

KYLE'S JOURNEY WITH NIGHT terrors began when he was just two years old. They were unpredictable; not every night would bring the same haunting scream. One evening, when he was about two and a half, I had just tucked him into our king-size bed after lulling him to sleep and felt a rare moment of calm as I settled down in the living room with my husband. I remember the clock barely ticking thirty minutes past his bedtime when I was jolted upright by a piercing scream. My heart raced but my husband sat silent, not budging an inch. My first thought was that my little guy had fallen off the bed.

In a panic, I sprinted up the stairs, skipping steps and tripping over them. As I ran into the room, I found Kyle sitting up in bed, tears streaming down his rosy, red cheeks, his cries echoing. Without hesitation, I scooped him into my arms, cradling him close.

"Baby, it's okay, you're okay. Mommy is right here, Poo Doo," I whispered, my voice gentle and soothing as could be.

I rubbed his back, trying to comfort him as he cried out in discomfort. It felt like an eternity before he finally calmed down, falling back to sleep against my chest.

This was not an isolated incident and while it became a part of our routine it thankfully only happened sporadically.

Then one chilling morning I was sitting comfortably in the living room when Kyle came barreling in, his screams piercing the walls. He was crying so hard he started to choke, even throwing up from sheer panic. I rushed to him, scooped him up in my arms, and felt his tiny body trembling against mine. My husband stood behind me, silent and mysterious. I could not tell if he was saying something to Kyle or what kind of expression he had, but it was the first time I felt the strange distance between him and my son, as if my husband was trying to shield me from something he did not want me to see or hear.

As daddy stood there, seemingly untouched by the moment, I felt the weight of it all pressing down on me. It was as if the gravity of what Kyle was facing had not reached him. I desperately asked my husband to run to the kitchen and get a cool washcloth to wipe Kyle's face and a thermometer to check for a fever. There was no fever. As I held Kyle tight, rocking him back and forth, I whispered softly, "Please, baby, tell me what's wrong. Mommy can't help you if you do not tell me." I took on his pain, as I brushed his hair back, feeling his warm cheeks against my skin. After several agonizing minutes, filled with coughing and sobs, he finally quieted down and fell asleep in my arms. I too drifted off on the couch while holding him close. I could never prove that anything harmful happened, but I have always carried quiet fears about what Kyle may have experienced when I was not there.

When he finally woke, he was ready for breakfast, seemingly unfazed by the morning chaos. My thoughts over what may have caused his night terrors tormented me. *What if there were things said or done in those quiet moments when I was not there, things I will never fully know, but somehow always feared?* It was the only explanation I could think of for the night terrors that plagued my son for years.

Why was this happening to my son? It is no wonder I became fiercely protective of him; I was a mama bear ready to defend her precious cub from any perceived threat. What do certain people not understand about that instinct? The love and concern I felt for Kyle was primal and normal, a deep-rooted need to keep him safe from whatever monsters haunted his sleep.

The question kept swirling in my head, for many years now, almost like an endless loop. What was behind those terrifying nightmares? I read that they are often linked to stress, or even genetic factors. I do remember having them when I was small, the same nightmare over and over, feeling so real. They lasted for years but eventually subsided and never returned. I also learned night terrors are not always at night and can occur when a child is transitioning between sleep cycles, particularly during non-REM sleep. But knowing the "why" did not ease my worry at all. Each time Kyle would wake up screaming, it felt like my heart shattered a little more, as if I was witnessing him battle something I could not see or understand.

I could not shake the feeling of vulnerability that came with being a parent. In those moments, I felt utterly powerless and protective. I became hyper aware of everything around him, always on high alert, analyzing every interaction he had, especially with his dad. I could not help but wonder if my husband understood the depth of Kyle's fears. Did he recognize the weight of our responsibility to keep our child safe, even from the things he did not fully understand? Knowing what I know now, I do not believe he ever truly grasped the depth of it all, or perhaps he chose not to.

While going through this emotional roller coaster with my baby, I often asked for advice from family, hoping to find comfort or maybe a shared experience. Some of them assured me night terrors were common in young children and that they would outgrow them. I also learned that empaths, which Kyle was, are highly susceptible to night terrors because they are highly sensitive to emotions and energies of others around them and are much closer to the spirit world than non-empaths are as small children. But those words felt hollow. Living through Kyle's agony, each situation felt like a reminder that I had to remain vigilant.

Over time and learning to adapt, I created a more soothing and ritualistic bedtime routine, filled with calming stories and gentle music, rubbing his back, hoping to ease the transition into sleep. Of course, I always made it a point to check on him throughout the night since day one, just a gentle touch to reassure both him and me. Little by little, those night terrors became less frequent, and I found myself breathing a little easier. Honestly, for many years after that first time, we rarely slept apart from one another.

Still, the memories of those frantic days and nights lingered, a haunting reminder of how fragile childhood can be. I realized my instinct to protect Kyle was not merely a reaction to his night terrors but defining my role as a protective mother. I also learned that being a protective mom was not just about shielding him from physical danger but also being a safe haven during his darkest moments and understanding what caused Kyle's fears. It was about building our bond that would help him feel secure and understood, listening, loving, and being present no matter what nightmares came his way, even when his fear felt overwhelming. I made sure that my son felt my immense love for him and that he was never alone in his battles.

MOTHER'S REFLECTION:
I Was the Light in His Darkness

There were monsters I could not see, dreams I could not interpret, and fears I could not name. But Kyle knew that if he cried out, I would always come. Every time. Without question. That is what being his mother meant.

It was not about understanding everything. It was about being the safe place he could run to in the middle of the longest night.

10

MAMA'S BIG BOY

WHEN KYLE BEGAN CRAWLING out of his crib at just eight months old it amazed me to see how he was able to climb out without falling or hurting himself. I was so curious about how he was doing it that we set up a camcorder to capture his escape. The footage left me awestruck. There he was, methodically figuring out how to climb over the side, a little escape artist in the making. I burst into laughter, marveling at his early problem-solving skills. My kid was a genius!

After his daring escape, he would run into our bedroom and tug on my arm to pick him up and cuddle him in our bed. I could not resist his sweet little face. He wanted to sleep with mommy and daddy, and I did not blame him for wanting to be close to us. How could I possibly resist? No way! However, I soon realized that I needed to take some safety precautions. We put up a baby gate in the hallway to ensure he could only come into our bedroom and nowhere near the stairs or anywhere else in the house.

As he grew older and transitioned to a toddler bed, our nightly routine turned into something so special. Reading a short bedtime story then holding his hand and singing to him as he drifted off to sleep. Every night he would insist on me lying on the floor next to him until his eyelids grew heavy, so I did, then I would sneak off to my bed. It was not very long before he would wake up and notice mommy was not holding his hand any longer. He would shuffle into my room and nudge me awake so we could start the cycle over again. Other times he would end up snuggling with me in our bed.

It was a special bond between mother and son, and I cherished those moments with him. Even when I was too tired to take him back to his bed, I never regretted letting him snuggle with me. It was a reminder of how much he needed me, and I was happy to be there for him.

Around the age of two, Kyle crawled into our bed one night, nestled between us, and reached out with both hands, his tiny right hand finding his daddy's, his left curling around mine. "Goodnight," he whispered, pulling us all together in that small, sacred moment. This symbolized his love and need for both of us.

I replied, "Goodnight, Poo Doo. I love you so much."

Innocently, he asked me, "Mommy, what is love?"

I was not sure how to explain it to a toddler. I told him that love was when your heart beats so fast and you care for someone so much that you want them to be happy and be with them all the time. Surprisingly, he understood completely and replied, "I love you, Mommy, I love you, Daddy. Goodnight." He held my hand, and we cuddled together, as I rubbed the sides of his eyes until he fell asleep, which did not take long. It was a beautiful moment that I will always cherish, filled with love and warmth between our family.

MOTHER'S REFLECTION:
The Shape of Love

I remember how fleeting these early years were. Each moment spent together, each question asked and answered, shaped our relationship in ways I never anticipated. This is the importance of being present, of cherishing laughter and the cuddles, and nurturing the bond we share. Love, in its purest form, is not just a feeling but a collection of moments that created the foundation for our lives together. As I watched Kyle grow, I have always held tightly to those treasured memories, knowing they will always be the heartbeats of our family story; of his story.

11

WHAT KYLE HAD TO
LEAVE BEHIND

THANK GOODNESS FOR MY mom and dad. When Kyle was a little over two years old, we had to make some tough decisions. My parents wanted me to stay permanently at home with Kyle, but we were already losing our home after my husband, our sole means of survival, quit his career after going into a deep depression. Even the affairs did not seem to lift the heaviness he carried. Whatever he was searching for, it did not bring him closer to peace, or to us.

We had no choice but to move and we returned to the old neighborhood where I was born and raised. My parents bought us an old, run-down house right around the corner from where I grew up and a block over from my brother. We had to leave our beautiful new home, and with it, Kyle's brand-new swing set. I wanted to bring it with us, but my husband would not allow it. Letting it go felt like leaving behind a piece of Kyle's joy.

The home we left in Smithville was literally across the street from the golf course and lake, which was specifically why I wanted Kyle to learn how to swim. Only being made to move to the other side of town. This was not the future I had imagined for myself or my son. But once I began to see how deeply my husband was struggling, I could not find another way forward. I prayed that Kyle would be spared the weight of his father's choices, and I held onto hope that somehow, our marriage and family might still find healing. Through it all, my family stood beside us, offering the support we so desperately needed.

I got through it with the help of my mom and dad. Kyle was too young to realize where he was, so the move affected him less than me. The house needed to be completely redone both inside and outside to be safely habitable for a child. So, I told my husband that if mom and dad were going to save us by providing a house, he would have to make this place livable for our son.

We remodeled the entire house. Once we were done, it was truly a nice clean place to live, other than a few roaches here and there from the neighbor's house. They would leave bags of trash outside for months on end and the roaches were endless. Even quarterly pest control treatments did not get rid of all of them. It was disgusting but as far as I knew, out of my control. My focus was keeping my space clean and safe for my son and family. I wanted us to still be a happy family despite our current situation.

Kyle got the master bedroom. I decorated it so nicely, and there was plenty of room for all his toys, TV, and a toddler recliner and for sleepovers with his cousins. It felt like the least I could do, especially after his father uprooted us away from the beautiful bedroom by the lake that Kyle had loved so much.

Living in this little house in Grandview I did my best to make it a home a special home for Kyle.

Even when he got older, he would remind me of the snakes and bugs coming from our next door neighbor. No one should have to live like that and yet, there we were, navigating the consequences of another person's choices I could not justify. I tried to understand, to make sense of it all, but in the end, no excuse could make it right. Not for me. Not for our son. Nothing was more important than me being a full-time mommy and raising my son like millions of other good moms out there and nothing felt more important than my husband stepping into the role of mentor and protector for our son. But as time passed, it became painfully clear that those needs were going unmet, and I was left trying to fill the gap.

MOTHER'S REFLECTION:
What a Home Really Means

Those turbulent times shaped not only our family dynamics but my understanding of resilience. I learned our home is not merely a physical space but a feeling, created through love and support, even in the most challenging circumstances. While my husband's mistakes brought pain and upheaval, they also revealed the strength and importance of my family. I sometimes reflect on how these experiences influenced my parenting. They instilled a deep sense of responsibility in me, more than ever before, to create a safer environment for Kyle. One that would counterbalance the instability he faced. In the end, I held onto hope that, even during the surrounding us, love and determination might still carve a new path forward.

12

MY BABY HAS THE FLU

WHEN MY LITTLE MAN was four years old, we had to take him to the emergency room due to dehydration. Despite my best efforts along with vitamins to take care of him, he was extremely ill with the flu and had been vomiting and running a fever. He refused to drink liquids, or even suck on a popsicle, so the nurses needed to administer IV fluids. Unfortunately, we got an inexperienced nurse who unsuccessfully stuck him twice.

Kyle was screaming and crying, looking at me with wide, pleading eyes as if to say, "Help me, Mommy."

At that moment, I felt a surge of protection and stopped the nurse, demanding a more experienced one. I refused to let them hurt my son repeatedly because they could not find a vein.

As I kept apologizing to my baby and holding him tight while rocking him in my arms, I told the new nurse, "You get one stick."

She sort of laughed it off, but I was deadly serious. She got it on the first try.

One of the nurses brought Kyle a stuffed bunny to cuddle, hoping it would help ease his pain. It did dry up his tears a bit, and he eventually fell asleep in my arms. We had to stay in the hospital for about three hours until he received enough fluids, and his temperature went down. No more pain for my little man.

This happened two years in a row, but thankfully, never again. I am so grateful my son got better in the end and was back to his rambunctious self once again. It broke my heart that he was so sick. My guidance always came from a place of love and wanting the absolute best for him.

MOTHER'S REFLECTION:
One Stick, One Mother's Promise

That night in the ER, watching Kyle suffer, something fierce rose up inside me. I was not just his comfort; I was his defender. My quiet "You get one stick" was not anger; it was love, sharpened by my exhaustion and fear.

I did not have phlebotomy training at the time, but I had instinct. The kind only a mother can carry.

Kyle's tears dried, but mine did not, not really. Because moments like that never leave you. They become proof that love is more than gentle, it is unflinching when it needs to be.

This story may be small in the scope of his life, but it is etched into mine forever.

13

EARLY LEARNER

As a devoted mom, I believe I exemplified love, perseverance, and dedication. I consistently focused on Kyle's needs to ensure a successful future for him. Throughout, I encountered numerous obstacles, some within my marriage and from his family, that could have easily disheartened me. I passionately believe I was being guided by a higher power, Almighty God. I knew I needed the patience of Job to assist my son in his proper development, and I am so grateful that God granted me the special gift of nurturing, and the grace I required to fulfill this role that I dreamt of for so long.

When Kyle reached the age of two, we began participating in "Parents as Teachers" which involved teachers making monthly visits to assess his learning progress. The teachers would make monthly visits to our home and observe him draw, skip, and jump, assessing when he would be able to start preschool if I chose to let him go. Every assessment indicated he was ahead of schedule in his development and learning. That is because I was a proud, full-time momma and dedicated every minute to teaching and nurturing him. I wanted Kyle to be eager to learn new things every day, so I made up games for us to play. I was told he could start preschool early if I wanted but I did not want him to. I wanted to hold onto my baby Kyle a bit longer, cherishing our moments together.

Kyle showed an aptitude for academics when he began reading at the age of three. I know it is hard for some to believe, but it is true, because I spent every minute with him playing and teaching. My son was never neglected by me in any way. Every moment I spent with him, whether playing or teaching, I knew I was investing in his growth. When he saw that his cousin, who was a year older than him, had started to read, he wanted to catch up and he did. He exceeded my and everyone else's expectations in reading and writing, and many other skills and I wanted to foster his very bright mind.

My husband worked in internet technology when Kyle was a toddler and would often bring work home with him. Kyle was an avid learner, so my husband would try to teach him how computers worked. Kyle picked this up very quickly and was soon reverse engineering anything my husband brought home, even experimenting with his small cars and construction toys to see if he could take them apart and put them back together. It was nice to see my son's mind grow while enjoying some quality time with his dad. Both were so smart in ways that I could not even fathom. It made me happy to see them together like that, although it was an extremely rare occurrence. How I wished it would have stayed a healthier relationship throughout his life.

As the years went on, the dynamics shifted. Kyle and I both found it increasingly difficult to engage his dad in one-on-one quality time. My husband seemed, from observation, disinterested in developing any common interests or learning new things to share with his son. This disturbed me and Kyle seemed to felt the sting of rejection from his dad more times than I can count.

I realized how crucial it was for Kyle to feel supported and cherished not just by one parent, but by both of us. My devotion to Kyle has always been steadfast. But I also understand our parental involvement was a shared responsibility that would shape my son's self-esteem and sense of belonging. I did my very best to nurture his talents and passions and I knew the love and support I provided him would always be a foundation. I hoped my husband would one day realize the precious opportunity he had to bond appropriately with our son as I continued to guide Kyle on his journey, both academically and emotionally, but I longed for the day when he would feel loved and valued by both of his parents.

MOTHER'S REFLECTION:
God Trusted Me with His Mind

I used to worry whether I was doing enough, if the hours spent reading and creating were shaping the boy I prayed for. But now I understand. Kyle was not only gifted, but he was also entrusted to me. I was given the heart and the grace to guide him. And even when others missed the beauty of who he was, I never did.

That was my calling. That was my joy.

14

KYLE'S FIRST VACATION

I THOUGHT IT WOULD BE good for us to get away from everything, to be a family of three for a while and gain some perspective. After my husband moved us from our home, the upheaval that followed left us dazed. It was not just a change of address, it was a shift in everything we had known, and the emotional toll was undeniable. We needed a break from everyday life if I was going to forgive my husband and move on, a reset, if you will.

We chose a budget-friendly cruise to the Bahamas. Kyle was in his element, reveling in the excitement of the big boat and the joy of playing in the sand at Paradise Island. I captured every precious moment on video. Looking back, I am so grateful I did. Now I have dozens of movies highlighting my baby, my little boy, and eventually, my young man. Each video is a bittersweet reminder of how quickly time passes; he will never truly be far from my heart.

I think the cabin steward received great satisfaction and expertise in crafting towel animals for Kyle, which added a touch of magic to our trip. Yet, I believe Kyle's happiest moments were when we arrived back at Pompano Beach, Florida after our cruise for a couple of days of beach time. One evening he discovered a tiny crab shell, which he lovingly named "Crabby." That little shell became his constant companion, accompanying us everywhere. However, one evening, we made the mistake of leaving Crabby in the rental car while we enjoyed dinner at a Mexican restaurant. After dinner, when we got to the car and opened the door, a wave of odor hit us like a brick wall, an unfortunate consequence of leaving aquatic life away from the sea for too long. We were seriously not aware this was going to happen. Kyle's dad was getting irritated by the smell and decided Crabby needed to return to the beach for safety. Kyle's heart broke as he said goodbye to his little friend, tears streaming down his face.

"Bye-bye, Crabby," he said, feeling sad and tired from the day.

As we walked back to the hotel from our car, Kyle's sobs echoed through the night air. I tried my best to console my sweet, sensitive boy who was getting so sleepy, but his dad grew even more frustrated with both of us; Kyle in his sorrow, and me in my empathy toward my baby boy.

At just three years old, Kyle was navigating a world where he found empathy for almost everyone and everything, an openness he carried throughout his lifetime. But his dad. It was a painful lesson in emotional disconnect, one that would follow Kyle through years of struggles. He seemed to carry a silent longing for his dad's understanding that often went unmet. That night, as Kyle snuggled with me, falling asleep in my arms, his dad retreated to the bar near the pool, seeking solace in a beer instead of his family.

When we returned home from our trip, life returned to a semblance of normalcy. The vacation, though a refreshing escape, felt like a fading dream. Reality would soon set back in, and I found myself consumed with the responsibility of maintaining a clean and safe home for Kyle, which is all I wanted.

My baby's first trip served as a reminder of the profound impact that emotional presence, or lack of, can have on a child. A parent who is emotionally unavailable can create a void in their child's life that results in feelings of isolation and misunderstanding. Kyle's empathy, a beautiful quality, was often met with emotional distance from his dad, and as a result, he learned early on that his feelings might not matter. All parents need to be more aware and emotionally present regardless of their own issues.

MOTHER'S REFLECTION:
What Stayed with Him

I once believed the vacation would be the memory, sandcastles, towel animals. sea life, but now I see it was the silence that stayed with Kyle. The moment when his tears were met with frustration instead of comfort.

I gave him my arms. I gave him my heart. But part of him still waited for something else. Something I could not give.

15

BACK TO WORK AGAIN

I **TRIED TO DO WHAT** I could to make the best of our unpleasant situation. At that point in our lives, my husband was working but did not bring in much money and we were not able to buy food on our own. My parents were helping as much as they could, but I took a part-time job cleaning offices at night.

Kyle hated Mommy going to work but not as much as I hated leaving him when I promised myself, I would never leave him alone with his dad after the experiences when Kyle was a baby. Yes, I was angry at my husband for putting me and Kyle in this horrible situation. At times, it felt like he did not fully grasp the weight of what we were going through. The fear of leaving my son alone with him tormented me daily as I had to withdraw the promise I had made to myself just a couple of years prior. The resentment toward my husband was unbearable at times. But he was currently trying to build a new career, so as his wife, I needed to support him in that effort and hope he would better himself and our family unit.

I had extreme mom guilt but did not have much of a choice. I had to work. Someone had to put food on the table, and it was going to have to be me for a while, with my parents picking up the slack. I did not realize then that I was witnessing the beginning of a pattern, one that would unfold over many years, marked by emotional highs and lows I struggled to understand. I made sure I called my little man every night while working to assure him mommy was coming home and that she loved her boy. Although I often worried about leaving Kyle in his dad's care while I worked, I knew that if we ever divorced, Kyle would be left alone with him for entire weekends, and I would never know what would happen to my son. This way, I could at least return home to him every night and wake him every morning. Moms all over the world go through the same ordeal. I was no different than any other devoted mom wanting to keep her child safe and yet keep the family flowing.

One night when I called, Kyle told me he was hungry, and said his daddy was not talking to him when he asked for something to eat. Kyle was only four years old.

He said, "Daddy won't make me something to eat or play with me, Mommy."

I was furious inside. I was working to provide for us, and yet hearing Kyle say he was hungry, and he had asked daddy with no response, shattered me. He was only four, and I was not there to fix it. The helplessness cut deeper than the anger.

I could not do it all, working and making up for what he should have been doing. My husband needed to step up to the plate and be a father. I stuffed my anger down for Kyle and told him once again I was so sorry, and I would speak to daddy later.

Every time I called, my husband said he was watching TV, something that seemed to consume most of his time. It often felt like he had checked out emotionally, slipping into one of those detached states I had come to recognize, while Kyle remained in the background, playing alone, and needing more than he received.

This was getting ridiculous and dangerous for both Kyle and me. I assured Kyle I would be home as soon as possible, and I would make him something to eat and play with him. I asked him to go into his room and lie down, and mommy would sing him to sleep until I got home and that is what I did. I sang "Hush Little Baby" to him over the phone as I dusted office desks. Before I knew it, he was sound asleep because when I stopped and called his name he did not answer. I did everything I could on many occasions to calm my son and assure him his daddy loved him even though he could not see or feel it. At least I hoped for this, but actions prove someone's love for another, words just prove of who they pretend to be. Most times I doubted the level of commitment my husband was willing to give to parenthood or to our marriage.

At times, it felt as though my desire to stay home and be a devoted full-time mom stirred something unsettled in my husband, perhaps even resentment. I could not name it then, but the tension was unmistakable. I felt as if he created conflict just so I would have to go back to work. Despite the challenges with my husband, I was determined to be the best mother I could be. I poured all my love and energy into raising my son, even as I struggled with the demands of motherhood. It was not easy, but I was grateful for the support of my parents and their willingness to help me in any way they could.

Looking back, I realized there was a learning curve to parenting, and I made a few mistakes along the way. However, I never lost sight of my love for my son and my desire to see him thrive, which was my number one goal.

I knew I loved my son more than life itself. My actions and words reflected the love I poured into our son. In comparison, his dad often seemed emotionally distant, much like the environment he came from. That disconnection, both around him and within him, made it difficult to read anything from him.

The night of Kyle's disturbing phone call, I waited until I got home to talk to my husband but by then I was so mad I could not even look at him. The lack of responsibility was staggering. It often felt as though the safety and well-being of our child took a back seat to whatever was on the television. I went straight to Kyle's room and got in bed with him and hugged him. He was asleep just like I had left him on the phone. He woke up and said he was hungry. This flared the anger in me toward my husband again and I could have easily lashed out instead, not saying a word. I did not want my son to see my pain, so, instead I focused on the task at hand. Feeding and comforting Kyle.

Mommy would fill in the holes my husband left open. I made him a simple meal of some fish sticks and applesauce with ice cream for dessert as a small but well-deserved treat (and a few extra calories). He was satisfied after that. I read him a book, and we fell asleep in each other's arms.

How I despised being away from my baby to clean offices and picking up my husband's slack. I lacked respect for my husband for doing what he did to us. He often seemed caught in a cycle of decisions that, from my perspective, did not take into account how they might affect our family. Another night, I arrived home after yet another long shift of cleaning and walked in to see my precious three-year-old son standing in the kitchen near his little desk, the one Santa Claus had brought him the prior Christmas. Kyle was holding a piece of paper in his hands along with a pair of adult scissors. He was so sleepy, swaying back and forth, forcing his eyes to stay open. His father sat in the recliner watching television, seemingly unaware of what Kyle was doing or even where he was. *What if my son had fallen on those scissors?* Fear surged through me. I dropped my purse, grabbed the scissors from my baby's hands, and scooped him up. He instantly fell asleep on my shoulder as I carried him to bed. *How could anyone sit so close to such innocence and not see the danger unfolding right in front of them?*

I was still deeply unsettled about leaving Kyle each night for work, especially after that incident. A quiet resentment had begun toward the circumstances, and toward the man who seemed unable or unwilling to protect what mattered most. I worried that each time I left, I was stepping into a silence that left both Kyle and me feeling unseen. I began searching for a way to make my leaving feel like something Kyle could understand, maybe even something he could feel proud of.

I made sure I brought him something small when I arrived home every night, so he had something to look forward to when I returned. He was too young to understand why I had to leave every night for a few hours, and I did not want him to know the severity of the situation we were in. This small gesture brought him a little bit of peace knowing I would be back, and he could expect something special when I returned. I would rather him associate me leaving with a happy return, even if it was something small leftover from work.

Sometimes I would bring him paper clips and show him how to connect them to make a bracelet and necklace. On one occasion, I brought him a stress ball that depicted the earth. One day as we were cuddled together watching a movie, he unexpectedly said, "Mommy, I want to make a rubber band ball." I laughed at the odd child-like request and told him, "Awesome, what fun, it may take us a while, but we can do it together."

Looking back, those years were incredibly tough, but they also taught me a lot about the lengths a mother will go to for her child. I learned that sometimes I had to make excruciatingly difficult choices to ensure the wellbeing of my son. My relationship with Kyle grew stronger because of the time and effort I put into being there for him, even when circumstances were less than ideal. While my husband's behavior was a constant source of frustration and, of course, fear, it made me focus even more on the importance of being a stable and loving presence in my son's life.

Through it all, I realized that my strength and determination were not just for me, but for Kyle, and that made every struggle I endured, worth it.

MOTHER'S REFLECTION:
You Are the Advocate

No child deserves to live in fear, nor should they feel obligated to endure disrespect or instability simply because they are young and powerless. As Kyle's mom, I desperately tried to observe everything regarding how my husband engaged with his son and how Kyle would react and even the shifts in my husband's behavior. I was not being paranoid; I was learning to trust my instincts when something did not feel right.

I am begging all moms to be their child's greatest advocate. You cannot afford to ignore the signs of a distrusting person no matter how close, relatively, that person is to your child.

16

My Love is Louder Than My Pain

WHEN I HAD PAINFUL breast surgery, Kyle was only three, maybe younger. We were at home, I was giving him a bath, and when I lifted him out of the tub, my back gave out. No warning, no chance to brace myself, just blinding pain and collapse. I crumpled right there on the bathroom floor, helpless. I could not move.

I yelled for my husband to step in. He took Kyle, dried him off, got him in his jammies, while I crawled on my hands and knees to the bedroom, each movement sending shockwaves of pain down my spine. I remember feeling a mix of shame and rage. Shame that I could not carry my son, rage at my own body for failing me when he needed me. I lay there on the floor until the spasms passed enough to drag myself into bed. But it never really passed, it just dulled into something manageable.

A couple of weeks later, I underwent breast reduction surgery. It was not elective. It was survival. Gravity had become an enemy after having Kyle, my huge chest was pulling my frame forward, undermining what little strength my back had left. The procedure was meant to give me relief, but in the process, it exposed just how much was resting on my shoulders that no surgery could lift.

When I woke up in that hospital bed, hurting, it was Kyle who reminded me why I had pushed through. He came into the room with daddy, and the second he saw me, his little face crumpled. He reached out to me, sobbing, clutching my arms, my hospital gown, anything he could reach. He climbed into bed, onto my chest, right on top of my fresh incisions, and the pain was instant and white-hot. But I did not stop him. I could not.

Even in that moment of physical agony, I chose my baby boy's comfort and love over mine. I wrapped my arms around him and held him tightly, willing myself to breathe through the pain just to love on my boy. My body screamed, but my heart was louder. He needed me, and I needed to be needed by him. His tears soaked through my gown. He could not form complete sentences yet; he just cried and held on as if letting go might mean losing me for good.

He would not go back to daddy. He did not want to. When the time came for them to leave for the night, Kyle fought. He clung to me and screamed the whole way down the hallway, his cries echoing in the sterile silence.

I remember telling my husband, "You give Poo Doo anything he wants! Please do not let him cry or be sad!"

I lay there, numb from more than surgery, my heart breaking into pieces I did not know how to stop. I felt helpless. My maternal instinct was clashing with my physical incapacity. This I could not win, being in the hospital.

That night, I called my parents. Begged them to check on Kyle, to maybe take him in while I healed. I asked my mom to go to the house and stay with him, just be there, so I would not have to wonder if he was being fed, bathed, *seen*. She did not stay like I hoped she would, but they did stop by to check. I clung to that, at least someone laid eyes on my son. Still, nothing could silence what I already knew. Kyle had not been cared for in the way he needed. His fear told the story his words could not. The agony of Kyle leaving my side; that was not normal. It was not just sadness; it was terror.

And I knew why.

I do not want to believe my husband ever crossed that unthinkable line, I pray to God that darkness never touched my baby, but I do believe there were times when Kyle's needs may not have been fully seen or met, especially when I could not be there to hold him. I felt the crushing kind of absence in my gut. It is the only explanation that fits.

The day Kyle was left strapped in his car seat in the garage, during the sweltering heat of summer is seared in my memory. After that, something in me shifted. I could no longer explain it away as simple forgetfulness. What I once hoped was harmless began to feel unsettling. Maybe, in his own way, he did not see the risk. But that did not make the consequences any less real, or any less mine to carry. Because when I am the mother, the one who should have stopped it. I should have been there, even when I physically could not carry it all.

MOTHER'S REFLECTION:
My Instinct Was Real

There is a difference between pain and burden. Pain knocks us down. But burden? That is what we rise under, day after day, with a quiet kind of strength only love can summon.

What I did not say in the chapter, but feel with every fiber, is how motherhood taught me to hold more than I ever thought possible. Not just my son in moments of joy, but the questions, the fears, the echoes of what I could not control. In choosing Kyle's comfort over my own, I learned that love will always outlast injury.

This is not a story about what attempted to break me, it is about what did not.

17

SNAKES

EACH SPRING BROUGHT THE expected swarm of garter snakes, so many that my little man could not play in the yard with his cousins at our new home near my parents. I was always on guard, watching as he played in the sandbox or on the swing set, ensuring he would not unknowingly stumble upon a snake while walking in the grass or picking up a rock. It was a source of constant embarrassment and shame that he had to live like that, following a series of changes that I did not choose and could not stop. Our lives were shifted in ways I never could have predicted. The fear of a snake darting across the kids' path made Kyle and his cousins reluctant to step outside at all, and I too was hesitant to let them play outdoors.

To avoid the unsettling situation, I would often take Kyle over to Momo and Popo's house just around the corner for lunch with his cousins. This was a daily routine, and one of the few reasons I appreciated living so close to my parents.

My parents had maintained this close-knit habit, and they were genuinely wonderful grandparents to Kyle and his cousins. They were also fiercely protective of their grandbabies. For example, Kyle discovered at the age of two that he could hold tightly onto my hands and walk up my legs to my stomach, then flip over. He figured this out on his own. He found endless joy in performing this trick, giggling as he showed off his newfound skill in front of Popo and Momo. But Popo would often fuss when I flipped Kyle over or carried him as a baby on my shoulders, worrying that I might drop him. I always reassured my dad I would never allow my baby to fall. My son knew that I would always keep him safe and trusted me up until the very end.

I reveled in the moments with Kyle and my parents, and Kyle did as well. I often found myself wondering why his dad did not seem able to connect with him in the same way I could. *Why is it so hard for parents to meet their child in that tender space where they simply want to be seen and known?*

I was both mom and dad in many respects, and it felt heavy at times. Thank God for my parents' immense support when my husband seemed to struggle with his luck and faith. They did everything they could for their grandkids, and each held an incredibly special space in my parents' hearts with a particular softness reserved for the only boy, my Kyle.

One day when we went to my parents home for lunch, the day seemed typically warm with the absence of any breeze in the air. As we got out of the car, I spotted Kyle's cousins walking down the street to meet us. Their mommy was behind them, keeping both eyes on them to make sure they made it safe. I noticed something unusual in the yard, the leaves were moving, though there was no wind. At first, I brushed it off as nothing significant but a few seconds later, Kyle shouted, "Mommy look!" He pointed at the grass, and before I knew it, he and the girls were screaming and jumping onto the porch. I rushed to open the front door, but they were already racing inside, with a mix of terror and anxiousness. I followed closely behind as my heart raced. I had to keep my composure as the mom, even though I was just as frightened.

My eyes were drawn to an area of the yard where I thought I saw a pile of snakes wrestling in the grass. I yelled for my mother and the kids to stay away from the door, I could not allow my mother to faint right in front of the grandbabies, as I had seen her fainting from the sight of a snake firsthand when I was younger, an event which seriously scared me silly.

Taking a deep breath, I called animal control, trying to sound calm. The officer explained that I was seeing a "breeding ball," a term that sounded as horrifying as it was. I told her I did not care what it was, I just needed her to come out at once. I could not bear the thought of my son or nieces being anywhere near that mess.

Not soon enough for me, animal control finally arrived with buckets and grabbers and quickly started to collect snakes. The officer explained that it was illegal to harm the snakes, so they would be relocating them to Longview Lake. She assured me she would return daily to round up as many as possible.

That night, both Kyle and I were haunted by nightmares. At just four years old, Kyle had expressed his desire to live somewhere else, terrified of the snakes that seemed to be invading our lives. I understood his fears all too well; I was scared too, worried that something like this could happen again or a more dangerous snake might find its way into our home. I assured Kyle that one day we would find a better place to live, free from the worry of snakes lurking around us. I promised him I would never let anything hurt him. Deep down, I was trying to convince myself of that promise, dealing with anxiety that our home might harbor creatures that could jeopardize our safety.

That experience taught me how to navigate fears for both me and my son. A hard reminder of unexpected obstacles that intruded on our lives, whether it was in the form of a slithering snake or a more complex emotional struggle. I realized I was not just protecting my son from physical dangers but also from the anxieties that can arise in an unpredictable world.

As the days turned into weeks, I found ways to help Kyle reclaim his outdoor space. After surrounding our house perimeters with moth ball granules, a recommended strategy for keeping snakes at a fair distance, we began exploring the backyard together. I focused on teaching him about the beauty of nature while respecting its creatures in their own element. I wanted him to learn that while fear might come knocking sometimes, it certainly did not have to keep us from enjoying life.

I understood that being a mother often means facing fear head on, not just for myself but for Kyle as well. I wanted to create an environment where he could thrive. One where fear would not overshadow his laughter and joy. I think those snakes were a catalyst for growth for both of us. A lesson in courage and embracing the unknown and finding ways to adapt and face our fears together.

Living in our little house in Grandview that my parents purchased for us, I poured my heart into making it a warm, loving home for Kyle. No matter how much time passed, he never forgot the snakes and bugs creeping in from the neighbor's yard, a reminder of the challenges we faced. No child should have to live that way.

Nothing mattered more to me than being a full-time mother, raising Kyle with the same love and dedication that so many good moms show every day, and nothing should have mattered more to my husband than guiding and protecting our son.

MOTHER'S REFLECTION:
Not All the Snakes Came from the Yard

Although I protected Kyle from the snakes in the grass, some dangers were quieter. Unseen. They did not hiss, they withheld. They did not strike, they ignored.

And even though I could not always name them, I never stopped guarding my son from the things that tried to darken his joy.

18

ABSENT FAMILY

I MADE SURE MY SON was remarkably close to my family. I also wanted him to be just as close to my husband's family, but it seemed they were not as motivated at all to be grandparents as my parents were, nor did his sister ever seem interested in building a relationship with her nephew.

It was so incredibly sad to see my in-laws so distant and not involved with Kyle. He was such a special boy. He was the first and only grandchild, yet it never seemed as though they recognized how extraordinary he truly was, or how fortunate they were to have him carry the Wiley name. This miracle child, so full of light, never seemed to be celebrated by them, the way he deserved.

Kyle never had a close relationship with anyone on his dad's side of the family. Looking back, it never seemed as though they genuinely wanted a close relationship with Kyle. There was a noticeable emotional distance, withdrawn, reserved, and hard to reach. Over time, I began to sense deeper struggles within the family dynamic. My husband once described his father as a bitter, lonely man who often drank heavily, and I could not help but notice how that atmosphere shaped the way they related to others, including Kyle. As Kyle grew older, he acknowledged this and asked me why they did not act like my side of the family, who were loving and generous and full of life and fun. I had no answers for him because I was trying to make sense out of their distant and strange behavior myself. Even when I tried to confront them on occasion simply asking why they were so absent I never got a straight answer from any of them, only defensiveness and secretive silence I could not make sense of.

My sister-in-law saw Kyle only on rare occasions, usually just his birthday or Christmas, and never seemed interested in spending meaningful time with him. Even though his grandmother lived only eight minutes away, she showed little desire to build a relationship with him. Even when Kyle stayed with her temporarily as he got older, after his father left again, his grandmother still did not seem interested in forming a meaningful bond. Instead, it felt as though she echoed the same patterns of emotional distance and confusion he had already experienced.

There were moments when her words felt more like manipulation than genuine care, and when money was offered in place of presence. It left Kyle with more questions than comfort; questions that I still could not answer if I were to be honest with him.

Kyle felt loved, wanted, and supported by my side of the family. My parents, along with the rest of my family, showered him with affection and attention, making up for the absence of his other side. We created our own traditions and memories, ensuring that Kyle knew he was cherished.

MOTHER'S REFLECTION:
The Quiet Grief

It was so sad to see the lack of interest from my husband's family, but it also reinforced the importance of the love and support Kyle received from my side. It taught Kyle and me both that family is not just about blood relations. It is about the bonds we build and the love we share. Kyle grew up knowing he was deeply loved by so many, and that the foundation of love and support helped him thrive despite the absence of his other side.

There is a particular ache that came from watching my son search for love in places that were void. I wanted to shield Kyle from that, but some emptiness cannot be explained only mourned.

19

WHERE IS DADDY?

As a baby and little boy, Kyle would go to his dad and ask him to play with him, but I can remember his dad always refusing, saying maybe later or that he was tired and needed to rest. This might have been true, but raising a child takes an effort that he did not seem to want to put in. Regardless of whether either of us were working, it is no excuse not to spend quality time with your child. This is what makes life and working all worth it. It would break my heart when my husband came home from work and walked right past us, and we would not see him for the first hour while he was in the bathroom on his phone or in his office.

I would watch my son's precious little face follow his daddy down the hall when he came home from work, waiting for his daddy to acknowledge him. That little face would light up as if to say, "Today, maybe Daddy will be different." As time went on that light would slowly fade and dim to a flicker of a dying candle. He and I both grew accustomed to the silence. While I played with my son, his father remained distant, physically present, perhaps, but emotionally elsewhere. I did not want my son to think that his daddy's behavior was normal, but in our house it was. As much as I desperately wanted it to be different.

My son confided in me one afternoon around the age of seven or eight, while I was in the bedroom folding clothes, that he hated his dad.

He wanted his daddy to play with him. To ride bikes with him, to play basketball with him. *He just wanted his dad's attention, but how could the Masters' tournament matter more than the little boy standing right in front of him, waiting to be seen?* Golf was only one of the unimportant and disturbing pastimes that kept his dad from bonding with his son.

Kyle was crying and I tried to convince him he did not hate his dad, but he insisted he did hate him and did not want him around anymore. He asked me to make him leave. A lot of moms would have ignored their child's request, but I put deep thought into it, absolutely I did. If I had left, again, I would be at the mercy of my husband and my great fear of something happening to Kyle when he was alone with his dad for extended periods of time. I was torn.

I found myself constantly making excuses for my husband's behavior and, looking back, I questioned why I did. There were many moments when I silently wished he would leave, his presence felt more like absence, his interest in us barely visible. And then, one day, he was simply gone. No warning. No explanation. Just gone, leaving both of us without a home, and me to pick up the pieces.

What kind of man, claiming to be rooted in genuine virtue and principles, would subject a wife or child to such an unthinkable and painful situation?

I had already spent most of my married life functioning as a single mother, so a separation would not change the reality by much. There were things my husband did that I felt were inexcusable and impossible to justify, but I always had his back. Because I had seen that things were not always so bad. I just had to wait until the waters settled. It turns my stomach when I think about all the times I stood up for my husband, only to be met with accusations I knew were not true and eventually left behind without warning or explanation. Things I would not tell another woman to stand for. But at the time I had a false hope that maybe, someday things would change. But they never did. They only got worse as the years went on as Kyle and I were always in the crossfire, trying to appease.

I remember one Christmas morning when Poo Doo unwrapped a toy car wash, his eyes lit up with excitement. He looked to his daddy, hoping to share the joy, but his dad remained in bed. This broke my heart. *How could anyone miss the chance to step into a child's world when all they want is to be seen and joined in their joy?*

Although I spent time making my traditional cinnamon rolls for my precious child, and after opening all the packages and getting up at the crack of dawn to see if Santa Claus came, it should have mattered and it did. I stayed awake long enough for me and Kyle to play with his new toy. Eventually he slowly faded into sleep and that was my chance to nap as well. We were spending the day with my parents and Kyle's cousins, yet I still had the energy to play with cars or games and read with my son. I knew these moments would not last forever, so despite whatever I was feeling, I was going to take part. I had a blast playing with my son and doing whatever he wanted to do.

One day my husband told me, "I can't wait until our son is a teenager so we can hang out together." I was shocked. *Did he just want to fast forward through Kyle's life, to have a buddy?* I never understood why he said that, until Kyle got older, then it was very clear to me. Over the years, I had witnessed patterns of behavior in him that felt immature and unpredictable, moments that left our son without the steady guidance and mentorship he so deeply needed.

Looking back on all the instances when Kyle would tell me how much he hated his daddy and wanted us to leave; I truly did not see exactly everything that was happening to him. I finally realized my husband may have repeated the pattern he experienced as a child.

When I took Kyle to a store with me when he was a baby, he was always so quiet, never a whimper. I could tell sometimes he wanted to cry or scream out like he was hurting but he did not. I would make sure he was clean and dry and fed. I always worried about his diapers being too tight or him being too hot or too cold. I noticed sometimes he would struggle at being quiet. I could tell he wanted to talk, to scream, to cry but nothing would come out.

I will never forget the moment my mother-in-law told me she used to let my husband cry in his crib for hours. She said it plainly, without remorse, as if it were normal. I stood there stunned, trying to understand how anyone could ignore a baby's cries for that long. Her words haunted me, and suddenly, so much about my husband's emotional distance began to make sense. She confessed to me years later that she told my husband to do the same with Kyle while I was at work.

Thank Almighty God that Kyle was nothing like them. He and I had so much compassion, empathy, love, joy, laughter, and excitement inside of us that they could not bear it. My husband would ask me on occasion how Kyle and I had so much joy, energy, and life in us. It was foreign to him. He wanted to experience our joy but could not. I am so thankful that God allowed my son to emotionally thrive and not allow other family members to repress him.

I realize how much strength it took to navigate those difficult years. My husband's absence and lack of involvement were painful for both of us, but they also taught me the importance of being not just present, but completely, one hundred percent, engaged in Kyle life. I learned that my love and dedication might make up for the shortcomings of others. Despite the challenges, I am proud of the bond Kyle, and I built. It was through the many trials that I discovered my resilience and the profound depth of my love for my son. These experiences have shaped me into a stronger person and a more devoted mother.

MOTHER'S REFLECTION:
The Power of Showing Up

I never stopped showing up for my son. When others chose silence, I chose presence. When he asked, "Where is Daddy?" I gave him what his father could not; answers, comfort, and the kind of love that does not turn its back.

Even when I did not have all the solutions, I made sure Kyle knew one thing: Mommy would never disappear.

20

HOLDING HIM TIGHTER

IN SEPTEMBER 2001, KYLE was not yet four years old, not old enough for school. I was genuinely enjoying the role of parent. I would wake up early every morning before him and drink my coffee while watching the news. I knew that once Poo Doo, one of my many nicknames for him, woke up, there would be no stopping for the rest of the day. We would either be going to the park nearby to drive his battery-powered Jeep, teaching him to create with play dough, playing in his sandbox, making mud pies with his cousins, or building with LEGOs. He was so full of life and energy, like a normal four-year-old. His never-ending energy kept me on my toes, and I loved every minute of it. Everything had a bright and innocent glow in Kyle's life, and I wanted to keep it that way for as long as possible.

Things changed drastically for me as a mother on 9/11. I woke up on that very ordinary morning, ready to take on the day and do my usual routine before Kyle woke up. He would usually come into the living room and sit with me. I would cuddle and rock him and he fell back to sleep. This morning was no different as I carried him into his bed. He slept for another hour or so.

As I drank my coffee and ironed a few work shirts for my husband that I knew I would never get done once Kyle woke up, I watched the local news. Breaking news flashed across the screen and immediately caught my attention. I remember seeing the tail end of a plane sticking out of one of the Twin Towers. At first it looked fake, like a toy plane. I thought it was a commercial for something, so I continued to watch. It took me a minute to realize it was not at all fake. I quickly pushed the record button on the DVR. I watched in complete horror, witnessing something I never imagined could happen. I was terrified.

I grabbed the phone to call my husband at work and as I dialed, I saw another plane fly right through the tower. I started to shake and thought to myself, "This is not real, this is a movie." I turned the channel, and the story was everywhere. It was clear. This was happening! I began to wonder how far this attack was going to go, thinking of my small little world in the Kansas City area.

My husband picked up the phone and I started to cry. I begged him, "Come home now!" I was scared. I wanted us all to be together. Something was happening in our country and if things were going to get worse, I wanted us to be together and safe. He said he could not get off work because he had just gotten there, and they were watching it happen also. Everyone in America was watching it unfold, I am sure.

He told me he loved me and promised he would be home in a few hours. I called my mom and dad, and they tried to assure me we were safe and told me when Bubber (Kyle) woke up to bring him over for breakfast. I remember hanging up the phone and feeling alone and frightened. I thought the world was ending. I unplugged the iron and ran into Kyle's room, crawled in bed with my baby and wrapped my arms around him, holding on so tight like there was no tomorrow. As he still slept soundly, I kissed his precious cheek, telling him how much I loved him and began to pray to God for our safety.

Kyle would never truly know what the world was like before 9/11 but I would. Suddenly the world felt scarier and smaller than ever before. This was going to be the world my son would live in, and I wondered if this was the worst it could get or if this was only the beginning.

The events of 9/11 were a turning point in my life as a mother. The innocence of our daily routines was shattered, and the world suddenly felt more dangerous and uncertain. Through it all, my love for Kyle remained a constant source of strength and hope.

Considering Kyle grew up with no clear memory of the world before 9/11, he only knew what he may have learned in school. I strived to preserve his joy and innocence amid our world's turmoil. The events that day seemed to ignite a sense of community and connection throughout our country, reminding me how fragile life is and to cherish each moment. As I watched my beautiful boy grow into a young man, my prayer was that he would carry the lessons of love and compassion and be able to navigate the world with resilience and appreciation for the beauty that persists even in the shadows.

MOTHER'S REFLECTION:

September Shift

9/11 did not just change the world, it changed how tightly I held my son. That morning, fear rewired something in me. I stopped assuming we had endless time, as we all should. I started cherishing every breath, every laugh, every ordinary moment with him like it was a gift. I just prayed that others felt the same.

21

GOOD BEHAVIOR

As A YOUNG BOY, when we went to the grocery store or Walmart, Kyle was always so well-behaved. I did not have to tell him to be, he just was. We would hear other kids crying and screaming and having their little temper tantrums in the next aisle, but he always kept his composure. He would tell me things that he would like to have, and I would say, "Poo Doo, why do not you put it on your birthday list or Christmas list for Santa?" At the end of our shopping, being such a good boy, I would always allow him to pick out a new Hot Wheel or Monster truck and at the checkout he always got a candy bar or gum. Just a small gift for good behavior that was well beyond his age. Of course, on occasion, I would take Kyle along with one of his friends or cousins to the store and let them pick out whatever they wanted. My son was not in any fashion a "spoiled brat" as some would say about children who get everything. He was indeed spoiled because he was my miracle child. I wanted my son to have everything that I had growing up with and much more. There is not anything wrong with that. Every decent parent should want better for their child.

Kyle's Hot Wheel collection got bigger and bigger throughout the passing years. When we lived at our home in Grandview, at age six before we moved, Kyle and I lined up his cars end to end throughout the house, and I believe we counted almost five hundred. I wanted him to hand them down to my grandson one day. I was recently told that he gave them to his older cousin's little boys. Some are still in packages in storage, but most are not. He loved his cars, and I loved to get down on the ground and play with him.

We would set up Hot Wheel strips throughout the house and race each other. Even though I enjoyed playing with Kyle immensely, I could not understand why I was the only one doing so. His dad should have been racing cars with him and playing tickle monster and wrestling with him and all the other fun things dads do with their sons. I had to get on the ground and show him how to tickle and wrestle with Kyle. When it should have been natural, he seemed to be uncomfortable and somewhat robotic doing this with his own son. Kyle was not having fun and would give up and walk away feeling sad. It was very plain that my father-in-law never shared those experiences with his own son.

Why did I not see it? How could I have been so blind at the time? I was so distracted by the idea of a happy family that I could not see the reality of it all. It will always be something I regret. That I let myself be blinded for so long.

My son was my world, and I made sure everyone that came around him acknowledged him, spent time with him, and respected him. I made sure that everyone knew how I felt about my boy. My husband knew of my profound love for my son and how much his protection, health, and wellbeing meant to me. Yet, it seemed to me, he could not always feel that for his own flesh and blood, our son.

I could not help the way my husband was raised and that his parents may have not been fully present. It made me so sad for him but all I could do was create beautiful, lasting memories with my own son and hope his dad would want to be a part of them. *When a child's love is offered so freely what keeps someone from reaching back?*

Throughout the years, Kyle had a beautiful childhood, full of laughter, love, and the kind of memories that linger in his soul, while some family members remained absent, missing moments they could never reclaim, he still flourished. *How could they not see the miracle unfolding right in front of them?*

They truly are not aware of everything they missed. I tried many times over to get them to join in and invited them to everything that was going on in Kyle's life. I never stopped inviting them to all his football, soccer, basketball, baseball, tennis games or swimming meets, or his Tae Kwon Do spar events and all the other special occasions and get-togethers.

He had most everything a boy could ask for and I made sure of it, including love and attention from me, but he longed for something I could not give which was authenticity and attention from his dad and the family he came from. *What child does not yearn to be seen by the ones whose absence speaks louder than words?* I could not make them want to be a part of Kyle's life and spend quality time with him, but I prayed that they would want to. Maybe things would have been different. He is now with his Heavenly Father, the one who can truly give Kyle everything he needs or ever dreamed of.

Mother's Reflection:
A Gentle Boy in a Noisy World

I am so grateful for the bond Kyle, and I shared. His good behavior and kind heart were a testament to the nurturing environment I wanted to create. I am proud of the loving relationship we had.

22

PRE-K

AFTER THE TRAGEDY OF 9/11, I really did not want him to go to preschool. I wanted him to remain as young and innocent as possible in my care. But since his older cousin started the year prior, he and her younger sister wanted to be big kids too. Popo called it "Pretty School." It was only half a day, thank goodness. It was hard enough to be away from him for four hours, but I did get a lot done at home at that time and the time away provided Kyle a healthy social life and a sense of normalcy. As much as I loved being with my son, I knew that at some point I was going to have to let him grow up.

The morning of his first photo at the beginning of preschool, he woke up with his precious little face numb and drooping on one side. I did not know what it was. I worried something was severely wrong. He said he was not hurting. I checked and he was not running a fever, but I called the doctor anyway. I thought it was better to be safe than sorry and check all my boxes. They told me that it sounded like Bell's Palsy. It was not an emergency, but I needed to get him in to see the doctor. They told me to let him go to school and bring him in afterwards. This gave me a sense of relief. At least it was not an emergency and was not contagious.

He had his pictures taken, wearing a big smile on his face, even with Bell's Palsy. What a happy boy he was. I got him to the doctor right after school and they said it was nothing to be alarmed about and it would go away within two days, which it did. Still, this was not a wonderful way to remember your son's first day of school. It gave a great start to an already memorable day.

I was already nervous and took extra care to make sure Kyle looked nice for his first school photos with his cousins which was during the Christmas season. He looked oh so handsome in his little suit and tie. On the way to school, Kyle asked me if we could go to McDonald's and play. I told him we would get the girls and go after school. He threw a small debate in the car, screaming and kicking the seat in front of him. I was somewhat perplexed because my little guy never threw tantrums, but he had a sudden burst of energy and needed to get it out in the ball pit. This was not what I needed at the moment, but it seemed the day was ruled by Murphy's Law.

I tried to assure him that we would be late for school and Popo, and the girls were waiting. I tried not to giggle in front of him because he was just as precious as he could be. I knew I had to be serious. He continued his little huff, and I gave in and took him to play in the ball pit at McDonald's for fifteen minutes. I timed it exactly right and he was completely satisfied. After that he jumped out of the pit, straightened his suit and off we went. We arrived at school just before the photographer was leaving and Kyle had his pictures taken by himself and with his cousins who were dressed in their beautiful red velvet Christmas dresses that Momo and Popo had gotten them.

There was a boy in one of the classes who was overly aggressive. Kyle had never seen this before, so he was scared to be around him. This boy would pretend to have a toy gun and shoot the others during recess. Kyle asked me one day what the boy was doing, pointing his finger at the other kids. I told him just to stay away from him and play with someone else. Other parents were complaining that the boy should not be able to play toy guns. His dad saw it at recess one day and laughed about it urging his son to continue to the point that he always had to sit in time out.

The child was clearly not being disciplined by his father properly. Playing with toy guns was not a big deal when I was a child but now society tends to think it will lead children to play with the real thing when they get older. School administration makes it a big deal and for good reasons as far as I am concerned. Kyle had seen his cousins bicker back and forth on occasion, but this was his first experience with an aggressive child.

With Kyle now at school on a regular basis, I truly tried to cherish the one-on-one time we had. Some mornings before school started, we would go into the courtyard at the church where he attended school and walk, just the two of us. Kyle would pick dandelions until he had a whole bouquet to give to me, his mommy. I would take them home and try to savor them in some water for a day or two displaying them proudly because Poo Doo had picked them just for me. It was a sweet thing that he had done that would make me think of him throughout the day.

On one sunny afternoon, I went to pick Kyle up from preschool and we planned to get the girls and go to the park and play. I entered his classroom quietly so I could watch him interacting with the other children. I wanted to see how he was doing without him knowing I was there. Sometimes children act differently when they know their parents are around. As I watched him from a few feet away, he was just as kind and caring to the other children as he was when I was near. Always sharing and talking.

I slowly approached him while he was playing at the bean table. He was so proud to introduce me to his new friend, a girl he was sharing the table with. When I asked him if he was ready to go home, he looked up at me and I saw pale red dripping from his nose. His nose had a small lump on the side of his right nostril.

Poo Doo said, "Mommy, is this my bone?"

I at once thought someone had punched him in the nose and it was broken. I frantically called out to the teacher, who came and told me no one had been mean to Kyle and assured me all the kids respected him. She looked at it a bit closer and realized my precious baby boy had stuck a bean up his nose. As the teacher tried to calm me down, realizing it was in fact, a bean, I tried not to alarm Kyle and asked him to blow as hard as he could. The teacher called the pastor and since I was in dismay mode, they took Kyle downstairs, told me to stay put and they would be right back. For about ten minutes they tried desperately to get Kyle to blow out the bean and finally succeeded.

We took it home as a memento and carefully wrapped it up, knowing it would hold a special place among our keepsakes. I imagined looking back on it someday, laughing with Kyle and sharing the funny memory it represented. I still have the bean packed away with other precious treasures, such as the first lock of his hair, his first tooth, and other cherished mementos from his early years.

The classroom leader later asked me to help in the classroom. This was exactly what I wanted. I would read to the children and help with their snacks and then lay them down for their mid-morning naps. Kyle did not like that I would pamper the other kids to get them to sleep. He wanted all the attention on him, and I had a hard time trying to get him to understand that even though mommy was there, he still needed to listen to his teacher and lie down with the other children just for a while, so I would lie down with him and rub his back until he fell asleep. Honestly, I do not think he ever really fell asleep too long. He had too much energy and was always wanting to play or just be with me.

Looking back at Kyle's early days in preschool, I am struck by how these formative experiences, filled with both challenges and joy, shaped our journey together. Each moment from the unexpected health scare to the simple pleasure of dandelion bouquets is a reminder of the delicacy between protecting my son and allowing him to navigate his own path. Watching Kyle grow, confront new situations, and thrive despite minor setbacks were tests of his independence which he passed with flying colors.

MOTHER'S REFLECTION:
Finding Comfort in Brief Moments

In these early years, every small victory and every new experience held significant weight. It was a time of transition, not just for Kyle, but for me as well. It was about finding comfort in uncertainty, celebrating, and cherishing the unique, often fleeting moments of our daily life.

23

BIG BOY SCHOOL

AFTER FOUR YEARS OF living in an old, cramped house, we had finally moved into our newly built home, a place that felt like a fresh start in every way. I was thrilled knowing Kyle would finally have the space to run freely, play, and grow without limitations. The house was bright, open, and full of possibilities, and I imagined him filling it with laughter, racing through the halls, and inviting friends over to share in his adventures. It was more than just a house; it was the beginning of a new chapter for our family, one where Kyle could thrive in ways that had not been possible before.

I dreaded Kyle's first year of kindergarten, which his Popo called "big boy school." The days were much longer than preschool, and I was already struggling with that. Momo and Popo went with us to take Kyle to his classroom on the first day. He was so excited to make new friends. To him this just seemed like just another thing compared to what it meant to us parents. My baby is growing up! Another milestone. We captured it all on video, of course.

I remember watching him walk down the hall to his class with Momo and Popo. They were such proud grandparents. My husband's parents were not there. Their absence felt like a slap in the face to my husband, Kyle's dad. I made sure to give my in-laws school photos of Kyle every year and he even made them gifts, yet not one single gift or photo was ever displayed in their home.

One day, I mustered the courage to ask my mother-in-law, "Why do not you display Kyle's photos or gifts?" She paused, her face blank, as if she did not understand the question. After a moment, she shrugged and changed the subject, leaving me standing there, holding an empty picture frame like it was something foreign and unwanted.

They just were not proud grandparents or parents. It was difficult for me as Kyle's mom not to see them excited and proud of their only grandchild.

I never even saw a childhood photo of my husband throughout our years together until a month before he abandoned us. He brought home a Ziploc bag of maybe five photos he found in his mom's basement to show Kyle and me. I felt so bad for him again but did not say a word other than to thank him for finally sharing them with us after all this time.

On Kyle's first day of kindergarten, the classroom was overcrowded with proud dads and grandparents, and moms trying to hold back the tears from thoughts of what it would be like not having their baby around them all day and I am sure, tears of happiness for their child.

Yes, my heart hurt. I was one of those trying to hold back the tears, but I was able to do it and not let my son see I was aching inside. I wanted him to be excited to meet new friends and have fun learning. I did not want him to worry about me. Like a lot of moms, I did not know what to do with myself all day. I could only clean and organize so much. Planning and preparing dinner did not take much time. I would sit and watch the clock and idle away my time until I could get my boy. When the time came, I rushed up to the school and stood in a large group of moms and dads anxiously waiting for the bell to ring and the doors to open. The joy I had when I saw my son come out the front door of the school. He would always run and jump into my arms, and I would pick him up and hug him so tight.

This was an everyday occurrence for many years, and I loved it until he got too heavy for me to pick up. Then I would bend down to hug him until he got taller, then it was eye-to-eye hugging without me reaching down or him reaching up. We were huggers. That is what we did. Unfortunately, I never once saw my husband hug his son. Not once. To me, it was like he just did not know how. It was not his fault. It felt like he grew up in an environment where emotional expression was not encouraged. *What happens when someone grows up without being shown how to love, can they still learn to offer it freely?*

As the first month or two went by, I got lonelier and lonelier at home while my son was at school, and my husband was at work. I would visit with my mom and dad almost daily for lunch and go shopping with mom on occasion.

One morning when I took him to school, I walked him in as usual and eventually would allow him to walk down the hall by himself as I watched closely from behind, instead of walking him all the way to the classroom making sure that he made it in the right room and was greeted by the teacher. Nothing about this morning seemed out of the ordinary, but Kyle began acting differently.

He gave me a kiss and hug and slowly walked down the hall but then stopped, turned, and ran as fast as he could, yelling "Mommy, mommy!" I was walking out the door but quickly turned to see him. He jumped into my arms and hugged me tightly. He wrapped his arms around my neck and squeezed it so that I could not loosen his grip. He was crying uncontrollably. Kyle's legs were wrapped tightly around my waist. He was not about to let go. He said "Mommy, I want to stay with you, please Mommy!"

I at once thought there must have been a bully in the class that was picking on him, or his teacher was being mean. I held him so tight as he sobbed and told him that he could not go home with me. He had to stay and have fun with his friends, and I would pick him up soon. I know a lot of moms will tell you the same, that it was so hard not to take him home.

The school counselor heard us in the hallway from the office and came out. She said that we could go into her office and talk with her so we did not upset anyone that might see us in the hall. I carried Kyle into her office. We sat down and I asked him if anyone at all was being mean to him, and he told me "No" right away. He said that he just wanted to be with me. He was homesick and loved his mommy so much and chose to be with me instead of his friends. The counselor told me that I simply could not stay all day with him, and I needed to leave, and she would talk with Kyle, and he would be fine.

In a way, he warmed my heart to hear that my son loved me so much. However, I understood what the counselor was saying. My son needed to grow and learn both academically and socially. If he were always with me, that would not happen the way it needed to. It was so difficult for me to walk away from him that morning. I gave Kyle a hug and kiss as he dried his eyes and promised him, I would be back to pick him up soon. I made it to the front door. My feet felt like they were sinking into the floor, rooting me in place. My hands shaking, my heart begging me to turn around and scoop him up. But I clenched my fists before going to my car and sat in the parking lot for a few minutes crying and trying to pull myself together, resisting the urge to rush back to school and get Poo Doo and take him home. I sat and prayed through it. Praying to God to protect my son and to ease his mind.

I do not know what the counselor said to him but when I picked him up that afternoon, he was different, smiling and as happy as he could be. He said he had a wonderful day; I had worried all day long about him for no reason. He was just fine.

One day Kyle came home and told me about "opposite day" they had at school and how much fun it was. We decided to have opposite days at home. I was all about making things fun for Kyle as long as they were healthy and safe. He would wear his clothes backward and walk backward and try to talk backward. We would have breakfast for dinner and dinner for breakfast.

He would just laugh at himself and me as well. The joy Kyle and I shared seemed to stir something in his dad, perhaps envy, perhaps discomfort, I cannot say for sure. He rarely joined in, and that refusal was heartbreaking. *How could someone stand outside the laughter of their own child and not feel drawn in?* It was as if fun had never been part of his own childhood.

I decided to start volunteering at his school. I needed to be able to make sure he was okay and happy. That he was safe. Plus, it gave me something to do between the hours of house preparations and waiting. I am sure he would have told me if something was wrong and, indeed, he did in his later years. I think I had a harder time being away from him than he did me. I would be so lonely during the day from missing Kyle and worrying about him and I would call my husband to console me but never once did.

Was my son having fun? Was he paying any attention to the teacher? Was he making new friends? Was everyone as nice to him as he was to them? The highlight of my day was dinner time when I had my two favorite men all to myself and we could share the day's news with each other, as all our stories were different.

The emotional rollercoaster Kyle's first year represented was a significant transition not only for Kyle but for me as well. Watching him step into a longer school day and new social experiences was a reminder of the bittersweet nature of watching my little man grow.

The difference in my parents' enthusiasm and my in-laws' detachment and the way they showed love and support was odd to me. While my parents celebrated every milestone with pride, my in-laws' indifference was a painful reminder of how our family dynamics affected Kyle's sense of value.

The day Kyle ran back to me was gut-wrenching and revealing, as he clung to me. It was a touching moment that his struggle with change mirrored my own difficulty in letting go. The counselor's advice to allow Kyle to adjust independently was a hard but necessary lesson for me in trusting his growth.

Volunteering at his school was, in a sense, my anchor for adjusting, yet it gave me a way to stay involved and ensure he was happy and safe. It also provided me with a sense of purpose during the day.

MOTHER'S REFLECTION:
Growing Up, One Hug at a Time

This time was as much about Kyle's development as it was about my own journey in learning to let go and adapt. (Although a good mama will never fully let go.) The end-of-day reunions, with our shared stories and hugs, became a cherished reminder of our bond and the joy we found in each other.

24

THREE PEAS

KYLE SEEMED UNSETTLED WHEN his cousins would fight, which happened all the time when they were toddlers. This lessened throughout the years. It scared him. He was always running to me and asking me why they were always screaming at each other, and I told him sometimes that is what siblings do. They love each other but are learning each other's boundaries. When they were at our house and started to fight, he would ask me to take them home because he did not want to play anymore. Most times, when they left, he would want them to come back over. I would have to say, "Maybe tomorrow, Bubber," then we would play a game to lift his spirits. He would soon forget about them coming back over until the next day came.

I was the bad Aunt Dee Dee when I had to take them home yet did everything in my power to make them happy and allow them to spend as much time with Kyle as possible. We would make tents out of blankets and chairs in the living room. I did crafts with them and taught them things no one else could. We had many adventures that left us all smiling and laughing.

I vividly remember one day, when they were noticeably young, five and six, I let them put makeup on me and curlers in my hair, and we all went to Walmart as I pranced up and down the aisles with them proudly displaying their artwork while they just giggled and giggled, dancing all around. We all had a blast together on that day filled with laughter.

I cherished every moment spent with them, determined to create happy memories and to make sure they felt loved and included in Kyle's life. For a long time, Kyle and his cousins were like a close-knit trio, with Kyle and both girls being inseparable.

Their companionship was one of his greatest joys and one of the things of which he was most proud. I wanted, as much as Kyle did, for them to be that close forever.

However, as time passed, and the Three Peas got much older, the dynamics began to shift. The older cousin grew distant, which deeply hurt Kyle. Though he was an older teenager, he felt her new life filled with love and new responsibilities had led her to exclude him. He believed that he no longer fit into her world and felt shunned, especially after she started having kids. She did not invite him around as much, which was extremely painful for him, especially since they had been so close when they were young. Kyle's sense of rejection was profound, as he missed time with his new second cousins and felt increasingly isolated.

When he confided in me, at this point, it felt heartbreaking to see him hurt that way, especially by someone he loved so much. I understood she had children of her own and they took priority, but I also felt it was almost as if she thought he was not good enough to be a part of her circle any longer.

I understood the relationship with his cousins and how that bond affected Kyle's sense of belonging. Their close-knit connection, filled with happiness and many adventures together, showed both the beauty of growing up amidst the challenges. His cousins had a deep impact on his identity, as he thought of them as the siblings he had always wanted.

Despite the heartache, Kyle continued to spend time with his younger cousin, though this connection too eventually ended abruptly after some heavy words were said to him that left my son beyond devastated. The loss of Kyle was particularly challenging for her as well, and it deeply troubles me daily to see her struggle with the absence of her cousin Kyle. My role now, as the "bad" Aunt Dee Dee is to comfort and support, and pray daily, and to remind them both that Kyle is at peace, and to keep the memory of their special bond alive.

MOTHER'S REFLECTION:
What Peas Can Teach Us

Kyle, his cousins, and I shared so many adventures. But the bond they built was more than play, it was family tie, safety, and connection. Even when it frayed, the love remained.

Now, I carry the memories. I remind them of the joy. And I trust that Kyle's peace can still echo in theirs.

25

ICE CREAM AFTER THE GAME

THROUGHOUT HIS MANY YEARS, Kyle was a regularly active little boy. Kyle was a kid with boundless energy that could never be spent. I knew very quickly that sports were going to have to be in the cards. Otherwise, I would be the one out of energy, not Kyle. His first experience with sports was Itsy Bitsy Basketball at age three. This was his first experience with a group of boys. He was extremely nervous and shy but got out there and made friends quickly (as I thought he would). Watching him run up and down the court trying to dribble was such a thrill for me. The coach was wonderful. He loved those boys and praised them often.

During games, all the parents sat on the floor to be at ground level like our boys. In one game, Kyle was doing great and then accidentally collided with another boy while trying to get the basketball. He fell. Kyle was not hurt but embarrassed and at once ran to me, and as I swept him up into my arms and cuddled him, he shed a few tears and hid his precious little face in my chest.

I kissed him and held him to calm him down a bit. I told him, "Mommy is so proud of her little man. You are doing a wonderful job, Kyle. Are you hurt?"

"No Mommy," he responded, still nuzzling my neck so he thought no one could see him.

"Me and Daddy are having so much fun watching you have fun with your new friends. Are you ready to go back out there and finish the game?"

"Yes."

"Ok Poo Doo, go have fun, remember Mommy loves you." As he got up from my arms and walked back onto the court all the parents and kids clapped for him for being so brave, strong, and getting back out there to finish what he started. I was so proud of him. We stopped at Dairy Queen after the game even though it was frigid cold out. He put in a heroic effort for such a little guy so if ice cream was going to make him smile, then ice cream it was!

Momo (my mom) paid for all three of her grandbabies to do gymnastics. They were the three musketeers for many years and had so much fun together mastering their skills in tumbling. I would take them to gymnastics class on Saturday morning. I wanted my son to be the best that he could be at everything he pursued so he could experience the joy that came with it. I hoped that one day he would discover his true passion, something with which he could absolutely excel.

How do we know if our true calling is to be a lifeguard or a circus clown or a professional trick rider or anything else unless we take an interest in it and try to do our absolute best? That is how I see it anyway.

We got him started in tee-ball, like most parents. He loved it. I had the honor of being one of his coaches for a couple of years. What fun we had watching Kyle learning to hit the ball and run the bases. He was as precious as he could be. The laughter and smiles from my son made every heartache I endured was well worth it.

He played baseball for several years after that, moving on to coach pitch and machine pitch. I continued coaching until I finally decided to watch from the bench with the other moms, making sure the boys were well hydrated and had snacks readily available after a hard workout. Again, Kyle was a natural at most everything he did.

Although he played soccer for a multitude of seasons, his heart was always in baseball. Like many young boys, he dreamed of becoming a professional baseball player. I encouraged him to keep playing and practicing every chance he got. I would take him to the batting cages as much as we had time for when we could not get to the field to practice. Sometimes spending thirty minutes, other times spending countless hours hitting ball after ball, trying to get his stance and swing exactly right.

When it came to Kyle playing sports, he excelled at all he tried, although he did not like the competition. He loved the activity and energy of it all and the comradery of playing with others but despised having to compete and deal with other kids' adamant about the game, mostly because some parents were out of control competitors themselves and grooming their children to be the same.

To most guys, sports are a way to prove their manhood or toughness, but Kyle had a distinct perspective. He simply wanted to have fun without the pressure of competition or the roughness of other boys.

Although Kyle carried a guarded spirit, his gentle heart kept nudging him toward connection. He hated conflict which is why he never pursued athletics past the point of him having fun then he moved on to something else.

MOTHER'S REFLECTION:
Play Was Never About Winning

Watching Kyle steer through his early sports experiences was heartwarming. His boundless energy and enthusiasm for activities like Itsy Bitsy Basketball, gymnastics, and tee-ball highlighted his zest for life and curiosity. It was clear from an early age that sports provided him not just with a physical outlet but also a way to connect with others and explore his capabilities.

26

POPO'S PASSING

KYLE WAS HALFWAY THROUGH his kindergarten year. I picked him up from school and he wanted to play with his cousins, so we drove to their school and brought them back to the house. It was a beautiful, warm day, and I thought they could go into the back yard and jump on the trampoline.

As my sister-in-law and my nephew were bringing the kids food from McDonald's for dinner, I was sitting on the couch in the living room. I got a call from my mom. She said, "Something has happened to Dad!" My world stopped. I must have looked as if something terrible had happened because my sister-in-law at once looked at me and said, "What is it?"

I answered, "Mom said that dad had a heart attack. He fell and hit his head."

I was to get to the hospital right away. Kyle's aunt took the kids back to her house, and I flew to the hospital, about twenty minutes away.

I never thought this would happen, looking back on my day with him. Dad loved to spend time with his grandson. My parents lived for their grandbabies.

He had told Kyle that morning that when he got home from school, he would take him and his cousins down to the pond near our house to go fishing. Popo was Kyle's fishing buddy.

My dad had picked Kyle and me up that morning and dropped Kyle off at school, as he did on occasion. I went over to my parents' house later to eat lunch with them. My dad had not felt well the past few weeks. He had a quintuple bypass many years earlier that left his legs in so much pain daily. He was having a challenging time breathing as the years went on due to congestive heart failure. But this day was different.

I asked him that afternoon how he was feeling. He looked at me so bright eyed and said, "You know, Dee Dee, I feel fair to midland, I think I'm gonna go out to the lake for a while and shoot shit with the fellers and after Kyle gets home from school, we will go fishing."

I got the biggest smile on my face knowing my dad felt so much better than he had in a long time. I told him I loved him and as he got up to leave, he gave me a hug. I stayed with Mom for a bit longer to help clean then went home to do some laundry before Kyle got out of school. I never in my wildest dreams thought that would be the last time I would ever hug my dad again and hear him tell me that he loved me. He never made it out of the hospital.

I drove out to the Longview Lake Marina a couple of weeks after he passed, to try and get closer somehow. I wanted to know exactly what happened. If there was any place to talk to God about my dad, it would be at Longview Lake.

Kyle did not get the opportunity to see his Popo before he left this world. My dad's passing affected him greatly. Kyle and his Popo were best buds and shared an incredibly special bond—a bond he desperately wanted with his dad as well. Unfortunately, neither his dad nor his paternal grandpa was able to match.

The evening my dad passed away, I left the hospital and had to go home and tell my little boy that his Popo went to live with Jesus. He asked me when he would be back so they could go fishing.

Trying to hold back the tears, I expressed to Kyle that his Popo would not be back. But he would see him again in Heaven one day. I told him, "I know it will not be the same, but Mommy will take you fishing as much as you want to go and then one day you will be able to fish with Popo again."

I did in fact, take my son fishing along with his cousins and many friends, throughout the years. I baited the hooks, and learned the fish loved cheesy hotdogs better than worms or stink bait (thank goodness). Now my son can go fishing anytime he wants with his Momo and Popo by his side.

This is the deep bond between Kyle and his Popo, a relationship of endless love and shared experiences. Popo's loss left Kyle grappling with the permanence of death, as he asked when his Popo would return. As a mom, trying to explain the loss required a delicate honesty and instilling hope in my son in the belief of a reunion in heaven with his Popo.

The promise to take Kyle fishing, as his Popo often did, honored that beautiful bond. I knew that taking Kyle fishing could somehow keep his connection and a memory with his Popo alive. I believe it helped my Kyle grieve in a healthy way and heal as much as he could.

MOTHER'S REFLECTION:
The Bond That Never Breaks

Kyle could feel Popo's presence as he shared this with me. What an incredible reminder of a bond like theirs; the love and special moments they had together will endure, transcending even death.

27

KYLE'S FAITH

I KNEW IN SOME ASPECT Kyle would struggle with the concept of death. After all he was only six when his Popo passed away. Not only was he grieving for the first time, but he was going through his first experience with death. The idea of something or someone no longer in your life was completely foreign to him.

However, I made sure that my son knew who God was from an early age. That way when he experienced something like this, he could have hope that he would see them again.

I used to tell Kyle that I never wanted him to love mommy and daddy more than he loved God because God was the reason he was here in the first place. I wanted him to stay committed to God and to thank him every day for his life and his toys and food and home. We would say our prayers every night before bed and thank God for loving us and keeping us safe and the other people that we loved.

I was never an overly religious mother; in fact, I loathe being called religious by people who do not really know me, and who or what I truly stand for. I am more spiritual than anything.

Kyle and I read our devotionals every night. We also started reading the Bible together when he was young, although we did not get through the entirety together, I know that he continued to read it on his own. Instead, we would pick out verses and discuss their meaning.

I wanted to ensure he never forgot where he came from and to whom he truly belonged.

From his baby years, we all went to church. When we lived in Smithville, we started out at the Emmanuel Open Door Bible Church. After moving to Grandview, we went to Raymore Baptist Church.

I tried to raise him in the church early on. Even though I went to church from an early age as well, I was a newly saved Christian and full of passion for Christ. We would read the Bible together and went to Sunday School every week. I made sure that Kyle received a new Bible every Easter with a devotional at Christmas.

I wanted my son to be a God-fearing man, and he was. Sure, not every moment of his life was perfect. No Christian's is, and the devil gave him some exceptionally large stumbling blocks to hurdle. We all want to challenge God's authority from time to time. Still despite everything that he endured, he showed his love for God in many principles throughout his life, even throughout the substance stage, which held on to him so tightly. I had the utmost faith and hope that he would overcome it one day soon and become a greater man with Almighty God's hands upon him along with Mama's.

I seemed to be the only one who had kept the faith and hoped that my son would one day redeem himself. I made sure my son was covered. He never forgot his faith; I was a proud Mama throughout. The need Kyle felt to please the people surrounding him in their contaminating behavior did not lessen his love for his Heavenly Father. He was just being pulled in so many directions by fake believers and users, it was hard for him to stay focused on the plans that God had for just him.

I did not want to force any specific denomination on my son because, frankly, God does not care what church we go to and religious, man-made rituals are not important as long as we believe and choose to follow Him and abide by Him. But I wanted to set the foundation for my son to one day discover his own spirituality.

When Kyle was four years old, he joined Awana and attended for several years. Kyle was excited to learn scripture and hear stories from the Bible along with a special craft or game each week.

The first church he started at was great and he had lots of fun and made many friends but when the Awana director became a bit too controlling, he did not want to go any longer and I do not blame him. I sure was not going to make him stay. The man teaching took the fun out of learning about God, and he was getting hurt while doing indoor activities with limited space that were meant for outdoors and he was scared to go back. Getting hurt at church is a little bit contradictory, do not you think?

The activity was supposed to be filled with support and community, but it seemed a bit inconsistent to the church's beliefs when Kyle would get hurt. So, I got him to join an Awana program at another church with his cousins. He enjoyed having fun and learning with them until they reached fifth grade.

My son did, indeed, love God and would attend church with us until he got older, but when daddy decided to stop, so did he. He did not forget God but just put him on the back burner for a while to explore other things, but he never once failed to remember to whom he belonged. He soon relied on his faith when the unspeakable happened.

I discussed with Kyle, in his tween years, about sealing his faith at some point but it was entirely his decision. He decided to take confirmation classes together with one of his church and school friends.

My beloved, God-loving son, was confirmed and baptized at the United Methodist Church in Raymore, Missouri in the presence of his dad, Momo, cousins, uncle, and aunt, and one very honored mom.

When I reflect on my journey of nurturing Kyle's faith from a youthful age, especially following the loss of his Popo, my goal always was to instill hope by introducing him to God early on and teaching him the importance of spirituality over unyielding religious practices. Our nightly prayers, Bible readings, and church attendance were foundational moments that shaped his understanding of faith.

As Kyle endured the challenges of childhood and adolescence, including peer pressure and shifting interests, I stayed hopeful that the values I instilled would guide him. Even when he distanced himself from church for a period, his faith remained in the background, a steady presence in his life.

Ultimately, seeing his confirmation and baptism was a proud moment for me, affirming that despite the difficulties, Kyle's love for God endured.

MOTHER'S REFLECTION:
Faith is Freedom, Not Force

My wish is that this chapter might show a balance of guiding every child in faith while allowing them the freedom to explore their own spiritual journey. Abusing a child to submit to rhetorical and rigid religion is sickening and nowhere near what Almighty God is asking any person to practice.

28

CINNAMON TOAST

KYLE WAS AROUND SIX when he wandered into the kitchen one afternoon wanting an after-school snack. His small voice broke the silence. "Mommy, I'm hungry."

I smiled as I turned to him. "What would you like, Poo Doo?"

He thought for a second then said, "Can I have a piece of cinnamon toast?"

"Of course you can," I said, pulling out a slice of bread. I toasted it, buttered it lightly, and sprinkled cinnamon on top, just the way I always made it. But when I handed it to him, his little face fell.

"Mommy, you know I do not like butter," he said, sounding disappointed.

I knelt beside him, holding the plate in my hands. "I do know that. I'm sorry Bubber, I didn't forget. Mommy will eat this one. Let's do an experiment. Mommy will show you why we use just a little butter."

I picked Kyle up and sat him on the kitchen counter beside me, his small feet dangling. Kyle knew he was not allowed to touch the toaster or any electrical appliance, so he watched and waited quietly but curious as I toasted two pieces of bread. When they were ready, I handed him a butter knife, letting him spread a thin layer of butter on one slice while leaving the other dry.

"We do this so the cinnamon sticks instead of falling off," I explained. We sprinkled cinnamon on both slices,and I had him take a bite of each one.

As Kyle bit into the dry toast first, cinnamon sugar scattered onto his shirt and the counter. He frowned, brushing at the mess. Then he took a bite of the buttered toast, and this time, everything stayed in place.

Understanding, his face lit up. "Oh!" he said, nodding slowly. "Okay, Mommy. I'll try it."

I told him this was why we need just a bit of butter, and the toast tasted better with cinnamon on it. Just as we were almost finished with our little experiment, his dad burst into the kitchen from his office, visibly, in a dark and unpredictable mood. He took one look at Kyle, then shouted at Kyle, "Why can't you understand this? I've never seen someone so upset over a piece of toast!"

Kyle flinched. He got scared and moved closer toward me as I tried to shield him from his dad's sudden wrath. I reacted instantly. I wrapped my arms around him, holding him close. Then, keeping my voice calm but firm, I quietly told my husband, "Please be quiet and leave the kitchen now."

His presence, his outbursts, his frustration, always seemed unsettled by the world around him. At times, even everyday moments, noises, happiness, love, even his own son's innocent curiosity, seemed to trigger Kyle's dad. What he said about the toast and the way he said it was so wrong, and he had no right saying anything at all unless it was encouraging. But this moment was not his to ruin. I told Kyle to ignore Daddy so we could finish what we started.

MOTHER'S REFLECTION:
Some Moments Are Ours to Protect

Kyle wiped the tears from his eyes and took another bite of his sweet cinnamon toast. I knew, in that moment, he was safe. Kyle should not have to walk on eggshells around his dad for fear of another unstable outburst but as you will read further, it happened more as the years progressed, and Kyle grew.

29

MENAGERIE OF PETS

We ALWAYS HAD LOTS of animals and Kyle was taught to be kind and gentle with each one of them. His first pet was a little gold fishy, of course. That is most kids' first pet. Then he moved up to another fish, the Loner fish, or a Betta fish they are officially called, I believe. They eventually passed on.

I always had cats and dogs in my life. When Kyle was born, I did have three cats who he loved. He wanted his own kitty. So, Popo's neighbors' cat had kittens. Kyle got to pick two of them out and named them Dancer and Prancer. Dancer stayed with us until he passed seventeen years later. Poor Prancer did not make the cut. Prancer, as his name suggests, was too active for his own good, and as much as I believed he would be fine and outgrow it, that sadly never happened. Kyle did not understand why he kept scratching him and did not want him in the house. Although I never believed in giving an animal away once I had them, as they are family members and we need to cherish them like we do our own children, I also did not want Kyle accidentally to get hurt by one of them. We did give him back a couple of weeks later so he could find a loving home soon enough, so I did not get too attached to him.

Kyle decided he wanted a dog. A Golden Retriever. After seeing a Disney movie, he fell in love. I told him to ask Santa for one. Santa (with Momo and Popo's help) did oblige, as usual, Kyle's request. Kyle named him Golden. Golden was such a joy, but like all puppies, he was rambunctious and undisciplined. He jumped on Poo Doo so much and wanted to play. Kyle would laugh at first and loved Golden's kisses and then he began to cry because Golden was scratching and hurting him. He did not know how to control this puppy, and neither did we. Kyle and I decided to get Golden into a puppy training class.

We took Golden to Man's Best Friend training course a couple of times a week. Kyle was told that he was the owner, and he would oversee training Golden. It would be his job to teach Golden to obey certain commands. It was exceedingly difficult for such a young boy, less than six, to do this so I would help. Wow, it was so difficult to train a dog. We spent countless hours with Golden working with him on each command. Kyle got tired of it and could not understand why the puppy was not learning fast enough. For him, learning did not require repetitive training that a dog did. So, he got frustrated easily and often felt his patience grow thin.

Golden was expensive to train, and we could not afford it. He was still jumping on Kyle. He got too heavy and would hurt Kyle unintentionally. His dad did not want to help with the dog, and eventually, our financial stability began to unravel *again*, patterns of unpredictable behavior from his father made it difficult to maintain consistency, and the strain began to show, so we opted to give Golden to a beautiful family that had two Golden Retrievers already. This man knew how to train them properly and we knew he would love Golden forever. On occasion throughout the years, he would let Kyle and me visit. They lived near a thirty-acre dog park in Olathe, Kansas, and Golden could roam as much as he wanted to with his new brothers. We would meet them at the park sometimes and Kyle would run and play ball with them. Golden was happy and that is all that mattered.

After we moved again to a newly built home in Raymore, Kyle decided he wanted to try a guinea pig. The store associate told us they do better in pairs. He was an incredibly good salesperson, so we got two. I soon found out these pets also turned out to be expensive. They required a huge cage with toys, and the cost of bedding, which had to be changed frequently, and the food got overwhelming. One morning I woke up to find one had passed away. He was very well taken care of. I knew we had to bury him, and Kyle wanted to have a funeral for him, so we buried him in the backyard and said a prayer for him.

Kyle was sad and said Blackie (the surviving guinea pig) needed a friend, so we got another one. Every time I passed down the hall, I would start itching and my eyes would water like I was knee deep in onions. I never thought anything about it at first. The more I would go to the office where the guinea pigs were kept, to check on them, the more my eyes would burn severely and swell up. Next thing I know they both passed away one at a time. This was devastating to both Kyle and me.

However, I did put two and two together and realized that even though I had never been allergic to anything in my life, I was very allergic to any guinea pig, and they were deathly allergic to me. It was then I had to tell Kyle that we just could not do that to the precious guinea pigs anymore. He was sad at first because they were so much fun to play with, but he understood and moved on.

We then moved on to the next pet, and this one made me nervous. Green tree frogs, YES, we must have! We bought an aquarium, many accessories, and two itty bitty green tree frogs which were no bigger than a minute. Why in the world would I sink so much money into two miniature frogs that just sat there all day on a tree limb? Kyle took them out occasionally, but they were so tiny, no bigger than my thumb nail. They were bound to be gobbled up by some very hungry cats or stepped on if he did not contain them and kept his door closed while they were out of the cage.

We needed to buy live gut-loaded crickets for them once a week for their food. It was going great until the pet store ran out of crickets and did not get their stock that week. They needed to be fed. Kyle's dad decided he was going to teach Kyle how to catch crickets. NO! NO! While well-intentioned, I thought this was a bad idea.

The frogs had to have "special" crickets. They must be specially treated, gut-loaded crickets with calcium supplements! OMG! He took Kyle outside, and they hunted for crickets. Not too many, just enough to fill up the frogs until the pet store could get stock in.

It was a Saturday morning when I woke Kyle up and wanted him to go outside and play because it was such a lovely day. He had a friend over, and we all hung outside riding bikes. I decided to take the frog cage outside to clean it because it was the perfect day to do it. I carried the cage outside and went to transfer the frogs into a separate critter cage temporarily but could not find them anywhere. I started to panic. They were bright green, lime, and they usually stood out. After removing everything in the cage I noticed they were not hopping around. I saw one sitting as still as could be on a limb and the other one in the sand just as still as could be but there was something different.

Their bright green color was a dark dingy brown and when I touched them, they did not move a muscle. This did not look good. They had passed away overnight, I guess. The crickets that dad had caught and fed them were the cause of their death. I told him NOT to do it because wild insects can carry disease and parasites opposed to the gut-loaded crickets with protein and calcium added. I apparently knew nothing, so I was ignored as usual. I, of course, had to break the sad news to Kyle and dad was nowhere around.

I was frustrated at the whole situation. I was the one who told my husband the repercussions of this plan, and he ignored me. Yet, I was the one who was going to have to take blame (nothing new) for his bad decision. While yes, his intentions may have come from the best place, they came at a large cost.

Kyle loved lizards. After seeing some at the pet store, he asked for one for his birthday. Kyle was such a good boy. He was always so wonderful and helpful and loving to me. Of course, he was going to get a lizard. He got Buddy, our incredibly special leopard gecko, for his birthday. He was nine or ten at the time. We had the leftover small frog aquarium that was perfect for a baby lizard.

For Christmas, Mrs. Clause got him an even bigger aquarium for Buddy, as he was growing. I still have Buddy, the lizard, one of the many cherished items I have left of my son. I have to say, Buddy is a good pet and nice company to have. He only required a few dollars a month to support. However, he is getting old now, over sixteen years old, and does not move around much anymore. I recently discovered that Buddy loves tropical Dubia roaches, which apparently contain much more vitamins and protein than crickets. I wish I had known this sooner. I promised Kyle that when he finally got settled into a place of his own and stopped moving around, he could take Buddy. Animals need stability just like children do.

I recently had a scare with Buddy which required an emergency trip to the exotic veterinary nearby. The cat next door ran in my house when I opened the door to go out and went straight for Buddy's cage, jumped on top and bent the screen. When I heard the commotion, I ran inside and got the cat quickly out of the house and looked to see if Buddy was all right. He was nowhere to be found. I frantically searched his cage, thinking that the cat had gotten to him. But I realized there would have been some remnants left behind if that had happened.

As I bent down to pick Buddy's water bottle up off the floor, there he was. White as a sheet. He at once shed his skin and was cold to the touch. I picked him up and wrapped him in a warm towel and laid him gently in his cage. As I started to cry, thinking I had almost lost the pet Kyle was counting on me to take care of, I was apologizing to my son above, promising I would not allow anything else to happen to Buddy.

I am not sure how he had gotten out of the cage in the first place as he had no signs of trauma from the cat. But it was a long drop from the top of the dresser to the floor, so I am not even sure how he managed to survive the fall with no fractures. His tail did end up falling off, which I found out is a normal thing that lizards can do from fear and autonomy. They can actually lose their tail very quickly if a predator grabs it and they can make their quick getaway. Buddy's tail quickly grew back, and he is as good as new.

He had not eaten for days. I started to panic because he always devoured the waxworms and mealworms, I gave him as a snack several times a week and then stopped. I had to take him to the vet as soon as possible. I could not allow my son's lizard to pass away too. After blood work and many tests on Buddy, we found out that Buddy may have gotten too much calcium sand in his digestive tract and was having a tough time passing it.

Well, I had to bathe him every day before work to get the dry shed off his fingers and toes so he would not lose any. I had to give him a food supplement with vitamin C and a laxative by syringe. It is a two-person job, but I have had to do it on my own. Do you have any idea how hard it is to get a lizard to open his mouth? I was able to bond with Buddy.

Now he is used to me taking him out weekly and bathing him in warm water and he loves it. This is just a small thing I could do for my son until he was ready for his lizard. No one is ever going to tell me that I do not love my son more than life itself. How many people would go to the lengths of spending over four hundred dollars on an eight-inch tetrapod for their child? Some, I imagine, would opt to have him put to sleep. I will continue to take care of him until his last days and love him for my son alone.

MOTHER'S REFLECTION:
A Promise Kept Until the Very End

My son's pet lizard passed away on May 22, 2023, after experiencing similar symptoms as a few years ago. Despite my efforts to care for him by supplementing his meals and supplying warmth and hydration, he sadly became unresponsive and stopped eating. He lived a long life of nearly seventeen years, and I am glad I provided him with great care. I buried him near his loving owner, Kyle, as I believe that is where he would have wanted to be.

30

COLORADO RUINED

SHORTLY AFTER WE FOUND Golden a good and stable forever home, Kyle got a stuffed puppy that he also decided to name Golden. He carried that stuffed dog everywhere and tried to take care of it as if it were a real creature. This was his way of getting over having to give up his real dog. We were vacationing in Colorado one summer and had to stop by the grocery store. My husband waited in the car while I, carrying Kyle, browsed the aisles with Golden the stuffed puppy. We quickly made our purchases and got back in the car. As we drove off, I heard Kyle rummaging in the back then he cried, "Mommy, Golden!"

Oh no! Turn the car around!" I pleaded, and after several tense minutes, my husband finally did, his voice tight with frustration. We returned to the store, but he stayed in the car, unwilling to help. *How could someone remain so detached when their child needed them most?*

We searched every aisle more than once, lost and found, and every inch of our car to no avail. It had only been a few short minutes. I found it extremely hard to believe that someone would take it that fast. I did not want to leave the store nor did Kyle. We spoke to a manager who helped us search, with no luck. I just could not believe that Golden had disappeared that quickly. Someone must have seen him and took him. Kyle was upset and began to cry. We went back to the car and did another thorough check but failed to find Golden. I tried to calm

Kyle down and was sympathetic to his pain. My husband remained unmoved. He just looked in the rearview mirror at a crying Kyle and said, "I can't believe you're crying over a stuffed dog. This is ridiculous!"

He never seemed to show empathy or emotion, only flashes of anger and detachment surfaced. *How does a child learn to feel when the example before him is so tightly closed off?*

Kyle continued to cry while I fumed at my husband. Our child was six and yet an adult man could be just as petty and cold to his son's pain and loss. My husband never even helped to look for Golden.

I knew only from conversations I had with my mother-in-law that my husband did not have aa nurturing and special childhood, and I sympathized with him. I wish I could have changed that for him. The way he grew up is the opposite of everything I believed in and experienced growing up and wanted for my beautiful son. To a child, there is a thin line between fantasy and reality. To Kyle that stuffed dog was real and he had just lost the same dog twice. I would let my son get other pets, but I would be apprehensive before we would get a family dog.

The pain my son felt losing his pride and joy was unbearable for me. I, along with Momo, tried throughout the years to find him another Golden but none would suffice. The smallest things, or things that most adults would say were petty or not that big of a deal, are important to small children. I knew how important Golden was and did everything to appease my son. Kyle would remind me of that day on occasion even when he got much older as it did affect him greatly. He again lost someone that he loved dearly.

For Kyle, the loss of his beloved stuffed animal mirrored the loss of a real pet, a touching indication of the attachments that shaped my son's world. The difference between mommy's empathy and daddy's dismissive attitude showed the importance of confirming Kyle's feelings. No matter how trivial they seem to any adult.

To Kyle, Golden was not just a toy but represented love and compassion. What his dad considered insignificant carried an immense amount of weight in my son's heart that seemed to shape his experience and reaction to the many losses in his life.

MOTHER'S REFLECTION:
Small Losses Can Cut Deep

I pray this reminds every parent to nurture and acknowledge their child's emotions and promote understanding amid their struggles. It seems to me that the losses Kyle experienced resonated through his life and influenced his future relationships as well as his feelings toward love and loss. Parents, please be vigilant and do not ever dismiss your child's pain as trivial.

31

KYLE GIVING BACK

I TAUGHT KYLE TO HELP others with less than he had to help him better appreciate what he did have. Yet, he took this on with much more vigor than I initially expected. I never underestimated the giving heart that God gave my son. It was one of the Fruits of the Spirit and God had planted a very bountiful garden within my son.

Kyle was taught good manners by me at an early age. He was taught to always say "please" and "thank you," to address others respectfully with "sir" and "ma'am," and to hold the door open for others or help someone with their groceries. As he grew older and became more independent, I was proud to see that he continued to practice these manners instilled in him early on. It was a testament to his kind and considerate nature, and I was proud in many ways to be his mother.

When he was little, around the age of seven or eight, he did not understand why there were people standing on street corners holding up signs that would say, "Help me, please" or "Homeless, please help, God bless." This made him sad. I told him there were many people that were not as blessed as he was, and they needed our prayers.

He saw a man in a car in front of us one day at an exit. Kyle asked me if we could give him something. As traffic started to move, we slowly approached him. Kyle rolled down his window and handed the man standing, who was quite elderly and dirty from head to toe, five dollars. This made the man smile and it made my son smile as well.

Kyle was hungry and wanted to stop at McDonald's. When we stopped, he felt the need to ask me if we could get the man something to eat. Kyle loved chicken nuggets and thought everyone should too, but he also thought the man would want a hamburger, so we got him both along with fries and a drink. We had to circle back around on the highway and get back on the off ramp where the man was standing. He was very obliged to Kyle and was tearing up as he spoke to me words I already knew, "Your son is a gift from God."

I replied, "He sure is, thank you."

However, Kyle did not want to stop there. He wanted to do more with something else in mind. When we saw someone else, we would head for the nearest drive-through, usually McDonald's, to get the person something to eat, pray for them and head on our way. The smile on Kyle's face for doing a good deed was so worth it.

The day we met the man at the exit, Kyle insisted we go to Walmart to purchase backpacks. Kyle wanted to make care kits for the homeless. He saw this on television one day and wanted to do it. He was so excited about this project and the fact that he thought of such an idea at a youthful age made me excited too. He called his Momo on my cell phone and was excited to tell her what we had planned to do. Clearly the compassion bug is contagious because Momo told him that we would meet her at Walmart, and she would help pay for it.

My mom and dad were always there for their grandbabies as well as anyone else who needed help. That is where my son inherited so much kindness and compassion. My parents were always lending a hand up for everyone including having a vast supply of pop and water, and even popsicles in a cooler on their front patio for the neighborhood kids and others who needed it, especially during the hot, summer months. As well as giving their clothing and collecting winter coats for the City Union Mission every year. This is where I, along with my son, learned to give back.

We spent most of the day picking out backpacks and filling them with water bottles, wet wipes, a notepad, and pens so that the homeless could journal on their path. I always told Kyle that we all have a story that should be shared. We also put some Lunchables and non-perishable snacks like pudding cups and granola bars along with plastic utensils in the backpacks.

We put a small pocket Bible in each and every one of them and distributed them throughout the Raymore, Grandview, and Kansas City area. We were going on an Adventure for Good, going from city to city looking out for homeless people on the way. As soon as Kyle saw someone standing by themselves, he would yell, "Mommy, stop!"

I think we handed out at least twenty-five that first day. It was a long, rough day for him, but he was so full of pride and joy that he could help another human being that was less fortunate than him. Kyle wanted to tell daddy and so did I, but we kept it as our little secret. Based on past reactions, I feared he would respond with anger instead of pride or instead not responded at all. He often saw kindness as wasteful, especially when it came to money he felt was his and his alone to gamble; even when my mom paid for most of it. *Yet, how could a father not celebrate the generosity of his own child?* She was as willing as I was to do anything to keep her grandbabies happy and content and help another human being. She jumped at the chance to help Kyle pay it forward to the less fortunate.

After that, my son was always looking for a way to give back wherever he could. He truly seemed to love helping his fellow man more than he did himself.

He was a true believer in kindness and helping others in any way he could and not expecting any payback. Kyle quickly learned to give back and volunteer at Harvesters Food Banks, handing out food to the line of people that would drive through. He also regularly sorted items at the Salvation Army and volunteered at Heart and Hand where he loved to make goodie bags for the inner-city children and gather school supplies for Scrapps.

As he got older and could drive on his own and would volunteer at Goodwill or even at the local humane society whenever time allowed in between school and work but said as much as he loved playing with the cats, he did not like cleaning out the litter boxes (honestly, who does?). He just wanted to walk the dogs and take them to the playground that the shelters had available.

When he got into a bit of trouble, this was one of the community services he had to endure. It was not the same as volunteering to do it. He was made to do it.

He would call me every time he helped to tell me how much he really did enjoy volunteering on his own, even sending me photos and video of the work he was doing. He felt so good being able to help another person but not as good as I felt seeing my son giving back to how God blessed him.

My boy tried so hard to be everything to everyone. He was so much like me in every good way. He was tall, thin, and beautiful. Kyle was outspoken and passionate about what he believed in. He would not back down and believed in fighting for animal rights and children's rights. Paying it forward was what I taught him, and he enjoyed the look on people's faces when he would do something good for them.

He wanted to make me proud. But the thing is, I was always proud of my son and made sure he knew it every single day. I do not think he told his dad much about the volunteer work he accomplished as he told me he thought his dad would not say much about it or even care, so we kept it to ourselves for the most part and shared it with only a select few. Kyle so wanted to make his dad proud. What was sad is that his dad did not seem to understand what that meant. *When a child's heart is wide open, how can those closest to him not see the beauty in that?*

As we took a walk together one morning, when Kyle was around the age of eight or nine, he wanted to stop and help one of our neighbors, an older man, who was mowing his lawn. It was early and summer had just begun but it was already getting hot. He saw the man getting worn out and wiping his forehead with his handkerchief. My precious little man offered to help him so he could rest. It certainly was not easy for Kyle at that age, but he insisted on finishing the man's lawn for him.

The old man gave Kyle an antique pocketknife that had belonged to his dad to keep as thanks for a job well done. The man said the knife was what he could do, though at least sixty years old, him giving such a special and treasured gift to my son, showed Kyle how grateful he truly was. He already had a collection, some belonging to his Popo and others that I gave him as gifts or ones that he bought on his own. I have carefully kept his cherished collection and other important belongings safe for him, until he was able to live independently again.

Kyle picked up walnuts out of a woman's yard because he knew it was a mess, and the grass was not able to grow. These small gestures of kindness from Kyle, I knew, came from the largest and softest heart. He really did care so much about others and their struggles.

Throughout the years he would ask me questions like, "How come all kids do not have what I have?" or "Why are there so many homeless families?" and "How come some kids do not have mommies and daddies?"

I did not really have answers for him. I wish I had. He was so deep in thought and wanted to learn more about how to help people. I did not really know myself other than some people were just down on their luck. Some kids' parents have passed on or some made poor choices. All I could do was say that we could not help everyone, but we could do our best to help as many as possible and we needed to pray for them. I understood his desire to help. It was difficult to see people in such a state. I knew though, that if he could, my son would save every person and animal in need that he saw. It is just who he was and a few of his friends confirmed his beautiful heart in memories I will share later.

I am deeply moved by my son's innate compassion and generosity. From a youthful age, Kyle embraced the values of kindness and empathy, going above and beyond to help those in need. His actions, whether it was giving money to a homeless man, creating care kits, mowing someone's lawn and asking for nothing in return, or volunteering at various organizations, among the other wonderful deeds, he showed a heart full of love and a spirit dedicated to making the world a better place. Despite the challenges and lack of support from his dad,

Kyle's unwavering dedication to helping others has been a testament to his beautiful heart and the values instilled in him. Again, Kyle's Momo and Popo shining brightly through the eyes of my son. His story is a powerful reminder that even small acts of kindness can have a profound impact, and I was always so incredibly proud to see his quest for selflessness and care.

MOTHER'S REFLECTION:
A Ray of Hope

Kyle's journey is a ray of hope, showing that true fulfillment comes from serving others and making a positive impact in the world.

32

HOMESCHOOL

I WILL ADMIT IT. I can be a little overprotective of a mom but will never apologize for looking out for my son's well-being as much as I could. Not only to my son but to any child I am given charge of. I was at my son's school every day checking in on him. I made sure he was being treated fairly and eating his lunch and making sure he read the little notes I left in his lunch box daily. His lunch box usually consisted of a jelly crimp sandwich, some chips, fruit, yogurt, and juice. He did not like peanut butter. Who does not like peanut butter? My son, of course. He did not like the crust so I crimped an "only jelly" sandwich, and he would give the bread crust to the birdies outside before we left for the day.

I felt the need and wanted to reaffirm to Kyle how proud I was of him through the little sticky notes I added to his lunch box and back-pack, reminding him how much I wanted him to have fun learning all he could. He loved the little notes. Every day's note had an affirmation as did all the text messages I sent him as he grew older. I never wanted a day to go by without my son knowing how much he was loved by God and mom, and I have not stopped.

He also loved me being there for him and the other kids. I would go in every day and volunteer to read to his class and maybe work in the office or help the teacher with her paperwork, also helping the children with their social skills.

One particular afternoon, when I was on the playground with Kyle and his friends, the principal came to me and said, "Mrs. Wiley, you really love your son, I have never seen a more attentive parent. You are so good with the kids. How would you like to get paid for being here every day?"

I was floored when she offered me a job as a paraprofessional. This was so perfect. I could help my husband with the bills and be with my baby every day. What could be better?

For a few years, I worked in my son's school district as an aide. Kyle and I had a blast being together although I did have to watch over the other kids as well and made sure that Kyle knew at that point, I was not there just for him, but also to protect and help his many friends.

The year he was heading into first grade I was leery in every way, even letting him go back to school. This was because I had seen some overly aggressive behavior at school. There was one boy, a fourth grader, mercilessly pounding on kids half his size. He seemed to dominate the school, not only the kids but the administration as well from what I observed. I was worried for all the kids as much as Kyle and felt the need to report this behavior. The administration simply took it as my helicopter-ness and ignored me. I took Kyle out after his first-grade year. Knowing that the administration did not take it seriously, if I could not protect them all, at least I could protect my own son.

I decided to do homeschool with Kyle in second grade. At first Kyle thought it was going to be all fun with his mom as the teacher. He soon came to realize that being at home would involve work. However, I came to realize that it was work for me too.

He was too smart and the lessons in public school were just too slow for him. He got bored with second and even third grade public school curriculum, so I had him in Abeka fourth grade curriculum, which was much more his speed and intellect. He thought it would be fun to be homeschooled and seemed to enjoy the challenge it gave him. I enrolled him in classes at a homeschool church where he learned so much more than in an elementary school. They offered him so much more as far as extra classes other than science and history. I was so impressed with everything my son carried out and knew that he would excel no matter what.

Kyle decided his musical instrument in home school would be the piano. So, of course, I found an older lady that gave private lessons. It did not last long. Not sure why. We could not afford a piano, and I certainly did not want to invest in one until I knew he would commit to learning, so I bought Kyle a keyboard. He did not want to practice on his keyboard much. Maybe he just did not click with the teacher. I did have a talk with him to make sure that everything was all right, and he said that it just was not as fun as he thought it would be. That was fine as long as he tried. Our homeschool journey was full of experiences that Kyle and I cultivated together. My protective nature led me to make the decision to homeschool my son. I thought I would ensure Kyle's safety and be providing him with a better education that matched his intellect and curiosity. Despite the obstacles, I believed homeschooling would allow Kyle to explore new learning opportunities and a love for knowledge, and it did. He could not get enough of the History and Discovery channels on TV. Kyle's enthusiasm and adaptability were so inspiring, and I am grateful for the time we spent learning and growing together. This part of our lives showed the importance of being present and proactive in my son's education and well-being, and the joy that came from supporting him in his unique path.

Kyle was in 4-H club when he was being home schooled. He learned archery, which was one of his favorite sports and he was excellent at it. We of course bought him targets and the best bow and arrow set for someone his age. Our next-door neighbor would help him as he already had a target set up in his back yard preparing himself for deer season. I was great at archery still after decades of my brother and I practicing in our front yard when we were about the same age as Kyle was.

MOTHER'S REFLECTION:
Learning on Our Terms

Homeschooling Kyle was not just about academic growth, it was about protecting his spirit, nurturing his curiosity, and staying present in each stage of his development. Our days were full of learning, laughter, and the kind of closeness that formed the deepest foundation. I would not trade that time for anything.

33

WANTING A SIBLING

KYLE HAD MANY FRIENDS throughout his entire life, but he just wanted a lifelong blood brother or sister. He wanted more than anything to be a big brother. Although he grew up with cousins who were more like sisters to him, but lived apart from him, my son just wanted to give his heart to everyone that he could, so it made sense that he wanted to be a sibling. However, after he was born, my husband, without consulting me, chose not to have any more children, even though I wanted one more. He ultimately won, as usual.

One day Kyle saw a commercial on TV about being a foster parent. He asked me what it was. He said he wanted us to do that. He wanted to be a big brother and be able to teach someone younger than him and be able to play together all the time. I honestly never considered this as a way to have another child. This would be a way, I thought, to make both my husband and child happy as well as another beautiful child in much need of a stable home.

I told Kyle I thought that this was an excellent idea and brought up the idea of adopting a child to my husband. He made it clear he wanted no part of it. He told us both that if I ever brought another child into our home, he would leave. *When love expands to welcome a child into a family, what kind of heart chooses distance over connection?*

This broke my son's heart and mine as well. My son was so young and had to witness his dad's resistance and experienced way too much disappointment from him. I told Kyle he would always have tons of friends. He would mention from time to time, still well in his teen years, how he longed for a brother. I do not know why he would bring it up, but I knew he still thought about how his dad once rejected the idea of another child and rarely made time for him. That kind of absence leaves a mark. *How does a person feel to be met with silence instead?* Even though he had many friends, there was still that special one missing. I have always felt bad not being able to give him that.

I am often reminded of my son's deep desire to share his love and kindness with a brother. Despite the disappointment and challenges my son faced, he wanted desperately to be a big brother because of his generous and caring nature. His story is an emotional sign of the importance of family bonds and the impact of his unfulfilled desires.

MOTHER'S REFLECTION:
The Brother He Would Have Been

I am proud of Kyle's resilience and his ability to find happiness and connection in his many friendships, even as he yearned for the sibling he never had.

34

THE LAUGHTER IN BIRTHDAY PARTIES AND SLEEPOVERS

I TRIED TO MAKE UP for the lack of video documentation from his birth by making his birthdays as big as possible. All his friends and family would be over, there would be a big cake, appetizers, and a table brimming with presents. At the end of the night, I would make a big dinner for the extended family, and we would all toast our glasses to Kyle with white or dark sparkling grape juice. (We never drank or had alcohol in our presence or our son's presence.) We would toast to the king of the day, our King Kyle. That was always his and my favorite part. He would just beam when it would come time for the toast in his honor.

Kyle was invited to his first birthday party for one of his kindergarten friends, at a skate rink when he was six. Well, he fell in love with skating. It was like he was born with wheels on his feet. It was a fast activity, and he had so much fun with it that he went every weekend and had a blast with his friends just as I did when I was his age.

He had one of his own birthday parties there as well. When they did the Hokey Pokey, Kyle was always one of the last people to skate because he was so thin and limber. He even won first prize quite a few times. Dad and I skated with him a few times. I was not as good as I used to be, falling down a lot more and sore the day after. Bubber and I would just giggle as he would help me up off the skate rink floor and to the bench to sit and rest awhile. I loved watching him skate. He would twirl and do all sorts of fancy moves. I never saw him fall. Not once. I miss his laughter. Even laughing at me when I made a fool of myself. It was a joy to see him smile and be happy and have fun.

I would always have parties for him and his friends on his birthday, with a new theme every year. The first year was teddy bears. One year was Scooby-Doo, another Ninja Turtles, then Yu-Gi-Oh, Spiderman and so on. I would take them all for an activity, like the indoor amusement park at the Great Plains Mall, Worlds of Fun, laser tag in the caves up north of the river, paintball, a sleepover at Great Wolf Lodge indoor water park, and more. Every year was a blast on his birthday and, of course, his two cousins were always there by his side to enjoy his special day with him.

During the summer months, I would set up our tent in the back-yard and let him have sleepovers with many of his friends. We would roast hot dogs and s'mores over the firepit and have popcorn, listen to music, and play games in the backyard until they were worn out, then they always wanted me to tell a ghost story once they settled down. I was not good at telling stories and only knew one or two but would read one from a book until they fell asleep. I remember waking up at times to check on them as they dreamt soundly, then a few hours later, rising early in the morning to prepare them a hearty breakfast, and finding them sleeping on the rec room floor and Kyle in bed with me. I guess maybe my storytelling was spookier than I thought.

Kyle's birthday parties and sleepovers remind me of the fun and excitement these moments brought him. His love for skating and the fun themes of his birthday parties showed his adventurous spirit and the strong relationships he formed with his friends and cousins. These experiences were not just about the activities but about creating lasting memories and a sense of belonging and happiness. I am oh so grateful for the opportunity to support and share in these happy moments with my beautiful boy, watching Kyle grow and thrive in an environment filled with love and laughter and happy times. Every parent should want this for their child. Nothing else mattered more to me than seeing my son happy, which was my happiness.

MOTHER'S REFLECTION:
Toasts, Ghost Stories, and Giggles

These memories of birthday parties and backyard sleepovers were Kyle's joy and mine too. Whether it was skating hand-in-hand or watching him twirl with fearless delight, every celebration was stitched with laughter, love, and belonging. Creating those moments was not just about having fun, it was about showing my son that he mattered, and that every year of his life deserved to be celebrated. I would give anything to hear one more giggle at a silly ghost story or raise one more sparkling grape juice toast to our King Kyle.

35

THE FRIENDSHIP THAT CHANGED EVERYTHING

KYLE WAS NOT RETURNING to his old school. After what happened, I no longer felt confident in the way things were handled. At the new school, he settled in quickly, falling back into routine and making friends, even though the environment felt just as uncertain.

One boy stood out. He was quiet, gentle, and seemed drawn to Kyle's warmth. Kyle came home each day with stories about new classmates, but this boy became a constant. Their personalities balanced each other, Kyle was adventurous and outgoing, while his friend was more reserved. Together, they brought out the best in each other.

Sleepovers became a tradition. Every year, Kyle would host a "get to know you" night with a handful of boys. I always made a point to meet their families. This friend felt like part of our family because he was often at our house after school and on weekends. It was as if I had a second child, and I welcomed him with open arms.

His family seemed to love him, but they appeared to be navigating their own struggles. I never saw their actions as intentionally neglectful, just overwhelmed. Their needs were different from mine, and I tried to offer what I could.

At Christmas, Kyle wanted to give him a gift. He said his friend did not have many toys. He picked out a model car, and when he gave it to him, the boy's face lit up with awe. That moment stayed with me. Later, when Kyle noticed how much his friend loved playing on our computer, I asked my husband to build one for him, something simple, with educational games.

One day, while they played foosball, Kyle came into the kitchen and said, "Mommy, he said a bad word." When I asked what it was, he whispered it in my ear. I was stunned, not just by the word, but by the fact that Kyle recognized it as wrong. I gently pulled the boy aside and explained that we do not use that kind of language in our home. He said, "But my brother says it all the time." I reassured him that while he may hear it elsewhere, it was not acceptable in our home.

Later, when we picked him up to play, his parents greeted me warmly. They stood together, drinks in hand, chatting casually. I did not say anything, but the moment unsettled me. It was early in the day, and their ease with drinking made me uneasy.

That afternoon, something unexpected happened. While the boys played, Kyle's friend suddenly began to hurt himself. Kyle rushed in, asking him to stop. Eventually, he did. Kyle was shaken and did not want to play anymore. I gently told the boy it was time to go home and asking him to grab his things so we would not be late.

When we arrived at his house and pulled in the driveway, he was reluctant to get out of the car. I was not sure why, but I did let him that we would see him in a couple of days. After he left, Kyle asked me what a certain word meant. I turned around quickly and asked him where he heard it. He said his friend told him. It made me nervous for the boy because the word had a troubling meaning, and I could not help but wonder what he might have been exposed to.

I went to the door, to talk to his mother. I was in short distance from the car so I could keep my eye on Kyle. I asked if there was anything I should know about because of what we witnessed at our house and what he had said to Kyle. She mentioned he had once been on medication, but they had stopped it due to cost. That detail stayed with me.

She also told me, "I have no idea why he would say that." I remember staring back at her, stunned. I could not understand how she did not see to be more concerned? From my perspective, there were many possible reasons, but none seemed to land with her in that moment.

Days passed without a visit. Kyle's friend called, but Kyle did not want him to come over.

"Mommy, tell him I'm sick," he would say.

I told Kyle I would not lie for him, and I did not want him to lie either. When I asked why he did not want to be friends anymore, he said, "He scares me, Mommy. He was hurt, and he hurt himself on the floor, and he told me a bad word."

I told him, "That was not right, but he needs your kindness and prayers. It is not okay to ignore someone who is hurting." Part of me ached. Kyle had been exposed to so much; things no child should have to navigate. None of it was the boys' fault. But I understood how overwhelming it must have been.

Eventually, the calls stopped. It broke my heart. Kyle was devastated too. They had been like brothers. Now they were strangers.

I had thought about that boy many times throughout the years, and I am sure Kyle did too. I often wondered how the sudden end of their friendship affected him. I prayed it did not leave lasting wounds. I share this story not to discredit anyone, but to show how deeply it impacted Kyle. He eventually made new friends, but the loss stayed with him. It was like losing a brother.

MOTHER'S REFLECTION:
Not All Goodbyes Come with Closure

Kyle's friendship with this boy taught him empathy, boundaries, and the complex reality of helping someone in pain. Losing that bond was heartbreaking, but it also showed my son's sensitivity and intuition, his ability to protect his heart while still offering kindness. Their time together shaped Kyle's understanding of connection, and though it ended too soon, its imprint stayed with him. Some friendships change us forever, even when they do not last.

36

TRIP TO TIJUANA

WHILE WE HAD DAYS with no cousins or friends over, and it was just the two or three of us, I would ask Kyle what he wanted to do. Sometimes we would play a game or do a craft. Other times, with a sparkle of excitement in his eyes, Kyle would ask to watch our wedding video among the dozens of other videos he could choose to watch. He was captivated by the beautiful memory of his parents' wedding. He liked to see Mommy and Daddy kiss at the end and would blush and giggle. I think most little ones do get a kick out of seeing their parents show love and affection toward one another. It makes them feel safe and secure.

After each viewing, he would actively say, "Mommy, let's watch it again!"

One day, he turned to me and asked, "Mommy, what does it mean to be married?" I explained that being married is when two people love each other so much that they want to create a family and spend their lives together, with God by their side. I reassured him that Mommy, Daddy, and Kyle are one unit, and that we would love each other forever. In his sweet little voice, he replied, "Mommy, I will love ew forever." The way he pronounced "you" was adorable and unforgettable.

At first, he did not fully grasp the depth of what I said, but as he grew older, he came to understand what it truly meant to be a family.

He made it a point to end all our conversations with those special words. His last words to me were, "Mom, I love ew more than anything in the world." I feel so fortunate to have many recordings of him saying that throughout the years.

Inspired by Kyle's enthusiasm, I thought it would be fun to take him to Cuvier Park in La Jolla, California, to the very cliff overlooking the Pacific, where my husband and I had exchanged our vows. It was a beautiful way for Kyle to connect with a pivotal moment in my life.

As we walked through the community of La Jolla, it reminded me how much I loved this area; one of my favorite places in the world. We enjoyed the breathtaking views of the Pacific Ocean, and the playful seals basking on the rocks at Seal Park. The live music at La Jolla Cove Park and delicious Mexican food at Old Town San Diego made it an unforgettable experience for us both.

Kyle and I developed a tradition of collecting seashells at every beach we visited. From the sandy shores of Hawaii, the breathtaking coast along the pacific in California, to the beaches of Florida and everything in between, each shell became a keepsake of our adventures together. It was more than just a collection; it was a tangible memento of our vacations together.

Before we left La Jolla to fly home, we decided to take him over the border to Tijuana. I recalled visiting the city with my parents shortly after my wedding. The fun of shopping, going to the markets, and the lively atmosphere were unforgettable, especially watching my dad haggle with the locals. I knew Kyle, with his curious spirit, would enjoy the experience just as much.

Not knowing what lay ahead, I had asked my husband to park on the California side of the border, but he made an impulsive choice and drove straight into Tijuana without hesitation. *How could someone disregard such a clear request, especially when safety and trust were at stake?* For the next hour, Kyle and I were engulfed in fear for our lives.

Despite our growing anxiety, Kyle's dad seemed to me, determined not to turn around. It felt like he was in a fog, disconnected from our fear as he drove deeper into the heart of Tijuana. At that point, we felt helpless, forced to navigate a complete circle for well over an hour, all while entering increasingly impoverished and potentially dangerous areas.

Kyle was very scared, of course, and so was I. He was pleading with his dad to turn the car around, desperately trying to express how scared he was, but his and my words fell on deaf ears. Being ignored was nothing new but nevertheless, disheartening; he was completely focused on maneuvering our rented convertible Mustang through the mayhem, straight into the heart of Tijuana and dodging oncoming traffic while doing so. The locals were going in complete disorder, ignoring all the oncoming cars, and driving on the wrong side of the road. We quickly realized that traffic rules seemed nonexistent in Tijuana.

Eventually, we found ourselves in a small town, driving through it at a snail's pace, the tension in the car very evident. With each minute, the reality of the situation was amplified, trying to find a safe way out and trying to get my husband to go faster. In that moment, it felt like he did not care how overwhelmed or unsafe we were. Kyle was terrified and desperate for a bathroom, but stopping was far too risky, and there was nowhere safe to pull over, so I handed him an empty water bottle to use in the backseat. After a long delay, we finally reached the border, where we waited for three hours in a small line of cars, growing increasingly hot and hungry. A little girl approached our window, holding a sign asking for money while her mother lounged in the shade nearby, and Kyle, saddened by the sight, started to cry and begged his dad to hurry. My husband finally reached the front of the line, instead of stopping as instructed; seemingly believing he could drive through the gate although no one else could, but he sure mistakenly thought otherwise. *What makes someone think the rules do not apply to them, especially when the stakes are so high?* He was quickly confronted by a guard who jumped in front of the car, weapon drawn, shouting, "Stop or you will be in for a world of hurt!"

I was filled with embarrassment and fear for all of us, as Kyle, a frightened little boy, watched a man point a gun at his dad's head, mistakenly believing we were criminals. The guard searched our car and asked Kyle if we were his parents. He was too scared to speak, tears in his eyes, looking at me as if he wanted to jump into my arms but was afraid to move for fear he would be hurt. I reassured Kyle that it was okay to answer yes or no, and I told the guard we looked exactly alike, which he accepted, though his suspicions remained due to my husband's dark skin and behavior as well as asking him twenty questions. Surprisingly, he answered them all correctly considering the mental state he seemed to be in and the hell he put us through.

The border guards truly were evil people. After the guard let us go, I had to repeatedly apologize to my son, suspecting that my husband would never take responsibility for putting our family in harm's way, and has not to this day.

This trip was not just about revisiting the past; it was about building new memories with Kyle and deepening our family bond. I enjoyed watching my son laugh and have fun. This trip was supposed to be a treasure trove of love and connection. What started as a lovely and peaceful vacation ended in terror and trauma for my innocent son.

MOTHER'S REFLECTION:

Fear at the Border, Calm in Mama's Arms

What started as a tribute to love, and connection turned into a terrifying experience no child should ever endure. To see a weapon pointed at his dad, to feel helpless in unfamiliar territory, to be ignored when fear was real, that is not just trauma, it is a betrayal of safety. My husband's irrational decision and a stranger's out of control, aggression stole the joy from our trip, but Kyle's innocence and trust reminded me of what love truly is. God does not operate in intimidation or cruelty, He dwells in gentleness, in comfort, in a mother's arms that promise protection no matter the storm. I still ache for what Kyle saw that day. But I know that the way I held him, reassured him, and prayed over him, that was God's presence.

37

TOO MATURE

KYLE, EVEN AS A little boy, wanted to work. He wanted to make money like Mommy and Daddy did. I told Kyle his job was to go to school and learn and have fun in the process. He would even get an allowance for doing so. He must have sensed the anguish in me even though I tried to hide it from him as much as possible. Honestly, I think he could tell we were struggling although I never said a word to him and made sure he always had what he needed and wanted. He saw more than he should have, moments that no child should have to carry and he overheard us talking about another paycheck lost to gambling. *How does a child make sense of that kind of instability, especially when all he wants is to feel safe and seen?* Even though Kyle did not really know what that meant, he knew daddy must have done something bad. When the bills were due, I had to go to my parents for help it seemed as if my husband did not care one iota about how his actions impacted our family or our son. At just eight years old, my precious boy carried himself with a maturity beyond his years. He wanted to help, he wanted to work, because he saw a need and felt called to fill it. In many ways, he showed more strength and compassion than the man he looked up to.

I told him, "No, sweet pea, you do not need to work for a very long time. Your job is to have fun with your friends." I constantly reassured

Kyle that his only two jobs were to continue to go to school and be with his friends, to just be a kid.

He loved to read and learn. He loved history, math, and science and excelled at them all. I wanted him to learn to read and write and work with numbers and play music and paint and all the other fun things that we do as children. I would cry sometimes because I felt so bad that my boy wanted to be so grown up already. I felt horrible. But I also knew I had to shield Kyle from the painful truths surrounding his father, secrets that were not mine to tell, yet they weighed heavily on both our lives.

During our breaks and on the weekends, Kyle wanted to sell lemonade and hot dogs at the pool. He got a lemonade stand for Christmas and could not wait to start making money even though he was already getting a great allowance for brushing his teeth and helping walk the dog and simply being the wonderful boy that he was (on top of getting excellent grades in school).

We took the stand to the pool during our lunch breaks and during the summer months. I would fill up a cooler and he would sell a cup of lemonade for fifty cents. I would cook a dozen or more hot dogs with buns and condiments and take them with us, and he would sell them for fifty cents as well. A hot dog and chips with drinks were a dollar. He loved it. This taught him responsibility and compassion for others.

With his charitable side, sometimes he would just give a cup of lemonade to people because they looked hot or thirsty. Of course, I would make up for his customers who did not have money readily available. The money he made went into his piggy bank and later he would either buy himself a toy at the dollar store or give it to a homeless person. The love and caring my boy had in his heart for others was astonishing.

During homeschool, I allowed him to do a harder job, a paper route in Raymore. He would not let up until I finally said "yes." It only lasted a couple of months. It was at the end of the school year and throughout mid-summer. He wore out quickly walking up and down the hills in a few subdivisions while dragging his little red wagon full of papers in eighty plus degree heat to get extra money to add to his already vast allowance. Even a couple of days of walking in the rain did not stop him. I think you know who ended up doing most of the work. But he did his absolute best, and I was so immensely impressed with him for persevering for so long. He quickly learned that just going to school and doing his homework was enough work for him to get paid a good amount for doing so. He soon got bored with homeschooling and wanted to go back to regular school.

The appeal of homeschool began to fade and he missed the routine and socialization that school provided. I think it would have been different for him if he had a sibling, he could share the school day with, but he was an only child and absolutely did not like it. The lack of division from home and school was taking a toll on him. He just got tired of mommy being the teacher. I understood this. He just wanted me to be his mommy, nurturer, back scratcher, and snuggler. Although I never gave up instructing my son right from wrong along with reading and many other things, against my better judgment, I chose to let him go back to school.

I was so tired of making all the decisions by myself when it came to Kyle. I did not understand why his dad would not help me. We were supposed to be a team cheering our son on through life together and helping raise him together. The care and presence I hoped for from his dad never seemed to materialize. It was as if I was literally raising my son on my own.

With Kyle's early desire to work and help, I am struck by his maturity and compassion. Despite the many protests he faced, Kyle's willingness to contribute and his entrepreneurial spirit were evident, and I admired him for it. His experiences with the lemonade stand and paper route taught him valuable lessons in responsibility and empathy. These moments seemed to present his generous heart and how important it was to allow him to explore his interests while ensuring that he enjoyed his childhood. Kyle must have gotten his work ethic from my mom and dad because his quest was one of resilience and adaptability in general. It was my honor in supporting my son's growth and development.

MOTHER'S REFLECTION:
A Childhood with a Grown-Up Heart

Kyle's enthusiasm to help and provide showed the depth of his character, and how much he quietly carried. His maturity was not forced by rules but shaped by circumstances he never asked for. He deserved to laugh freely, play wildly, and feel protected. And still, he chose to love, to give, and to grow. Supporting his journey was one of my greatest honors as a mother, even when I wished the weight on his small shoulders had been lighter.

38

First Experiences with Cops

KYLE WANTED TO SMASH his pumpkin a week after Halloween for one year. I was throwing it away because it was rotting, but he had seen one of his friends smash a pumpkin and he wanted to try it. Not understanding what the big deal was and guessing it was just a boy thing. I allowed him to. I told him to make sure to clean up the mess afterwards and he agreed.

As he smashed the pumpkin, a police officer was doing his rounds in his patrol car, looking for someone to pick on. He decided it would be fun to pick on an eight-year-old child. He stopped his car and got out and tried to tell my son to stop! I told him he was not going to speak to my child that way and asked him why Kyle needed to stop. He said what he was doing was illegal.

All I could think was "What a loser." It was not illegal to smash a pumpkin in his own yard, but the cop insisted it was. I told Kyle the police officer was wrong and was lying to him. I stood up to the oversized cop and told him to stop harassing a small child and pick on someone his own age and I would be reporting him to the proper authorities. He got in his car and left. Kyle continued to finish what he started.

Why do these shady police officers think they can harass people, especially children, because they have a badge? He was clearly out to cause a conflict that day. He must have thought an innocent child, or his mom, would buckle to his demands. Nope! Right is right, wrong is wrong, and the unethical being was wrong and I was going to call him on it. Later I found out that cop had tenure and was getting ready to retire. His twisted thought process led him to believe he could do whatever he wanted to whoever he wanted and would get away with it just as others in authority had done, including the coach that claimed to be a police chief. Many years later I found out that he had lied about being the chief of police.

I also coached his team for two seasons of soccer. We needed another coach as there were too many boys that signed up and no one else was volunteering. I thought it would be fun, and I would learn as I went along. The time Kyle and I spent together was so unforgettable. We were always so close and had so much fun together.

One year as he got older, I decided not to coach, to just sit on the sidelines and watch the game. The coach happened to be a police officer. I drove Kyle to his second practice, and he was reluctant to join the others on the field. I asked him why, but he did not really say much. He became shy and tense. This was unusual for him as pretty much anything with sports would have him ready to play. I reminded Kyle that he wanted to play that year, so he needed to be a part of the team and practice. He told me that he did not feel good. I knew my son. I knew there was more to it than that.

When the coach saw Kyle sitting on the hood of my car as I tried to talk him into getting out there with the other kids, the coach looked at Kyle from about fifty feet away and yelled in front of every parent and child that was witness to it, "Kyle, I'm a cop! Get your butt out here now!"

I was shocked. The fact that he thought he could use his position and authority as a cop, a position meant to protect the public, to threaten a child completely flabbergasted me. That action was completely unacceptable to me, and I now understood the reluctance of Kyle wanting to play.

I told Kyle to get in the car if he did not want to practice. I looked at the man, wanting to get in his face and embarrass him in front of all the kids and parents. I held back every ounce of enmity I had. I got in the car and left but not before telling Kyle how sorry I was that he thought this egoistic man could bully him. Kyle wanted to have fun, not be bullied.

I called the coach later that evening and told him Kyle would not be joining his team. I also told him that if he thought for a second that he could intimidate or scare a small child with his title, especially in front of the parent, he was sadly mistaken, and if he wanted to bully someone, I would dare him to bully me. He did not apologize or even acknowledge what I said, a typical narcissist. This guy took the fun out of the game, so Kyle did not want to play soccer that year.

Kyle spoke with the utmost respect to everyone in his life but after the experiences with several crooked cops harassing my son for no reason other than them thinking they could, my son became resentful toward them, just as he did his dad and a couple of other male relatives that do not deserve recognition, let alone praise, for the adverse treatment of my son. His early experiences with male authority in his life were nothing but criticism, intimidation, manipulations, and bullying. He soon realized he could not rely on any man to mentor him and love him as his Popo did, who was gone from his life in a blink of an eye. My son was getting thrashed around by so many corrupt men (I use the term loosely) that he did not know who to listen to and became reluctant to listen to anyone.

I fervently prayed for God to touch my son Kyle, and for Kyle to sense God's presence. There were days I pleaded for God to grant Kyle the ability to recognize His voice and for God to reveal the true character of these people. I needed God to help Kyle distinguish between negative influences that hindered him from living his best and fullest life. I prayed with all my heart for God to transform my husband into the man Kyle needed, someone who could guide him with love, wisdom, and grace. And if that was not possible, I begged for a virtuous, Godly man to enter Kyle's life and walk beside him. Too many of the males who crossed his path brought harm instead of healing, physically, emotionally, spiritually. How could they not see the precious soul they were entrusted with?

These awful experiences should tell anyone of the complexities of authority and the impact they can have on a child's development. Kyle's innocent desire to enjoy something as simple as smashing a pumpkin was met with unwarranted intimidation from an unstable cop, an experience that should have been lighthearted but instead cast a shadow over his understanding of authority figures. It was heartbreaking to see how all this negativity shaped Kyle's perception of men in positions of power, leading him to fear and resentment rather than respect.

I have always believed that respect must be earned and when someone chooses to belittle or bully a child, especially one as tender-hearted as Kyle, they forfeit that right. Kindness should be the bare minimum, not the exception. As a mom, standing up to that overbearing cop was a crucial to the importance of advocating for my son yet again, against an unjust authority who seemed to pull their weight around willy-nilly. However, the experiences with the soccer coach compounded Kyle's feelings of distrust. His reluctance to join in an activity he once loved was an indication of how deeply his interactions with these men (again using the term loosely) had affected him.

The essential part of positive male role model in my son's life or any young boy's life and the consequences that result from their abuse of power is devastating. I felt the need to teach my son to be strong and understand the difference between real authority and those who abuse and misuse. My intense prayers for Kyle were a deep desire for him to find guidance and support. I hoped that despite all he endured, there was still a way for him to heal and trust again. I also learned the critical role I played in helping Kyle through a world that can sometimes feel overwhelming, unjust, and just plain cruel.

MOTHER'S REFLECTION:

Authority Without Compassion Leaves Scars

These moments were not just isolated memories; they were defining experiences that should have never happened. When abusive power was used to intimidate instead of protecting, my son's trust was shattered. Kyle saw that firsthand. What should have been harmless, smashing a pumpkin or playing soccer, became moments of confrontation, confusion, and betrayal. The absence of tenderness from authority figures left a void that even my love could not fully fill. But I stood beside him, louder than their titles and fiercer than their pride, determined to show him that real strength comes from dignity, and that God's authority always begins with love.

39

ARKANSAS AND UNINVITED TRUTHS

ONE WEEKEND, KYLE'S GRANDMA'S family (on his dad's side), decided to go to Arkansas to visit Kyle's great-grandparents. All of them, cousins, and their parents, were going. At the time, Kyle was young and in grade school, eight or nine, I believe.

He came to me and asked, "Mommy, are you going?" I said, "No honey, I'm not invited.

He then looked at daddy and back at me, asking, "Why aren't you invited?" I responded, "Poo Doo I have no idea, but it is okay. Just go and have fun with your cousins. Have a fun time sweetie, and I will see you when I get back."

Although he was sad that I could not go, my husband made it clear that I was not allowed to join them, without giving me a reason so I stayed back and let my son enjoy the weekend with his three little cousins. When I would call to talk to him at night, my husband would make an excuse, like he was too busy that he could not talk to me. Well, I needed to make sure my son was all right, so I insisted on speaking with him. I was afraid in the back of my mind that something would happen while he was away. What were they saying or doing to him? He did call me at one point, to tell me that he missed me and would cry.

I would try to soothe him and let him know that he would be home soon, not to worry, and spend time playing and being happy.

When they arrived home, I asked him if he had a fun time, and he said, "Yes, but I missed you that's why we came home early. I wish you were there with me."

I reassured him, saying, "It doesn't matter now that I was not there. I talked to you every day to make sure you were okay, and you are home now, that is all that matters. I'm so glad you had a good time, Bubber."

Later I found out from my mother-in-law that I was invited, and my husband had not said a word about it. In fact, they had misled both me and Kyle about the trip and then fabricated another story to explain to their family why I was not there. This was a constant ongoing issue, with one misleading statement after another, whether intentional or not, that created separation between me and my child, Kyle as well as his family, showing no remorse for how it affected our son.

MOTHER'S REFLECTION:
Exclusion Speaks Louder Than Words

I may not have been invited, but my heart was still there with my son. The silence around that trip told a deeper story, one of avoidance, separation, and quiet decisions made without regard for the impact on a child. Kyle's sadness, his tears, phone calls, and his longing for me were signs that exclusion does not go unnoticed by a tender heart. I have always believed that family should operate with openness and love, not secrecy and division. That weekend in Arkansas may have been brief, but its message was loud and clear. My commitment as a mother was to protect Kyle, not just from harm, but from the quiet injustice of being pulled away from truth.

40

BAD TEACHER

AFTER BEING HOMESCHOOLED IN the second grade because we witnessed too much bullying by a certain student, I was reluctant to put him back in school but did it anyway after long talks with the administration, letting them know that I was watching and protecting my son no matter what.

We gave him his first cell phone at the age of nine and told him he would be able to reach us no matter what. If he felt uneasy or scared or just had questions, then he could call me or Daddy. It did not matter where we were. I assured him he could call anytime, and I would answer, and it was the same throughout his many years. I was *ALWAYS* there for my son, twenty-four/seven, no matter what. I always had my phone on just in case my baby needed me anytime. If the teachers were not helping him or answering his questions, then he could call me. If he was being bullied by a student or teacher and nothing was being done about it, then he could call me. The school assured me he would be in safe hands with a new teacher in the district.

She seemed nice at first but then as the months went by, she became stricter with the students. He called me one day from school and told me that she was being mean to him. I spoke with Kyle and tried to reassure him that Mommy had his back, and he would be okay, but he needed to focus on his schoolwork. He would tell me about a kid in class that would bully the other kids too, but the teacher ignored it. Every time the bully hit another kid or call one of the kids a name, they would let the teacher know and she would turn a blind eye to it.

I confronted her about the kid bullying Kyle, and she insisted she had it all under control. After speaking with other parents, I found out that she did NOT have it under control and in fact was not doing anything to help protect the other kids, repeatedly ignoring. I went to the principal, who did nothing. I went to the administrator, and he did nothing. This was what happened two years ago all over again, but I held firm to my beliefs. I was not going to back down.

I received a call from Kyle one day when he was at school. He said the teacher was making him read the same book over again for the third time. To this day, it felt like she may have been retaliating against me for simply being an outspoken parent and protecting my son and other kids. He said that the teacher made him stay inside for recess for not doing good on a reading report. My son had straight As, yet it was not enough for the narcissist teacher.

He asked me to come to the school and get him. I was on it!! I was there for my son no matter what it entailed. I was not going to let him down, ever!

I got to the school, bypassed the office, and went directly to his classroom where I walked in to find the teacher standing over him as he stood against the chalkboard, like he was trapped and could not get away from her. This was not okay with me; an adult should never use their physicality to intimidate a child, which incidentally happened increasingly from relatives on his dad's side. I almost lost it but stayed calm. I told her, "Step away from my son NOW please!" She backed up and I asked Kyle if he was okay, and he said yes but he was scared. Of course, he would be. This teacher was dominating him.

I asked her what her problem was, and she said he was lazy and refused to read the book again. I told her he had read it twice and it was just a hard book for him to understand, and he did well enough on his report that he did not need to read it again.

This was ridiculous. In no way was my son being lazy, and sheer persistence was not going to change anything. Clearly this teacher did not know the phrase, "Crazy is doing the same thing twice and expecting a different result."

She told me that he needed to read it a third time, and I was persistent in telling her for the last time that he had read it twice already and was not going to read it again and we were going to move on to the next book. As always, I talked to my husband that evening to call her to tell her this was going to end, and he was not going to read the same book for the third time. I did not want to hear any more about it. I told Kyle in front of the teacher that he had done a wonderful job with the book and that I was proud of him for calling me when he needed help. I asked him if he wanted to go home, and he said no, that he wanted to stay the rest of the day. I told Kyle that he could go outside and play for the rest of the recess. She insisted that he stay in. I overrode the corrupt teacher's decision to punish my son for something he simply did not do.

What a big boy he was. I told the teacher to back off my son and let him do his job as an eight-year-old kid. I told her he was a great student and an even better son, and he was not going to be bullied by her any longer. I could not believe he wanted to stay the rest of the day. When I picked him up from school, he said she did not bother him at all after that, and he was in good spirits.

We all inevitably encounter bullies throughout our lives, and some, sadly, persist throughout childhood into adulthood. The key lies in how we handle them with civility. The school administration's inappropriate and unacceptable behavior toward Kyle, who was evidently more mature than most of them, and other students as well as me, along with other parents for speaking up, was not going to be tolerated. They tend to want to intimidate parents into keeping quiet. I was not going to allow them to stifle this mama or my son.

They also have a duty to protect every child in their care, not just picking and choosing. The child bully also needed protection because he could have been going through something awful at home, or another bully or a personal struggle within himself that needed attention.

When both school administrator and parents protect the child or teenager who is being bullied, it creates a positive outcome for everyone involved. By teaching the bullies (students and teachers) about the consequences of the actions, valuable lessons can be learned. It is important for the entire staff to gain insight into effective disciplinary methods to address the needs of the bully. Kids do not bully because it is fun, they bully because they have pain inside yet lack the knowledge or ability to deal with it in a healthy manner. Maybe divine intervention played a role in this school's management. I hope so for the sake of future students.

MOTHER'S REFLECTION:
Advocacy Is the Assignment

Some adults earn authority through wisdom. Others demand it through intimidation. This teacher had the title, but not the character, and I refused to let her diminish my son's voice. Kyle's education was never meant to be a battlefield. When he called me, he was asking more than a question, he was asking for protection, for truth, for help. And I showed up. Again, and again. Because being his mother meant being his advocate, even when schools resisted, even when systems faltered. Every time I fought for him, I hoped the lesson he learned was not about how cruel the world can be, but how fiercely love stands up to it.

41

CORRUPT ADMINISTRATION

WHEN KYLE GOT OLDER and taller and did not want me to stand at the school doors and wait for him, I would pull my van up in front and wait for him. Every single day when I picked him up from school, the first thing he would do would be to jump in the van and give me a big kiss and hug.

I would always say, "How was your day, Bubber?"

"Good, Mommy, how was yours?"

Then one day he asked me first, "How was your day, Mommy?"

"Good, Poo Doo but I missed you. How was yours?"

If it was a not-so-good day, then he would tell me right away so I could address it with the principal or teacher before everyone left for the day.

I would periodically have lunch with my son. One afternoon I went for lunch and signed in at the office but was followed by a staff member. I asked her why she was following me; she said she had orders. She stood there at the lunchroom door and watched me the whole time I ate with my son.

As we were dismissed from lunch, I was going to walk him to his room as usual, and she stopped me at the door and told me I could not walk him any farther. I asked her why and she again told me that she had her orders.

I asked, "By whom?"

She said she was not at liberty to say. I was so upset by this. I gave my son a kiss and told him I would pick him up later.

I called my husband at work and again he did not have anything to say. Same old thing from him…nothing, merely indifferent. Whether I or our own son was bullied or not was apparently only my concern. I learned that the teacher had asked that I not be able to enter her classroom. I am sure it was because I called her out on the bullying issue. I was not going to sit silently and allow the school to keep me out and away from my son while he was there. I did not know what was going on since he had been bullied by the teacher prior to this.

I did my research and looked up a very reputable attorney who made it his calling to sue school districts. I told him my story. He sent the district a letter saying they were not allowed to keep me out of school and away from my son. They were hiding the bullying issue and did not want parents to "out" them. After the superintendent and principal received the letter, it was amazing at how quickly the doors opened wide for my son and me.

When the MAP testing began, the teacher told the children if they had any issues on a question to raise their hand and she would try to explain it better. Kyle came home and told me that he raised his hand to ask the teacher to explain a question before he put down an answer and instead of explaining it to him, she told him the answer. The next day, Kyle came home and told me she was giving answers to other kids as well. I told him that she was cheating, and she was not supposed to do that. A couple of moms called me and told me that their kids were telling them the same thing. I felt like these parents were wanting me to do something about it. Well, I did. I called the superintendent and so did the other parents and the teacher got fired for cheating on the MAP test. The class had to have a substitute for the remaining few weeks of the year.

So, this teacher who had given my son such a tough time in the past was clearly not acting in the students' best interest. I know my baby was a very honest boy and I was going to protect him no matter what anyone said or did to me. That is what a good mama bear does.

He finished his third-grade year and went on to have even better fourth, fifth, and sixth grade years with great teachers. Principal's honor roll or honor roll one year after another with near perfect attendance. I continued to be attentive to his safety and well-being at school and continued to volunteer on the PTA committee. I chaperoned his junior high dances and attended every single party and field trip from kindergarten on. Kyle was my pride and joy. I had a blast with my boy and made sure I never missed a special moment in my son's life.

In retrospect, regarding our experiences with the school administration, it is so important to stand up for what is right and protect our children. Kyle's honesty and openness about his school day allowed me to address issues promptly, ensuring his well-being. The challenges we faced with the school administration and the teacher's misconduct were difficult, but they reinforced my commitment to advocate for my son's safety and education. Despite the obstacles, Kyle thrived, achieving academic success and forming strong bonds with his teachers and peers. Children should not ever have to face issues in school alone. School is intimidating and pressurizing enough as it is. I cannot stress enough how important parental involvement is in a child's education, and the impact of a supportive and attentive parent in overcoming challenges in and out of school.

MOTHER'S REFLECTION:
A Parent's Presence Is Not Optional

When a school stops listening, a parent must speak louder. The administration may have tried to push me aside, but they underestimated the power of a mother who refuses to be dismissed. I was never fighting just for access, I was fighting for truth, safety, and integrity. Kyle's honesty was my compass, and his courage became my conviction. When authority behaves as if accountability is an inconvenience, it is up to those who care the most to restore balance. I did not stand in that school to prove a point, I stood there so my son would always know that his voice mattered, and so did mine.

42

I LOVE BOOBIES

WHEN KYLE WAS, I believe, in fourth grade he started collecting the rubber bracelets that were all the rage back then, and honestly, still popular today. I made many to memorialize Kyle's passing and gave them to many of his friends and family. They are used to promote self-help, and to raise awareness for different charities or promoting businesses, and much more, and can be a fun thing for kids.

He had an impressive collection, and unbelievably, I still have many of them tucked away in storage with his other things. One that stood out in my mind, and his favorite, was a black camouflage bracelet with "I love boobies" printed on it. It was meant to support breast cancer awareness.

Well, when Kyle wore it to school, you would not believe the reaction! A staff member expressed concern, and I remember thinking, "Of all people, I would have expected more understanding about the cause behind it." When Kyle came home and told me about it, saying that the teacher told him not to wear it to school, I was furious and a bit perplexed.

"There is absolutely nothing wrong with that bracelet, Kyle. You can keep wearing it!"

Despite my encouragement, the teacher kept insisting that he take it off, even keeping him in from recess when he refused to do so. This back-and-forth continued until Kyle was eventually sent to the principal's office. The principal called me, and we had a serious discussion about the situation. I made it clear that Kyle was an eleven-year-old boy and a straight A student who was flourishing in school. He was just trying to raise awareness for a reputable charity and having fun in the process. Oh no fun to be had if the principal had anything to do with it! It was infuriating to think that the school administration could believe this straight-A student was wearing it for any inappropriate reason.

I gave Kyle the choice to leave it at home while he went to school or to wear it for just cause. He chose to uphold his right. I stepped in when needed to fight for my son and his rights against an administration, in my view, was acting unfairly and crooked, which is unfortunately a familiar role that I refused to get used to. I have always taught Kyle to stand up for what he believes in, and he did just that. He did not waver, and it brought me so much pride. I even rallied some of the other parents to challenge the school's ridiculous decision. In the end, I sought legal support again, and a letter was sent to the school affirming Kyle's right to express support for a charitable cause. It was unacceptable to me that they seemed to be interpreting the bracelet in a way that, in my view, missed its true purpose and message.

Kyle also needed to write a letter explaining why he was justified in wearing the bracelet and what it meant to him. We won the fight! Kyle truly was a beautiful human being, such a remarkable boy and later, young man. He knew that what he was doing was right, and he had to prove it to the school system.

It is disheartening honestly, to think how the administrators tried to pressure Kyle into submission, but their efforts fell short. I raised Kyle to stand up for just cause and to help those who are being mistreated or exploited and that is exactly what he did. I could not be prouder of him and admired him deeply for it. As I often say, "Fighting for what's right is essential even if we are standing alone." Kyle certainly did not stand alone. He stood tall for a cause that mattered and had me and many others in his corner supporting him all the way.

MOTHER'S REFLECTION:
Pride Is Not Measured by Popularity

When my son stood up for what he believed in, he was not defying rules, he was honoring truth. That bracelet meant something to him. It symbolized support, awareness, and the kind of light-hearted compassion that only a child can offer so earnestly. To see authority distort that intention was disheartening. But Kyle did not bend. He held steady in his convictions, with grace and quiet strength. As his mother, I stood beside him, reminding both of us that doing what is right does not always mean being liked. It means being true. Kyle showed me that standing tall can come in the form of a small wristband, and it can echo far beyond the classroom.

43

COPPER MOUNTAIN

KYLE HAD A DEEP passion for snow skiing, and he especially enjoyed snowboarding. During winter, we would visit Snow Creek Ski Resort in Weston, Missouri, where he could truly experience the thrill he loved, as opposed to snowboarding down a church hill near our home. It was also at this resort that Kyle earned yet two other Scout merit badges, one for skiing and one for snowboarding, adding to his impressive collection of achievements.

One year we embarked on a memorable trip to Copper Mountain Ski Resort. Kyle and his dad had an absolute blast, immersing themselves in the breathtaking Colorado Rocky Mountains as they skied tirelessly. While I did some skiing myself, my main focus was capturing my son's joyous descents on video. I also indulged in some shopping and treated myself to my first Starbucks experience, despite the overpriced coffee.

As a part of our itinerary, I arranged for a horse-drawn sleigh ride through the mountains at dusk. It led us to a magnificent open tent where we enjoyed an incredible evening dinner amidst the falling snow and the shimmering stars. This experience became the highlight of our trip for me, a precious moment when our family came together, just as it should have always been.

When I often think about our trip to Copper Mountain, it fills me with warmth and gratitude for the moments we shared as a family.

Watching Kyle revel in his passion for snowboarding and skiing showed me I needed Kyle to pursue what he loved, while I captured his exciting descents on video that allowed me to freeze those memories in time.

MOTHER'S REFLECTION:
Winter Joy

The horse-drawn sleigh ride was a serene contrast to the breathtaking days on the slopes and reminded me that the most cherished memories often arise not only from thrilling adventures but also from quiet moments of connection.

Ultimately, this trip taught me the value of embracing both excitement and simplicity in Kyle's life. I hope to carry this lesson forward, encouraging all moms and dads to create new adventures with their children while cherishing the moments that may just bring them closer together.

44

LOSING HIS
CLOSEST FRIEND

KYLE RETURNED TO HIS previous grade school for the remainder of third and fourth grade. He always made friends easily, but one boy stood out, someone he connected with deeply. They lived in various parts of town, so Kyle only saw him after school when I could pick him up, or on weekends when he stayed with us. We made countless road trips to bring friends back and forth. I did not know many parents who did that as often as we did.

Kyle and this boy fit together like puzzle pieces. His friend had older siblings and spent many weekends with us. For Kyle's eighth birthday, we gave him a battery-operated dirt bike. He was not quite ready for the real thing yet, though a few years later he earned both a full-size bike and an ATV. His friend once asked if he could have a bike like Kyle's, explaining that his family might not be able to get him one. I told him he would need to ask his parents first.

It was the summer before fourth grade, hot and heavy with anticipation for the Fourth of July. We planned to pick up Kyle's friend one morning, but when Kyle called, he said his mom had gone back to sleep and his older siblings were watching him. Once she woke up, we could come get him.

Later that afternoon, I got a call from his mother asking if we had picked him up. Panic set in. I left Kyle with his dad and drove straight to a nearby park, searching the streets with his family. Hours later, a family member called to say he had been in a terrible accident and was in the hospital.

We told Kyle immediately and rushed to be with the family. I did not know what we would find, and I did not want Kyle to see anything traumatic. But his father disagreed and allowed Kyle to go in. What we saw that day will stay with me forever. It was too much for a child. I feared it would haunt Kyle, and I believe it did.

Kyle shed quiet tears but stood strong. He held his friend's hand and whispered, "Wake up. I love you." A single tear slipped from his friend's closed eyes. Though he could not speak, I believe he heard Kyle's voice and felt his love. That moment gave them both a kind of peace.

Kyle was stronger than I was that day. I held the boy's other hand and, through my own tears, promised, "If you open your eyes and get better, I will get you that dirt bike you wanted." We waited, hoping for a sign. Then we said our goodbyes, told him how much we loved him, prayed over him, and left.

The rest of the day was quiet. I tried to keep Kyle busy, but the weight of it all was heavy. We prayed constantly. The next evening, his friend passed away.

I had to tell my little boy that his best friend would not be coming back. I said he would see him again one day in Heaven, but not for a long time. Kyle was quiet, maybe in shock, trying to absorb it all. It had happened so fast.

He asked me to lie down with him. We cuddled, and he held me tightly as I stroked his hair, trying not to cry. I reassured him that his friend was safe now, and that even though he would miss him, they would meet again someday. Kyle said he loved me and fell asleep in my arms, drained from the grief.

Over the years, we visited his friend's resting place from time to time. His parents gave him a framed photo of the two of them, which he kept in his room for many years. I still have it, along with other mementos.

In the spring of 2019, Kyle and I returned to the cemetery. It had been a while, and it took time to find his resting place. We brought balloons, wrote messages of love on them, and released them into the sky.

Kyle was older now, but I could still see the pain in his eyes. He tried not to cry, but I saw the anger and confusion beneath the surface. He could not remember exactly what had happened, but the loss still tormented him. We said goodbye and went out to dinner.

Just the two of us. We talked about our plans to move the following year. Kyle could always share his feelings with me, something he told me, he did not feel comfortable doing with his dad. His father had been taught to avoid emotion, but Kyle knew he could be open with me.

The loss of his closest friend left a lasting mark. In the days that followed, we did our best to support him, not by avoiding the pain, but by helping him navigate it. Reassuring him that his friend was at peace gave him space to grieve.

Visiting his friend and releasing balloons became a way to honor the memory. As Kyle grew older, the pain remained, showing up in quiet moments and deep reflection. I could always sense his emotions, even when he tried to hide them. It was a maternal instinct, not every parent has it, but I was grateful I did.

That time together gave us a sense of normalcy and a chance to look ahead, to a new home, a new chapter, and a bond that only deepened through shared sorrow and love.

In Loving Memory of Our Little Friend

To the boy who brought laughter and light to Kyle's world, your presence was a gift, your friendship a blessing. You are remembered not for the pain, but for the joy you gave so freely. You are missed. You are cherished. You are held in love, always.

45

THE BRACES
THAT GOT AWAY

KYLE'S TEETH BEGAN TO grow a bit crooked in grade school, which led me to make the decision to get him Invisalign braces. I wanted only the best for my son, and I hoped that these clear aligners would provide a more comfortable and less noticeable solution than traditional metal braces. Despite my good intentions, Kyle absolutely hated them. The dentist had presented him with a choice: Invisalign or the more traditional titanium braces. Faced with that dilemma, Kyle reluctantly chose the Invisalign, but it came with strict instructions. He was to take care of them diligently, including remembering to remove them before lunch at school. I made sure to reinforce those instructions at home, reminding him how important it was to keep track of his braces.

However, despite our best efforts, on many occasions, I would come home to find Kyle without his braces. I would ask, "Poo Doo, where are your braces?" The response was often the same: "Oh no! I left them at school!" This realization would send us into a mini panic as we would rummage through his backpack, hoping to find them hidden among his school supplies. More often than not, we ended up sprinting to the school as fast as we could, trying to make it before everyone left and the doors were locked for the day.

I cannot tell you how many times I found myself in the lunchroom, digging through the trash cans filled with leftover lunches from hundreds of kids. It was a daunting task, navigating through the remnants of half-eaten sandwiches and spilled juice boxes. Fortunately, the janitor, who had developed a soft spot for Kyle, would always lend a helping hand. Together, we would sift through the garbage, hoping to uncover the elusive braces.

Despite our efforts, there were two instances when we had no luck at all, and we had to replace the lost aligners. Thankfully, the dentist was understanding and quite fond of Kyle, so he generously provided a new set at no additional charge each time. I still keep the ones that were not permanently lost in safekeeping, a testament to the journey we shared. All in all, we spent thousands of dollars on his beautiful teeth, but I was grateful for the dental insurance that helped ease the financial burden.

MOTHER'S REFLECTION:
What We Salvage Together

I used to think braces were just about straight teeth. But those frantic dashes to the school, the trash can treasure hunts, and the quiet teamwork with a kind janitor taught me otherwise. They were lessons in love disguised as inconvenience. Kyle learned responsibility, and I learned patience. We both learned that parenting is not just about doing what's best, it is about showing up, again and again, even when it is messy. I still keep those salvaged aligners tucked away, not just as dental memorabilia, but as reminders of the journey we shared. The laughter, the frustration, the bond; it is all here, sealed in plastic and memory.

46

A VERY HURTFUL NEIGHBOR

ONE NEW FRIEND STOOD out. This boy was living around the block with his grandparents and his mother. He was a boy facing some difficult circumstances at home. A boy without a father. His grandfather wanted to be a role model for him. They did the best they could, but the boy obviously had anger issues. I was a little nervous about this friendship, but I tried to give the boy the benefit of the doubt. Because I doubted much had been given to him and I hoped Kyle and his circle of friends would be good for him. He was a neighborhood boy so in this case it was a relationship of proximity.

Kyle wanted someone nearby to play with as all his other friends were in different subdivisions, so he befriended a kid we frequently saw at the overflow pond while we were fishing. They became friends. Not close but just friends. The boy showed bouts of anger here and there and when he did, I would talk with him about it. I allowed him to vent to me and did my best to calm him when he got angry, but I did not want that around my son. He knew that if he started to get angry then he needed to go home. One day this neighborhood boy came over and asked my son and another friend if he could join them on the trampoline, and that was the last time he would ever be in contact with my son.

I was in the kitchen making them an after-school snack, watching them on the trampoline from my kitchen window to make sure they were safe. I heard a scream from Kyle's friend and ran out to see if everyone was okay. My fear was that someone had fallen off even though there was a net around the trampoline. (I always feared one of them bouncing too high and falling off.)

I ran outside as quickly as possible and around the corner, I saw the neighborhood boy and my son on the trampoline. This boy was on top of my son strangling him. Kyle's face was bright red and his arms flailing, trying to break free. Kyle's friend was trying to pull him off and as soon as he saw me, he let go. I grabbed his arm and pulled him off my son and off the trampoline. The strangler fought loose and started to walk home. I told him to stop at once. I was trying to see if my son was okay, but I was not going to let the strangler go. Kyle had turned beet red as this boy was draining every ounce of oxygen from his precious body. He quickly started coughing and crying hysterically. His friend and I carried him inside as best we could and got ice packs for his neck. I held him as I was yelling at the boy to stop in his tracks. I remember rocking my son back and forth and rubbing his head just as I did when he was younger and upset about something as he was crying out of fear and pain. I was trying to be strong and not cry myself or run after the boy.

I screamed at the boy to stop and come back. He ignored me. I called my husband and told him that the boy had tried to kill our son, and he was to come home now! After getting my son calmed down and settled down a bit, having his friend keep an eye on Kyle, I went outside, and the boy was still walking home as slow as he could go. I warned him not to take another step, or I would have to call the cops. Looking back, I wish I had. I should have called them and regret it to this day. He finally stopped in his tracks and turned around and walked toward the house. I told him to come inside and sit down because his grandparents or mom were not home at the time, and I was afraid that he would go get his grandfather's gun and hurt himself or one of us. This boy was a loose cannon, and this was the worst that I had ever seen, yet I knew it could get worse.

He sat inside on the couch as I shook uncontrollably trying everything in my power to contain myself. I had to control my contempt for this boy but at the same time was so empathetic toward him for being so lost, angry, and confused. This is when I hate being an empath. My son was as well. I called my husband again so he could talk me down as Kyle and I were both crying. We were both so afraid of this boy, but I was not going to let him walk away and hurt himself or someone else.

As he was taking his time, I kept telling my husband, "Please hurry and get here, please." I did not understand why he seemed so nonchalant about what had just happened. His son almost passed away, yet he had no urgency to console him or confront the other boy. As soon as he pulled into the driveway, I hung up the phone and when he came inside, I told him to get this boy out of my sight. I adore children so I was hoping and pleading for my husband to intervene. Believe me when I say it took every ounce of strength and prayer in me.

He drove the boy home and sat with him until his mom got home and then spoke with her. I do not know what was said as my husband always felt the need to keep certain things from me, the important things. I do know that a few weeks later, we saw the boy at the pond as we were fishing and he apologized to Kyle, though in my heart, it was hard to reconcile, considering he almost killed my son.

Kyle, being the sweetest boy on the planet, forgave him but refused to say another word to him or even look at him and wanted to go home until he left. The boy was moving away with his mother, and we would never see him again.

I had recurring nightmares of this event for a long time. Seeing my beautiful son lying on his back with someone on top of him taking every breath from him was devastating. The look of fear on my son's face as he was near death. I will never forget.

My son had nightmares for many nights after that. All I could do was to console him, sleep with him and rub his back until he fell asleep and told him that everything would be all right, and I was never going to let anything happen to him. I was overprotective after that day, even more so than before. I was not going to allow another deeply troubled child to hurt my son.

I will never know if that one incident on the trampoline played a part in my son's choice to start smoking pot to take the pain away. Deep down, I know it played a supporting role, but not the leading role that led him to substance. I sometimes think that he wanted to try it to let others believe that he was tough and could handle anything. Wanting a sense of control and power, to take him back from a time when he was helpless.

Only later did he realize he could not handle what the pot did to him but was too far gone in his struggle to stop, which led to much more lethal things in his effort to make the pain go away.

MOTHER'S REFLECTION:
Friendship Should Not Hurt

Kyle opened his heart to a boy who needed kindness, and for that, he was met with violence. That is the part that still stings, honestly. He was trying to be a friend, to include, to care, to give someone a chance. I cannot forget the look on his face, or the confusion in his eyes when pain came from a place where acceptance should have lived. It was not just a physical violence; it was a betrayal of trust. I will never stop wishing that moment had gone differently, and I will always admire Kyle's ability to forgive, even when the cost was almost his life.

47

ON THE ICE

KYLE'S FIRST EXPERIENCE ON ice turned out to be his last, at least for a while. I am not sure why the ice terrace always opens on a school day, but we woke up super early on a chilly morning, excited to take Kyle to the Crown Center Ice Terrace for his inaugural round on skates. Despite the cold, the sun was shining, and we felt it was a well-deserved treat for him. As a straight-A student who never missed a day of school, he had certainly earned a bit of fun.

True to form, Kyle was a natural on the ice, just as he was with everything else he tried. He glided around effortlessly, having a blast as he completed a few rounds. However, the mood shifted when we heard sirens getting closer. Initially, we thought they would pass, but they only grew louder.

A staff member began directing people to clear the rink, and we soon learned that someone had fallen, and another skater accidentally cut their finger with their skate. They were even searching for the severed finger on the ice. Understandably, this scared Kyle quite a bit and he said that he did not want to skate anymore. He quickly took off his skates and declared he was done. Rather than taking him to school that day, we decided to take him to Freddy's Train Station at the Crown Center and then back home. We wanted to end the day on a positive note, steering clear of the fear he had developed about getting hurt on the ice.

As the years went by, the memories of that chilly morning faded, but apparently his love for ice skating did not. Eventually, an ice rink opened at Town Center Plaza, and I was thrilled to hear that Kyle wanted to give it another try. I remember the first time we went together; it felt right, like everything had come together. Watching him glide around the rink again, I could see the joy in his eyes as he skated alongside a couple of his old friends. It was as if he had regained his confidence, and he was once again the natural athlete I had always known him to be.

I would make sure he bundled up, while I sipped on my hot chocolate, cheering him on from the sidelines and soaking in every moment of his laughter and excitement. Those nights were so frigid, but they were also filled with warmth from the happiness of sharing those moments together. After he was done, we would head off to On the Border for some Mexican food and to warm up a bit.

Kyle had come so far from that initial scare, and it was touching to see him embrace the sport and enjoy it once again. As he got older, he was spending more time with friends and less with mom, so I sure cherished our time together. They offered a glimpse of the wonderful young man he was becoming, along with the thrill of ice skating, he had healthy fun spending time with family and friends. It was a beautiful reminder that sometimes, even after that scary experience years before, he could find happiness on the ice.

MOTHER'S REFLECTION:
Skating Past the Fear

Kyle's journey back to the ice was not just about recreation, it was about restoration. Fear had cut into something he once loved, and for a time, it stayed with him. But healing came quietly, with confidence and joy skating alongside his courage. Watching him glide across the rink again, I saw not just grace, but growth. It reminded me that strength does not always roar, it can show up in a pair of skates, a warm laugh, or a child deciding that fear no longer gets the final say. He found happiness again, and I found hope with every lap he took.

48

BONES HEAL, HEARTS REMEMBER

I STILL HAVE KYLE'S ARM casts from when he was a young tween. He was practicing Parkour or on his BMX bikes when he broke both arms, luckily not at the same time. One year it was his right arm and the next year, it was his left. He was all boy and enjoyed all the rough, daredevil things that boys do.

I really thought he was serious about Parkour, so I got him into a Parkour class at a gymnasium not too far away where they had an obstacle course set up for simulation and allowed them to practice. I would set up the camcorder in the backyard and the two of us created small obstacle courses for him to practice his numerous skills. He enjoyed it, but was reluctant to go too far with it, since he had already broken both arms, and gone head-on with a skateboarder which I will tell you about next. He loved the action but did not enjoy the physical pain that came along with it.

We took Kyle and one of his extremely expensive trick bikes that he got for his birthday, to Lee's Summit skate park one evening. It was so crowded. There were many kids with skateboards, bikes, and inline skates. Kyle was nervous but warmed up eventually and had a ball riding his bike up and down the ramps. Next thing I see out of the corner of my eye, is my son colliding with another kid. I, of course, panicked and ran to save my son while his dad followed, casually.

Luckily, Kyle was wearing his pads and helmet which had a small crack in it. When I reached both, I saw that he had not collided with another kid, but a young adult. We needed to call 911. When the ambulance came and eventually took the young man away to the hospital, we left, as Kyle was too shaken up but not hurt, to continue.

I called the hospital later that evening and they allowed me to speak to the young man. He said that he had broken his pelvic bone in the collision. He said he had just gotten home from being deployed overseas for several months and that skateboarding was what he missed most of all and could not wait to get back to his passion doing what he loved most. He talked to Kyle and told him not to worry at all, and everything would be taken care of. He told Kyle to get back out there and keep practicing his tricks and never give up on his dreams.

It still bothered Kyle greatly that the other person got wounded and not him. I do not think that Kyle ever wanted to go back after that. He just did not like getting hurt, but who does? Kyle was so afraid he would hurt someone else. The nice young man managed to survive his time overseas in combat without getting hurt but met his match at the skate park that night.

I spent so much money on trick bikes, hundreds of dollars' worth, along with his dirt bike and ATV and many other toys and opportunities. I wanted Kyle to have everything I had as a child, and better. Not that I wanted to spoil him, but I genuinely wanted him to experience every wonderful opportunity available to him.

I felt the more fun things he experienced, the better his chances to decide what he really wanted to do with his future as far as education and a career. After all he was my miracle baby, and I knew that he was here for an incredibly special reason. I wanted him to be exposed to all the wonderful things that he could be doing if he took it seriously and worked at it and did not give up.

MOTHER'S REFLECTION:
No Harm Intended

That day at the skate park, Kyle saw the power of impact, not just on the body, but on the spirit. He did not get hurt, but it wounded him anyway. He was always gentle, always thoughtful, and the idea that someone else suffered because of a moment they shared shook him deeply. He was not reckless; he was growing. Exploring. Figuring out how far he could go without crossing a line. I saw a side of Kyle that day, compassionate, haunted, and brave and I still hold gratitude for that young man's kindness, for helping my son let go of guilt he should never have carried.

49

MORE SPORTS

KYLE HAD MANY INCREDIBLE years of baseball and soccer in the summer as well as football and basketball in the fall and winter months. He won an exceedingly substantial number of awards, trophies, and certificates that I was quite honored to share with others and very proudly displayed throughout our home. Kyle was proud of himself also, as he should have been.

When Kyle felt down about not carrying out something he strived for, I would confirm to him that, no matter what, I was so honored he started an honest effort in many things that many kids do not have the opportunity to. I also reminded him that he should do everything with diligence and not be ashamed of trying his best. My son worked feverishly hard in everything he did. God saw this and so did mom.

Kyle, and with some convincing, along with daddy, decided to try Taekwondo. That was quite a workout for him and required good discipline as he had to do many exercises to warm up before class. Students would have to practice their techniques and different forms of striking. They would both change into their uniforms and equipment and spar on the weekends out in the front yard getting ready for testing or tournaments. We spent so much money on equipment and lessons. For many months, Kyle developed great discipline but when they reached their high blue belt, his dad decided to stop.

My husband told me he wanted to quit, saying he did not want to spend any more money on it. The higher the belt, the more expensive it was. I assured Kyle that he could continue no matter what the cost. I wish Kyle would have continued as he was so good at it, but he followed daddy in quitting. When Kyle first started, he told me he wanted to go all the way to black belt. He would break Styrofoam in the front yard while I held it, as a steppingstone to breaking boards with his bare feet and hands. When I asked him to continue, he told me that his dad told him we could not afford it, and he needed to find something else to do. That was not how I saw it, we could afford, especially if it was something that Kyle was passionate about, I was determined to support him and help him excel and a decent parent would never put that burden on their child. No child should feel responsible for a parent's choices.

Adding to that pain, his dad wanted him to quit. He did not seem to support Kyle's desire to excel. I sometimes wondered if it was because he had not had similar opportunities growing up. Every parent needs to strive to lift their child higher, to inspire them to be better than they were. It is our job to open doors, to create pathways to success and to encourage them to dream bigger and achieve more than we ever could. I struggle to understand my husband did not seem to want more for his only child.

While Kyle enjoyed the sport and discipline, I think the real reason he enjoyed it was because it was time he spent with his dad. He wanted the attention and affection so badly from him. Kyle was starving for positive attention from the male role model in his life. When his dad quit repeatedly, that chance of connection was gone.

Kyle came to me and said, "Mom, how come Dad wants to quit? Why doesn't he want to spend time with me?"

All I could do was console him and try to convince him to continue but he was reluctant to do it if his dad was not going to be by his side and cheer him on. So many times, my son was disappointed. I continued to support and be there for my son regardless of what his dad was thinking and doing.

Kyle did, however, learn enough to defend himself if necessary and did come to the point a couple of times where he had to do just that. Kyle was aware he could hurt someone seriously with the skills he had learned but told me he did not want to hurt anyone so in turn he got hurt instead. This was the empath in Kyle. A boy who had compassion and cared so much for another human being whether they hurt him or not, and many did hurt him for no good reason up until his very last moments on earth.

MOTHER'S REFLECTION:
The Spirit Behind the Sparring

Kyle did not just chase medals or belts, he chased connection and when that connection disappeared, so did the motivation. I saw how much he needed encouragement, not just to succeed in Taekwondo, but to feel seen. He wanted his dad's attention. His presence. His belief. And when it did not come, the discipline Kyle had built could not erase the ache of being left behind. Yet even then, he chose gentleness over aggression. Compassion over domination. That is the kind of strength that no trophy could ever capture.

50

Sky Bound Memories

THERE WAS A FUN hobby that Kyle and I shared: Weather chasing. It is not a hobby I thought I would enjoy as much as I did, but it was fun, exciting, and most importantly, it brought my son joy, and I would do anything to see pure happiness and excitement in my son. It all started when Kyle was small. He and I would spend many days in the front or backyard or at a nearby park, admiring the sky and searching for different shapes and animals in the clouds, then in the summer evenings lying on a blanket in the driveway, just relaxing. As he got older, we lay on the dirt bike and ATV trailer in the driveway. Just the two of us unwinding and enjoying the crisp night air while sharing our day with each other.

"Mommy it's so pretty...look at all the stars Mommy, and God made all this didn't He?" I still remember his sweet, curious voice saying to me.

This was where Kyle fell in love with the beauty of God's creation and since then he was always curious about it. So, when a commercial came on TV advertising for storm spotters in our area and offering training, Kyle and I jumped on the chance.

Next thing I knew, we were both in City Hall for hours getting certified to be storm spotters for our area. Let me tell you, without hesitation, we were one of the first in the area and Kyle was so proud of that. Kyle oversaw record-keeping of our local weather and would report any major storms that came in our area. This was a milestone that Kyle was incredibly proud of. He even got to tour the weather center in Pleasant Hill, Missouri.

As soon as we got the necessary equipment in the mail, Kyle began taking detailed and copious daily records. He absolutely loved it and continued this practice well into his teen years. When he was fourteen, he called in a tornado like the one we experienced all those years ago. On the television, I could hear, "Kyle from Raymore has spotted a funnel cloud. If anyone is in his area, please find a safe place and take cover." At that moment I did not think I had seen my boy look prouder of himself. I do not think I'll ever forget that look of hearing his name on the weather. Sadly, his dad missed most of the special moments with Kyle because of his lack of interest in the family unit.

MOTHER'S REFLECTION:
Awe in the Sky

Kyle's heart belonged to the clouds, not just in wonder, but in responsibility. What started as stargazing became storm spotting, and he rose to the role with pride. I watched him take ownership of something so vast and unpredictable with a calm and confident spirit. Hearing his name broadcasted on the weather, I knew we had done something right, that his name stood for vigilance, passion, and care. He saw beauty in every shifting sky, and that same beauty lived in him.

51

Beyond the Greens

After Taekwondo, he thought he wanted to try something more relaxing like golf. Daddy loved golf. Surely his dad would want to spend time with him if he played golf. This was his dad's somewhat healthier go-to sport.

I bought Kyle his own set of clubs and everything else he needed to be the best he could be and enrolled him in golf lessons at Eagles Landing. I would take him there a couple of times a week for his lesson.

Kyle liked it at first but said it was too slow and boring. Kyle was more interested in sports that involved speed and high intensity. Golf is a game where you are alone with yourself and the conversation in your head. It was not the best fit for Kyle, but he still tried to please his dad even though his dad never tried to please him.

He pretended to enjoy it to be able to have something in common with his dad and was exceptionally good at it. He got bored easily and just wanted to drive the cart from hole to hole and watch his dad, although as he got older, he would go play with his dad or a friend from time to time.

Kyle and I would play nine holes at a course nearby and on occasion went to Top Golf for snacks and just to relax and hit some balls, and at times we would play miniature golf at a nearby fun center. Eighteen holes was too much for me as I found golf too slow as well, but it was always fun spending time with Kyle.

We both were energetic people and enjoyed a faster pace, so Kyle took tennis lessons so we could play tennis together. Kyle gave me a run for my money, literally wearing me out on the tennis court. Yes, he was faster than his much older and out-of-shape mom, but we had a blast laughing at ourselves.

He also joined a bowling league, of course getting his own ball with his name on it, and of course, earning another award along with the swimming team. He was also natural at all of them, quickly learning all aspects of every sport, gaining him yet more plaques, trophies, and ribbons which were displayed throughout his bedroom and other areas of the house.

Kyle loved athletics but did not like the competition. He lost interest in sports when it came to competing with others, saying, "Why do we have to compete? Why can't we just have fun playing the game?"

Neither one of us could play a simple game of Monopoly with his dad, without it lasting for hours on end until we were both falling asleep at the kitchen table. The competition was relentless. Kyle got so tired of it, so he stopped playing it with him.

We loved to take our bikes out to Longview Lake on the weekends and ride along the sixteen-mile trail. After school we would ride along the trails in our neighborhood and walk the dogs or take them to the nearest community center and walk the trails. We tried to stay as active as possible. Sometimes I ended up walking the dogs alone while he socialized and had fun at the skate park nearby. The time I spent with my son was remarkable and unforgettable. Oh, how I cherish and desperately miss all those precious moments.

MOTHER'S REFLECTION:
Joy Without Rivalry

Kyle chased only connection. Whether it was swinging a golf club to feel closer to his dad or pedaling beside me on a lakeside trail, he found joy in movement, not in medals. He was a natural athlete, but even more, he was a gentle soul who asked, "Why do we have to compete?" That question still echoes in me. Because for Kyle, play was never about winning, it was about being together and in that, he won every time.

52

ROOM TO BREATHE

KYLE HAD ALWAYS BEEN restless. As he got older, the urge to break free from the neat edges of suburbia turned into an obsession. He dreamed of open land, where he could ride his dirt bike and ATV without limits, where he could carve paths through trees, build his own ramps, and push himself past every hesitation. It was not just about riding. It was about breathing.

I understood that feeling, maybe more than I wanted to admit. He had a couple of friends that went to his school but lived much farther away in the country. We had built a beautiful home, a place where every corner held memories, where every wall stood firm against the storm's life had thrown at us. But beauty is not the same as freedom, and freedom, well, freedom was something Kyle craved so deeply that I could not ignore it. My husband seemed to see things differently. Moving just because Kyle wanted space? Not happening. I knew that debate well, it was not the first time we had it, and it would probably not be the last.

Kyle had a way of wearing people down though, with a mix of stubbornness and charm that was impossible to deny for long. After enough pleading, reasoning, and let's be honest, relentless persistence, we got Daddy on board with a compromise. If we could not move to the country, we could at least *go* there. That is how we found ourselves packing up gear, loading up the ATV and dirt bike, and heading to Deep Water in Clinton, and later, Perry Lake. A place where the trails stretched wide, and the air was fresh with the scent of adventure. Kyle would finally have room to be wild, but in a way I could, somewhat, control. Letting him ride through neighborhood streets was not an option. Not because he would not have done it safely, but because I knew the world would not always be kind to a teenage boy on a dirt bike looking for escape. Out in the open, though, away from the traffic, away from the rules that boxed him in, he could find something close to the freedom he longed for.

I would be lying if I said I loved every minute of it. Dirt, mud, the occasional moment of panic when the ATV got stuck, none of that was my idea of fun even though it was. *But watching Kyle? That was different.* The way his whole face lit up as he rode, the thrill in his voice when he pushed past the fear of a tricky hill, the way he laughed when I got stuck, all of it was worth every uncomfortable moment for me. Sometimes, he would invite his cousin along, someone who loved the dirt, loved the thrill, loved the messiness of it all. Maybe that was part of the magic of those trips. They were not just about the rides, or the trails, or even about Kyle finding the space he needed. These were awesome, precious memories. Ones I knew my husband would never get to have with our son, had we not been proactive.

We were not able to give Kyle the countryside he dreamed of, but in those moments, surrounded by trees and trails, covered in dust, and sweat, we gave him a taste of the freedom he had been chasing all along. For me, watching him with his cousin, laughing with him, even when I was covered in mud and mildly terrified, I found my own kind of freedom too.

MOTHER'S REFLECTION:
The Trail Between Us

There is a kind of trail that does not show up on maps. It is made of effort and compromise, of dust stirred by an ATV and quiet glances between a mom and her son who just needed space. I may not have loved the mud or the mess, but I loved what it gave him. That was the real terrain we covered together: the stretch between restraint and release, between being safe and feeling alive. Sometimes, letting him lead the way meant rediscovering myself, too.

53

CANADA

MY SON WENT ON to the fifth and sixth grade center making many new friends along the way. Kyle never seemed to have a problem in any area of his life from socially making friends to his academics. He was the perfect student and the perfect child. He had many wonderful experiences in school despite the losses and obstacles in his life. I did my best to make sure of this. He loved learning and what made all the difference in the world was the teachers he had. I could tell that if he had a good, attentive teacher he would thrive. When he had a know-it-all teacher, who thought they could intimidate kids, he was not doing well, and I quickly intervened to advocate for him. Honestly, there were only two or three that needed talking to.

Some would say I was a helicopter mom, but I was in no way going to let my son be discouraged or mistreated by an adult that was supposed to be teaching him curriculum. I knew I had the final say in my child's education and upbringing and was not about to let any teacher tell me anything different. Most parents are too intimidated to speak up for their children and their safety and education and it needs to stop. *How can some parents stay silent when their child needs them most?* I was in this all by myself and both Kyle and I seemed to be losing respect for his dad as he refused to stand up for our son's rights.

Kyle was a very conscientious student, conveyed by many of his teachers. He was that way at home also. When Kyle faced challenges with difficult teachers or struggled with lessons and studying, I made sure to address it right away and help as much as I could with homework. Dad helped with math and science, and I helped with English and history, and we both helped in his art projects and science projects.

Kyle kept a positive attitude throughout and was so proud of himself and his achievements as he should be. I told Kyle to always make sure that he thanked God for giving him opportunities to excel and guiding him, which I know he did as I listened to him speak to God nightly.

Witnessing my own child grow and acquire new life skills and academic knowledge was an absolute joy for me. It deeply touched my heart to see his enthusiasm for school and his eagerness to learn more every day.

I cannot emphasize enough how crucial it was for both my husband and I to come together to support Kyle in achieving a successful future, despite any issues we may have had, to be able to sow the seeds that would nurture Kyle into a remarkable young adult who could make difference in the world and pray that it would be carried on to our grandchildren one day. Although I did, in fact, embark on this journey mainly on my own, I am certain that my son had a significant, positive influence on many individuals during his brief life. Kyle achieved remarkable things and undoubtedly left a lasting imprint on his family, friends, and colleagues.

My son worked hard in school to disprove an earlier teacher's belief in him. He was popular and helped several students with their homework. So much so that he was recommended to be a part of People to People, an ambassadorship program to Canada for excellent students. He could not come recommended enough. He got to tour Canada coast to coast for two weeks and made some great friends. He would call me every night to let me know he was okay and having a fun time.

On occasion, he would tell me he wanted to come home because he missed me. I would assure him that the opportunity he was given was something that few kids, or any of his friends, had and we would be together soon enough, and he needed to enjoy himself and not worry about mama. This was the first time I had let him be away from me for so long but how could I take away such an awesome privilege from him because I had the mom jitters? I was not about to deny my son that opportunity.

However, my mom jitters were not completely off because Kyle came back different. Somehow, he seemed older. Like something had happened. One of the dangers of being an empath as my son was, is that it attracts a lot of people, and not always good ones. If people are toxic enough, it can be like you are drinking their poison with them. While all these kids might have been diligent students, they were still kids with their own troubles. I just wondered whose troubles he brought home.

Kyle's journey through intermediate school was marked by much growth. He thrived academically and socially, making new friends and excelling in many ways.

I will continue to say that my son needed both his parents' support and advocacy, as do all children because it plays a crucial role in their success. We must make sure they have the best environment to learn and grow. My involvement in Kyle's education was simply being a dedicated parent. His many achievements, including the People-to-People ambassadorship program is a testament to his hard work and the solid foundation I tried diligently to provide. I encouraged him to believe in himself and his abilities and this helped him fly seamlessly through new experiences with the utmost confidence and self-esteem.

MOTHER'S REFLECTION:

When Advocacy Becomes Legacy

*I did not just fight for Kyle's education; I fought for his light.
Every time I stepped in, it was not to control, but to protect
the spark that made him thrive. Watching him earn a place
in the People-to-People program was more than pride,
it was proof that belief, when nurtured, becomes legacy.
He flew across Canada, but he also flew past doubt, past
discouragement, and into the kind of confidence that only
comes from being truly seen. That is what I gave him. That
is what he carried.*

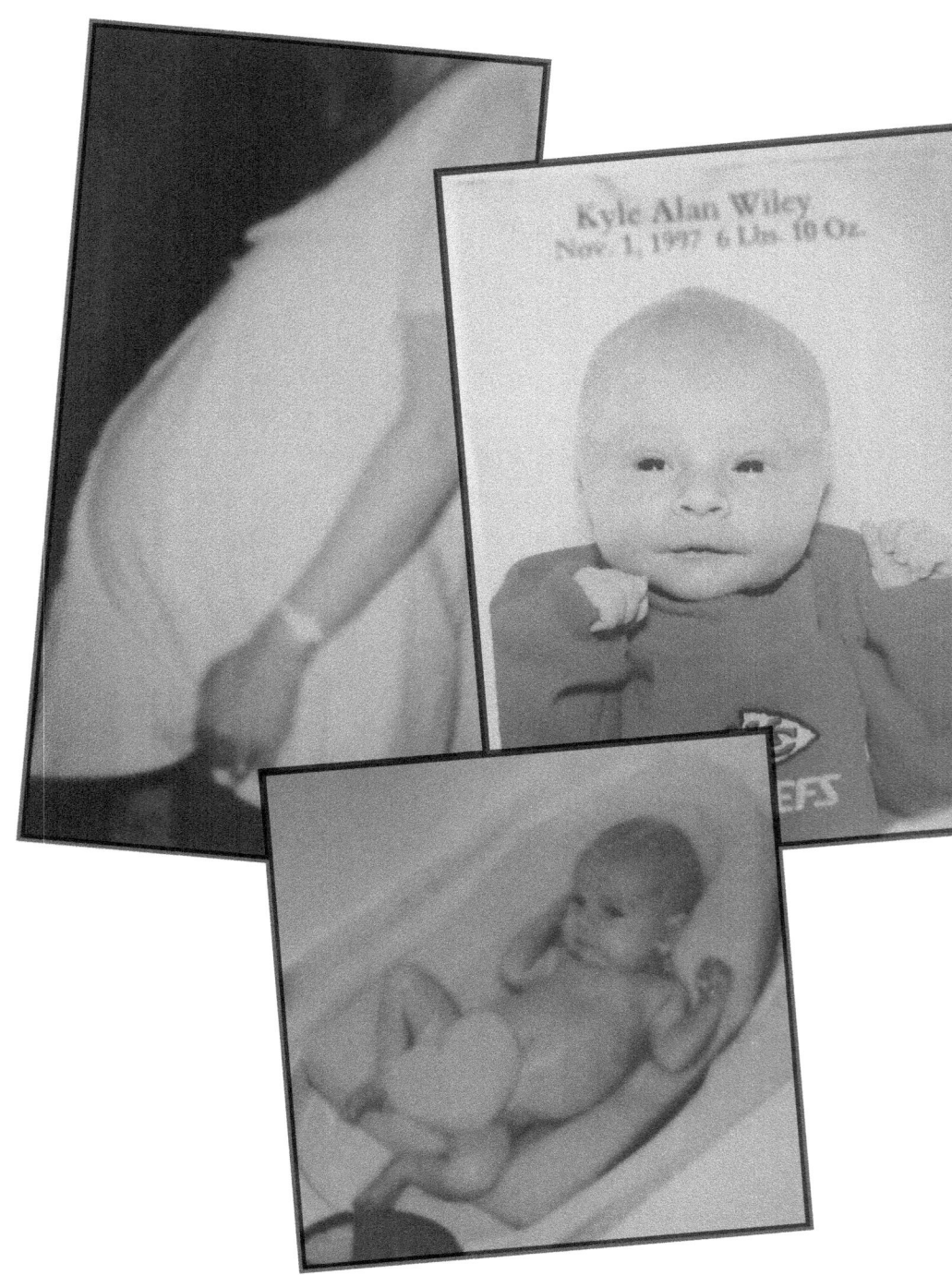

Top Left: Baby shower; eight months along. Celebrating the bump, the love, and the journey ahead.

Top Right: November 1, 1997. Wrapped in Chiefs Red and Day one of forever.

Bottom: One month of magic, wrapped in bubbles and bliss.

Child of Light

Child of Light, I Bless You!
I think of you, I pray for you,
not in terms of what I think you need,
or what I think you should do or be or express.

I lift up my thoughts about you,
I catch a new vision of you,
I see you as a child of light
I see you guided and directed by an
inward Spirit that leads you
unerringly
into the path that is right for you.

I see you strong and whole;
I see you blessed and prospered;
I see you courageous and confident;
I see you capable and successful
I see you free from limitation or
bondage of any kind.

I see you as the spiritually perfect
being you truly are.
Child of light, I bless you!

Daily Word May 13, 1975

Above: Two months old. Every time I looked into your eyes Kyle, I heard God whisper, "He is mine and He is yours."

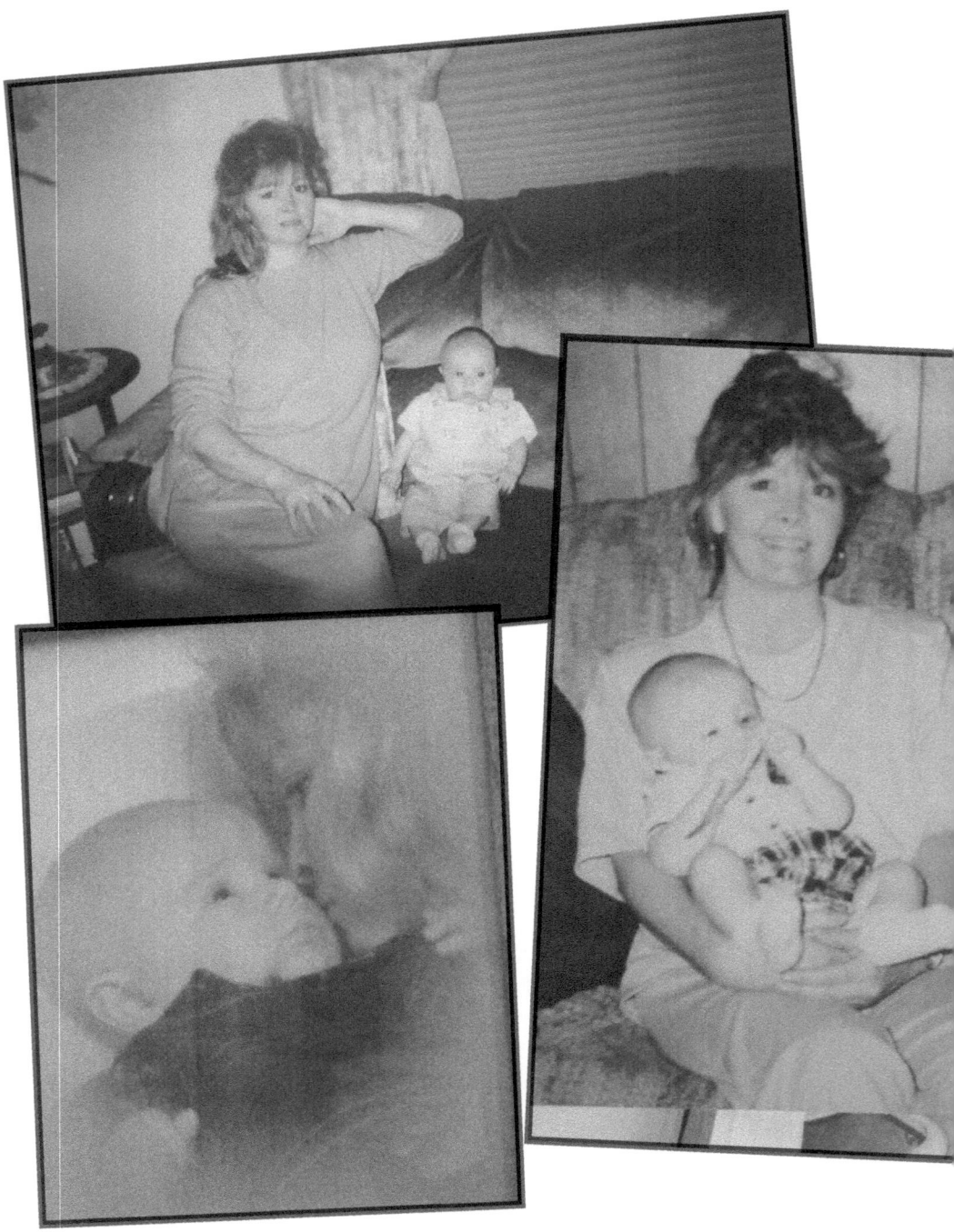

Top: Three months. Baby Kyle learning to sit up, and my heart was memorizing him.

Bottom Left: Three months old. This is the face that made me believe in eternity.

Bottom Right: First Easter, five and a half months old. That little outfit was handpicked. That little boy? Heaven-sent.

Top Left: Summer of 1998 with his Popo. Kyle was barely seven months old. One taught me how to survive. One showed me why.

Top Right: He was the caboose on this family train and being the only Grandson, Momo spoiled him soft and loved him strong. That is what committed grandmothers do.

Bottom: Two years old, where Kyle felt safest and most loved: in Mommy's arms.

Top: At two, winter gave him a friend, and me, a moment etched in forever.

Bottom Left: First sport at three years old, Kyle and Itsy-Bitsy basketball. Tiny hoop, big heart, and my little boy was already chasing joy.

Bottom Right: Family photo at age three. The bond was unbreakable, and the love already lifelong.

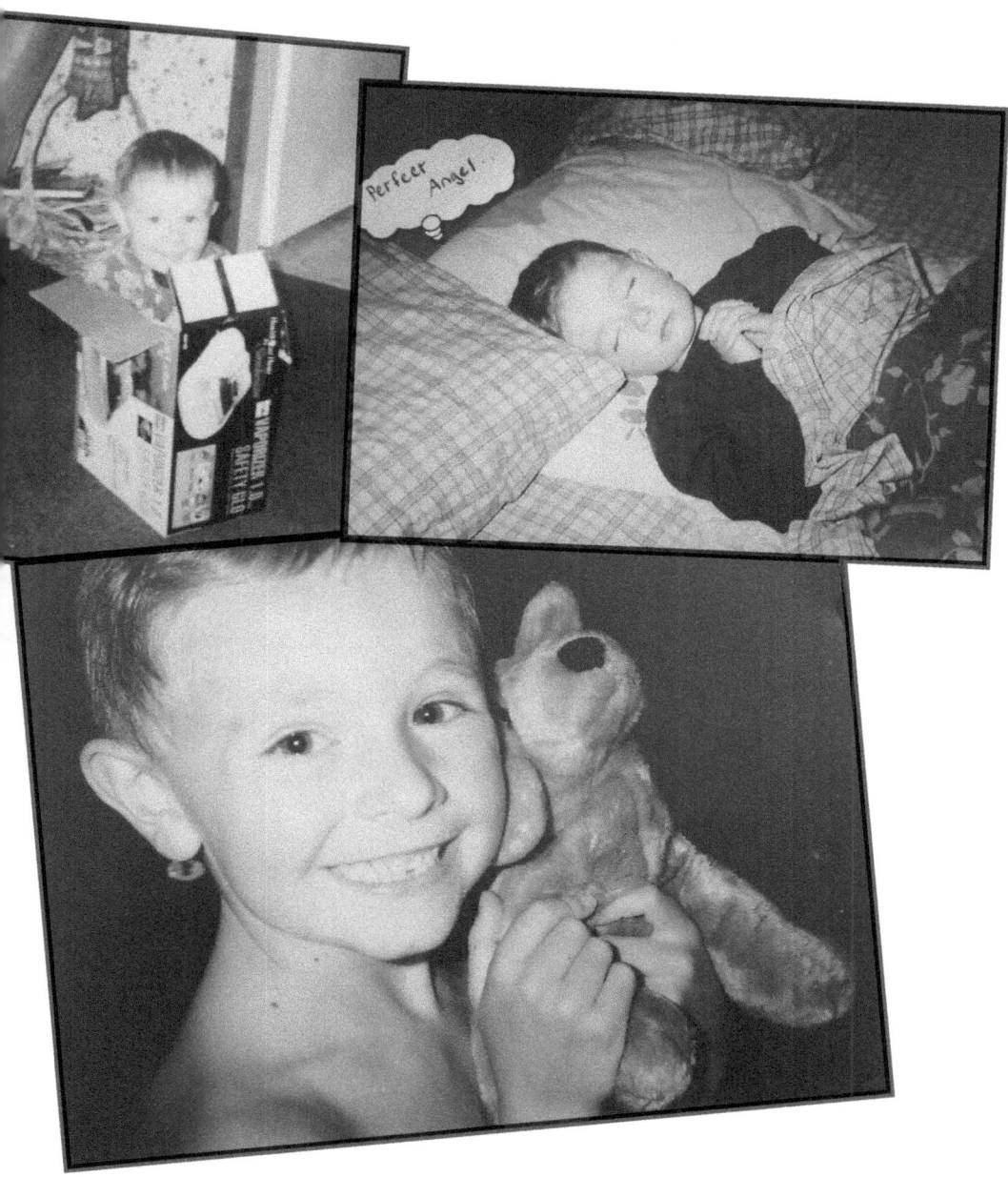

Top Left: Four-years old. Fit check complete. No room for doubt, just imagination. Who needs toys? (Though he had a ton of them.)

Top Right: Four-years old. Dreaming in the arms of grace. I still cannot believe he slept like this all the time.

Bottom: Age five. Kyle's pride, joy, and plush soulmate, all in one frame. He is glowing.

Top Left: Age seven. A Branson Thanksgiving filled with wonder, and a smile brighter than the ornaments.

Top Right: Age seven. Easter morning light, and the bond that never broke. Just us. Always.

Bottom: November 1, ninth birthday and unstoppable, Kyle, his new ride, and a driveway full of dreams.

Top Left: Summer, Age nine. Playground bars were his first training ground. Parkour began right here. Believe me, he climbed far more than monkey bars.

Top Right: Nine-years old. Stars, stripes, and swagger, Kyle lit up the lawn like the finale on the Fourth of July.

Bottom: Summer, age ten. St. Louis and a summer glow, Kyle leaned like the Arch, daring the skyline to tilt with him.

Top: November 1, Kyle turned eleven and tore into the day on his first real dirt bike. Wheels spinning, nothing but grass and glory ahead.

Bottom Left: Field Day, age eleven. When the games were goofy and the friendships were real. Laughter echoed throughout.

Bottom Right: Bridle Ridge Band, December at twelve-years old, my little Kenny G took the stage. A saxophone in his hands, and all my pride in the front row.

Top Left: Summer, at eleven-years old. Earning every splash; one merit badge closer to Scout greatness.

Top Right: San Diego, age twelve. Summer, open sky, nothing between Kyle riding shotgun with the top down and the ocean breeze.

Bottom: Age thirteen. Toes in the sand, heart wide open. Daytona Beach gave him a horizon worth chasing with his friends.

Top Left: Kyle at fourteen. Yellowstone and Big Sky, Montana. Still laughing. Still whole. This photo holds a pause. My son and I standing in awe of the land, seemingly unaware of how much we would soon carry.

Top Right: Fall at fifteen and oh so cool, confident and heart steady. The look that told me he was everything: He was perfect, and I saw it.

Bottom: Kyle at the top of his groupies, always striking like only he could with swagger and pose. Behind the grin, there was more, but this moment was his.

Top Left: In July, seventeen-years old. With his main sidekicks. His style was sharp; his faith was deeper. Kyle did not question it, he just knew, and he never walked alone.

Top Right: Eighteen-years old at the Royals game. Kyle, sending me a selfie and smiling with his friend. "Thanks, Mom. This day was perfect." Baseball was his thing; I just gave him the tickets.

Bottom: November, Kyle at twenty-years old. Worn thin and dressed in hardship living with his dad but glowing the moment he saw me. I held back tears of happiness. Our hugs were always something I could not let go of.

Left: Twenty-years old, Surrounded by his friends. His go-to look, tank, cap, cross. That was Kyle, simple, bold, faithful. He did not need much to shine through that bright and beautiful smile.

Right: Age twenty-one. Not posing, just pausing, a strong faith, looking up like Heaven had something to say, Kyle found a tranquil moment only God could hear. I wonder what his thoughts were?

Left: Kyle's confident smile and gaze is somewhere just beyond the camera. It almost feels like he is waiting or reflecting on something; as if the past did not have the last word.

Right: Age twenty-one. That bright, vivid smile from ear to ear and sparkling eyes. That is perfection, and it is all him. Each time he visited mama, my heart remembered to beat again. This is the young man everyone loved and adored. My beautiful young man.

My Love, My Life, My Everything

54

JOURNEY TO EAGLE SCOUT

HE SPENT SEVERAL YEARS as a scout and outdoing every rank, starting in Cub Scouts as a Bobcat then Lion, Tiger, Wolf, Bear, and onto Webelos Rank. He eventually gained himself the highest achievement in Cub Scouting, earning the Arrow of Light rank. This is where he learned his duty to God and how to be reverent and graduating from Cub Scouts.

Moving on to the Boy Scout of America Advancement, he began at Tenderfoot rank then advanced to Second Class, First Class, Star, and then Life.

I wanted to provide Kyle with every opportunity he needed and wanted. I emphasized to him that the activities and sports he was involved in would be invaluable throughout his life. He also recognized the significant role that God played in his life. Kyle understood the values instilled by the Scout program and how it positively affected him, offering opportunities for personal growth, courage, and perseverance as he developed into a young man. I longed for Kyle to pursue his aspirations and continued to encourage him, and if some might have wondered whether these goals were too ambitious for someone his age, is that not what makes the pursuit so worthwhile?

He began going on canoe trips and camping once a month. Every summer he would go to scout camp down in Warsaw, Missouri for ten days. His dad would spend the first couple of days with him to make him comfortable then he would need to go back home to work. I went for a couple of years for the first two days and could not handle it after that. Looking up at spiders hovering just inches over me, I tried to sleep on a piece of plywood while attempting to keep my mouth closed so the spiders would not find their way in, and getting very little sleep is not my idea of fun, but I did it for my little man to reassure him that he would be safe and have an enjoyable time. Once he felt secure and comfortable, then I would go back home.

Even though I knew he was learning and growing, eight more excruciating days away from mom were too long and the aching in my heart would linger until I could pick him up and take him home with me again.

One of our family camping trips with the scouts took us canoeing on the Elk River in Noel, Missouri, with Kyle and the scout troop. The boys were learning how to navigate the river, and each younger scout was paired with an experienced older scout to help them understand how to row properly without tipping over, how to avoid hitting submerged objects and also how to save themselves if the canoe were to capsize.

My husband and I shared a canoe, assuming he knew what he was doing and had absorbed the detailed instructions from the scout leader. It quickly became clear that my husband was not paying attention and was going to do it his way. At first, we floated peacefully down the river, but soon we needed to row and steer through the currents.

Kyle and his mentor along with several other canoes were far enough ahead, paddling effortlessly, and thankfully Kyle did not see what was about to unfold.

We were headed straight for a tree stump jutting out over the riverbank. The scout leader shouted for us to row on the right side, which would steer the canoe left and away from the bank. I listened to my instructions while my husband did the exact opposite. Given everything, we had endured over the years, I did not want to believe he was doing this purposely.

The leader, along with me and several scouts yelled at him to correct his course but he ignored everyone, yelling at me they were wrong. I debated jumping out of the canoe, but he kept rowing faster, as if he were on a mission to hurt me permanently. The canoe at that point was moving far too fast for me to jump out.

We collided head-on with the stump as a thick, knife-sharp tree root caught a chunk of my hair, just barely skimming the right side of my face and inches from going through my eye. As the canoe flipped over, I was yanked under water by the tree root and trapped. I managed to find an air pocket and feel my way to the edge of the boat, but the weight kept me pinned underneath as it was too heavy for me to lift.

Two scouts were able to pull the canoe off me, grabbing my hand and pulling me up to the bank of the river. Everything happened so fast, as I gasped for air and choking on water, I had a panic attack and was unable to catch my breath and slow it down. I looked up and saw my husband standing there, motionless. He did not flinch. He did not reach out to help me. He stood there. If *a man stands frozen while his wife nearly drowns, it is hard not to question his intentions.* I thanked God that Kyle did not witness what transpired that day.

We still had to make it back to the campsite. Refusing to get in a boat with my husband, the assistant leader took me in his canoe allowing me to rest for the remainder of the trip.

My head throbbed with a migraine that would not let up, so I had to go back home. I told Kyle to stay and enjoy the rest of the weekend, and he could ride back with a friend, but he insisted on coming with me. He knew something had happened and was worried. I wanted my husband to stay but he was persistent in going home as well.

I was terrified on the drive home and too scared to sit beside my husband, afraid of what he might do to either of us, so I sat in back with Kyle. From that day forward, I was always on high alert, watching every move my husband made. His behavior spiraled, and his self-care deteriorated along with his depression and mood swings. I did not know what else to do but love him through it and try to convince him to seek help, but my pleas were ignored.

Kyle still loved baseball, but he started spending more time with the scouts. The scout activities included crafting different things. I still have all the work he accomplished, some of it includes a butterfly house, a bird house, a work bench, a cookbook holder, a lanyard I still have hanging from my rearview mirror and much more that I still utilize. It also included working on his merit badges (which were grueling at times), camping, meetings, etc. Scouts, baseball, and schoolwork became too much so he decided to give baseball a break. He focused on accomplishing many merit badges, loops, and patches. Everything from skiing, bowling, woodcarving, gun safety, car maintenance, canoeing, as well as mastering the bow and arrow and many, many others.

One of the merits I was most proud of him earning was one where he had to bike fifty miles along the Katy trail. A full marathon to and back. It was open to the family, so we all decided to join. Let me tell you I struggled. Saying that I made it a quarter of the fifty miles would be generous. I had to stop at one of the break centers and hitch a ride with a scout leader back to start and let the boys do their thing. Kyle, however, with little break, finished the whole thing by himself. Even with his natural athleticism, I thought he would need a breather, but no, my twelve-year-old boy earned himself yet another merit.

One year I went down to camp with him, we had a tornado. The sirens went off and the entire camp had to seek shelter. We had to run in as fast as we could downhill and hide inside the giant drain tunnels, they had just installed, standing in calf deep water just waiting for the tornado to go overhead. I remember all the boys being so scared and my little man was trying to be so brave as we held on to each other and shared how much we loved one another and reciting the Lord's Prayer together to somewhat distract him. We made it through. That same year after we had left, another scout troop of boys, unfortunately, and very sadly, was not so lucky during a devastating tornado.

I had left after two days and then got a call from one of the scout leaders saying Kyle had to be air lifted to Children's Mercy Hospital where I met him. He had so many tick bites that it had made him sick and in so much pain. They gave him some medicine and sent him back to camp.

The next year was the same thing. H. Roe Bartle Scout Reservation had different camp sites. It was the luck of the draw I guess when it came to which troop would go to which site. He ended up at the same one two years in a row. I was told he got so many tick bites because it was a grassier area than the other sites. All I know is that my son got extremely sick and was rushed to Children's Mercy again where I met up with him. His entire body was stiff and hurt terribly and he was running a fever. The doctor said that he would be fine, gave him some antibiotics and steroids, and sent him home. The scout leader told me that if he did not return to the camp then he would be kicked out. After all those years of hard work and discipline, earning merit badge after merit badge and patches galore, he was going to be kicked out for getting overwhelmed in ticks. I put a stop to that real quick.

After the boys got back from camp he continued in many activities with the scouts. Those damned negative influences pushing and pulling him, oh so slowly, crept in and stole my son's motivation and without the much-needed guidance and leadership from his dad, he struggled to get back to where he once was.

My husband told me the scout leader had come to him and told him that my son was not a scout because he could not handle a few tick bites. Not true! The bites made him so sick that he needed to be airlifted back to Children Mercy. My son endured so many obstacles throughout his many years in scouts and was a true warrior. Even earning his Order of the Arrow which, I was told, is exceedingly rare.

I hoped my husband would never say anything to Kyle about that conversation as I knew it would devastate him. I found out later that he did confide in Kyle about the conversation with the scout leader, but I also later learned from Kyle that his dad discouraged him from finishing, even though he was so close to being an Eagle Scout instead of encouraging him to finish what he started. *What kind of father pushes his own son to give up, just because he could not face his own unresolved struggles?*

A parent not wanting their son to succeed and do better than them is so wrong on so many levels. His dad could have helped him with it. He should have encouraged his son. Kyle could have experienced a true father and son bonding time. He was only three months away from his Eagle but due to the lies he was told and a newfound sport of getting high; to suppress the pain that was inflicted on him by so-called adult leaders, he just did not have the enthusiasm he once had after the disparaging news.

The main man in his life just kept letting him down time after time. I prayed long and hard and tried my best to encourage Kyle to finish what he started, trying so hard to help him plan his Eagle project, but the burn he endured did not allow him to complete it.

To this day, I maintain that it was not Kyle's scout leader whose belief in his scouting ability was in question, but rather the discouragement, negative influence, and harsh words he received from home. I honestly believe these factors along with emotional letdowns may have contributed to Kyle seeking solace in substances, masking his true potential.

After absorbing all he learned in scouting, Kyle recognized the profound impact of the values instilled by the Scouts. These experiences brought immense joy in his life and with many opportunities to grow into a young man embodying courage. In turn, it also transformed into boundless kindness that he shared with everyone he met. It is true that one of the most valuable things we possess is what we can give to others. Kyle touched the lives of many people by generously offering his kindness and unconditional love.

Kyle's journey toward becoming an Eagle Scout was loaded with challenges, not just from the demands of the program, but from the very person who should have been his biggest supporter, his dad. The disappointment of his lack of encouragement subtly emerged, casting a shadow over what should have been a time of celebration and growth. Instead of standing behind him, he seemed content to let his own fears and failures dictate Kyle's path. It was a painful realization for Kyle, who had always tried diligently to look up to his dad.

Why would a father want his son to follow in his footsteps of quitting? It was a question that haunted Kyle, and me as well, especially as he was nearing the finish line of his scouting journey. He had spent years working hard, earning a vast amount of merit badges, and developing skills that would serve him well as he continued his life. Yet, the negative words from his dad were always in the back of his mind, sowing seeds of doubt that seem to overshadow his achievements.

MOTHER'S REFLECTION:
Almost An Eagle

Kyle was three months from Eagle. Three months from the highest honor a Scout can earn. But the weight of discouragement, especially from the one person he longed to impress, was heavier than any merit badge. He had the skills, the heart, the discipline. What he lacked was the support and still, he gave kindness. Still, he gave love. That is the legacy he left behind, not just the patches and ranks, but the quiet strength of a boy who kept giving, even when the world gave him reasons not to.

55

D.A.R.E.

K YLE, ALONG WITH HIS classmates in intermediate school, participated in the D.A.R.E. program, a multi-week initiative designed to educate children about the risks and consequences of drug and alcohol use. The program aimed to equip kids with knowledge and reinforce the importance of parental involvement in keeping them safe. While I was always a hyper-vigilant parent, watching over Kyle as closely as I could, I soon learned that even the most watchful eyes could not shield my son from everything.

One evening, after reading devotions together before lights out, Kyle was lying in bed, as we were discussing the night's lesson; a reflection on peer pressure. It was a simple yet profound topic, one that I knew held immense weight in any child's life.

"The D.A.R.E. program is boring," Kyle suddenly admitted. Then, after a pause, he asked, "What is addiction?"

I took a slow breath, making sure I came up with the right words, realizing this was more than just a casual question, it was a moment that required mom's care, complete honesty, and depth.

"Addiction," I told him gently, "is when something takes control over you, when you can't easily give it up, even when you know it's hurting you."

I glanced toward the doorway where my husband stood silently watching us. He was a man entangled in his own destructive habits.

Turning toward him, I asked advisedly, "Honey, tell Kyle how bad it can get if he does not listen, if he does not walk away from people trying to pull him toward something dangerous." But he did not respond. He simply looked at us, then turned and walked away into the other room, saying nothing.

What could he say, how do you warn your son about a danger you have not escaped yourself? A man trapped in his own addictions, incapable of warning his son about the very dangers he was drowning in. A father should protect his child, guide him, prepare him for the battles ahead, but instead, he remained silent.

And in that silence, Kyle received the loudest message of all.

Even after taking the D.A.R.E. program in school, he still did not believe marijuana could negatively affect him.

But is that not how we all think? That the bad things, the consequences, will not happen to us?

Until they do.

MOTHER'S REFLECTION:
A Quiet Warning

Kyle asked what addiction meant, and I gave him the best answer I could. But the silence that followed, that was the answer he remembered. A dad's silence in the face of truth speaks louder than any warning. It told Kyle that danger can live quietly, that sometimes the people we look up to are still fighting battles they cannot name. I wish he had heard a different message that night. I wish someone had said, "You are worth protecting." Because he was. He always was.

56

CHANGE IS NOT ALWAYS GOOD

WE NOW ENTER THE age when boys started to change. Kyle was always a great kid, but he started acting up a bit and I quickly found out why. Another kid in school was taunting him. Boys would get jealous of Kyle because he was popular. He was sweet, gentle, funny, smart, sociable, talented, and good looking. Oh no, I am not just saying that because I am biased as his blessed mommy. He truly was a wonderful kid.

There were two boys that were just not going to let Kyle be happy because they were not happy. Kyle had everything they did not, and it made them green with envy.

One Saturday afternoon I was sitting on the couch relaxing for a bit when I got a call from one of Kyle's sixth grade teachers. She asked to speak to my husband. I asked her if there was anything I could do to help because he was my boy too. She said yes, maybe in a bit, but she needed to speak with Kyle's dad first. I called out to him. He picked up the phone and walked into the other room, so I did not hear the conversation. When he finished talking to her, he came into the living room and told me that he and Kyle would be back in a little while. I asked them where they were going and he said, "Do not worry about it, we will be back." They both took off. I just sat there wondering what the heck had just happened.

I got another phone call, and it was the teacher calling back. She said, "I am sorry for not speaking to you before, but I needed to tell your husband something right away." She told me that her daughter, who was friends with Kyle, was on Facebook and saw a video going around of two kids fighting Kyle. I started shaking as she told me this. Someone hurt my son.

She said when her daughter came across it, she immediately told her mother, who called to talk to my husband. I started to cry thinking that my son had been beaten up. He had come home from school the day before with a slightly busted lip and faded black eye but had told me a story about how he got hit with a baseball. I did not question it because he never got into fights.

My husband and Kyle came rushing in about an hour or so later and my husband was so high, not on drugs, but a high he gets from his sporadic episodes. It was like he was high on his own pride. He had this broad smile on his face, kissed me, and said, "You would be so proud of me Deanna. You should be proud of Kyle too."

I said, "I am always proud of my son, but what happened?"

He went on to tell me that two boys had set Kyle up the day before as he was walking home from a friend's house in the subdivision across the street from ours. When he passed the one boy's house, this boy was in the front yard and claimed to want to make amends with Kyle. As soon as Kyle stepped in the yard, one boy grabbed him as the other boy started to hit him.

Another kid videotaped the entirety on their phone and posted it on social media for all to see. My baby had been set up, manipulated, lied to, and abused by two reckless kids. I was furious at those boys but wondered what my husband had done to fix the situation.

My husband and Kyle had gone to one of the boys' houses and was told by his father that he no longer lived there and was staying with his grandpa. He gave my husband the address and they went over to grandpa's house. My husband asked to speak with the boy and when he came to the door, my husband told the boy to immediately take the video off Facebook, right then and there. My husband never stood up for me or his son and never did again after that day, so this was a surprise to say the least. Grandpa made the boy go in the house and take the video off and apologize to Kyle.

He was right. I was proud of my husband and even impressed by his action and authority to protect Kyle. This was one of less than a handful of moments in three decades where I was reminded of the person my husband could be if he only tried harder for our son's sake alone. His protective authority and leadership were short-lived.

I was also proud of my son being the bigger boy and the godly boy he was raised to be. Several years later he told me he did not fight back because he knew that he could have hurt them badly with what he had learned in Taekwondo, so he just froze up. He broke boards with his bare feet and hands, so he could have defended himself, even breaking bones, but knew it would not have been a fair fight. Two against one is never a fair battle, especially when it is dark versus light.

The bullying had slowed down quite a bit after that incident. For what reason? I do not know. Maybe it lost its allure, they found a new target, or the perpetrators feared the repercussions. Life had returned to its normal ebb and flow, which meant Kyle was a happy kid making many friends again.

My son made friends with everyone. Even the ones that needed it the most. He knew everyone needed a friend and was the best friend to many. He did not deserve what he got from so many kids and others that took full advantage of him. He was raised in the church, and he knew how to be nice to everyone and forgive them even if they were not nice to him. He knew we are all called to love our enemies and neighbors. His dad and his untrustworthy cousin were trying to instill grudges in Kyle and never forgive anyone simply because they could not. This was not right, and Kyle knew it.

Kyle did not want to hurt anyone even though they hurt him and his empathy for others continued up until the day he passed. Many people tend to take advantage of and use someone like my son because of his compassion and love for others. Something that they do not nor will ever have. He was hurt by a multitude of individuals who claimed to care for him, including close family members and close friends, all of whom exploited his trust for their own benefit. The pain he experienced stemmed from those who should have supported him but instead prioritized their interests over his well-being. Whether they can or will admit it or not is irrelevant. Kyle was not fully aware of what they were doing to him either. I have no fear of speaking the truth as Kyle and I were stifled to not ruffle feathers for years.

Kyle's extraordinary capacity for kindness and compassion shone brightly, even as he faced adversity. Yet neglect, bullying, and trauma were an unbearable weight on his shoulders. My son longed for empathy, support, and presence from the ones he loved. I pray his legacy serves as a reminder that every act of kindness can make a difference, and every gesture of love can be a lifeline. In Kyle's memory, I wish that we all will work harder to build a world where compassion prevails, and no child will bear such a heavy load alone. Is it not just evil, watching kids so poisoned by jealousy that they turned on kindness itself?

MOTHER'S REFLECTION:
He Was Targeted

Kyle's compassion was his superpower, and his vulnerability. In a world that often punishes gentleness, he stood firm in grace. He did not retaliate. He did not seek revenge. He chose restraint, even when others chose cruelty. That kind of strength is rare. And it is heartbreaking that it was exploited by those who could not understand it. But Kyle's legacy is not in the pain they caused, it is in the love he gave anyway. That is the kind of light that outlasts darkness.

57

DETENTION

I WILL ADMIT THAT IT was not just forces pulling Kyle away, there was so much ache inside him. Internally things were pushing him out and I fear this heartbreak helped seal his fate. One day after coming home from walking the dogs, I noticed the air felt charged. However, I found Kyle's dad chasing him into the kitchen. I found Kyle pointing to his dad, and my husband, with a red face, bulging eyes, and fists clenched ready to swing, like a volcano ready to erupt. I had no idea at the time what caused the fight (and I still do not to this day, something his dad will forever keep secret, guarding it closely). I just knew that Kyle said he caught his dad doing something horrible, but he would not tell me anything else. Whatever it was, it lit a match.

I immediately jumped in to defuse the situation. I knew for all my husband's sins, hitting me, at that point, would not be one of them. But for good measure, I got in between the two of them and faced my husband. "Do not you even dare touch our son. Do not even think about it."

I kept my eyes directly on my husband and he knew I was serious and would protect my son no matter what. At this, my husband unclenched his fist and stormed into the living room, but Kyle was not ready to give up. Fueled by years of disappointment and silence, he followed his dad into the living room and gave him a small poke.

Things once again got heated. I did not know what to do but if I had the power of hindsight, I would have told myself not to do what I did.

I can regretfully say that I called the police. I was looking for a mediator only to resolve the situation. If things turned violent, like they would, I knew I could not physically break it up but would physically fight my husband if he chose to hurt Kyle. I wanted the cop to be a mediator. I needed him to keep my son safe. When the cop came, I ran to the yard to explain the situation with Kyle and his dad following close behind.

The crooked cop (he was no officer of the law), not a protector, not a peace maker, was stiff and seemed ready to fight at a moment's notice. As soon as I began to explain what happened, he interrupted, not with concern for Kyle but with accusation. He began questioning my husband and I at once, asking if Kyle had touched either of us.

Why would he ask us that? This evil being was ready and willing to pick on a young teenager instead of the real issue; instead of the instigator. Kyle, out of fear at this point, was hiding in the car. He had locked himself in the car and despite my pleas he would not come out. Kyle was afraid of both the shady cop and his dad, he knew neither one had his best interests at heart.

How could he not be afraid, when the two men in front of him, the ones who should have protected him, must have felt more like threats than safety?

The cop asked if my son had hurt me and I said, "No, of course not. He obviously was trying to protect me."

Wondering why he asked me that, and the fact that my answer seemed to go over his head, things got more heated when the cop fully turned to my husband and asked one last time if my son had touched him. *Why was he so persistent in asking him the same question instead of asking my husband if he had any intention of hurting our son and wanting to get the full story?* I will never cease to believe he was not in any way a decent police officer but very corrupt, to say the least, and indeed out to seek pain on someone, a young boy, instead of helping him.

"Yes," my husband said, as I witnessed no emotion whatsoever and no flicker of concern in his eyes.

I felt as if the air had left my body. Angry tears poured from my eyes as the cop pulled my son, scared and heartbroken, from the car and clasped cuffs on his wrists like he was dangerous which was so far from the truth. I was so angry at the cop and my husband. For the first time I had anxiety that made me shake from the inside out.

The touch that got Kyle arrested was a mere child's touch, yet the victim, was an adult man, fully willing to hit his own child and have him arrested. *Could he not see that his son was in pain? How do you explain a person whose presence offered no safety, only shadow?* He needed reassurance and love, empathy; something that should have and could have been given. I begged the cop to arrest me instead. He was cold and empty, not hearing a word I had said to him. I looked to Kyle's dad, hoping he would intervene and explain things more honestly, but he stood silent. My words fell into a void.

To this day, I have no faith in the police or the justice system in general. Nor do I have any faith in my husband considering what we both endured. If a man is willing to let his son, and his wife, be arrested, just to protect his own secrets... what else is he capable of?

He refused to tell me what the confrontation was all about although a few years after that, Kyle did confide in me that he caught his dad doing something that he should not have been doing, and he threatened Kyle to keep quiet.

My son did tell me, "It would just hurt you more, Mom."

That is when Kyle stood up, not just for himself, for me too and for that, he ended up in detention. This is a system where boys like Kyle are punished for protecting the truth.

Now, after years of all the chaos that we endured, nothing shocked me anymore when it came to my husband's behavior, but that did not make the heartbreak any easier.

MOTHER'S REFLECTION:
When Protection Becomes Punishment

Kyle stood up for me. For truth. For what was right. And for that, he was punished. Not by the law, but by the silence of those who should have defended him. That night, the system failed him. His father failed him and yet, Kyle still chose restraint over rage, love over retaliation. I will never forget the look in his eyes when the cuffs went on. It was not fear, it was heartbreak. I will carry that moment with me always, as proof that my son was brave in ways the world never understood. The pain they delivered will echo back, the guilty, the hidden, none are exempt.

58

BROKE AND REBUILT

W HEN WE TRIED TO defend ourselves against the horrible things he did to us, we were falsely accused of horrible things, deflecting, at best. I regret not knowing who my husband really was. If I had known many years ago, I would have saved my son from so much heartache.

Kyle was given two weeks in juvenile detention, and those two weeks killed me. Sentenced for a child's desperate act to hold someone accountable. All I did was cry. We visited when they allowed us to. He said everything was fine, trying to put on a strong face, but I could see some things were broken and one of those things was his trust in me. I did my best to advocate for Kyle but also made a mistake in thinking that the very cop was there to help us and thought his dad would step in and protect him or at least defend him. Instead, they seemed to join forces.

I could understand somewhat that Kyle needed me to do more, and I feel I failed him, but what could I have done against two people that cared more about control than truth? That is the nicest thing I can honestly say about either of them. To punish a scared helpless teenage boy, while ignoring the deeper abuse behind it, was the cruelest betrayal of all and totally unforgiving.

During one visit Kyle looked at me and asked, "What is going on Mom?"

I was not sure what he meant honestly. I did not know what to say because I was not sure what he meant, and I did not yet understand everything that was happening beneath the surface until Kyle had told me something I had already sensed. I felt that his dad may have been reshaping a story behind closed doors, painting my son to be someone he was not to protect something he did not want exposed. I later came to recognize, with the help of professionals, that this was not miscommunication, it was emotional manipulations. Subtle, painful, and disorienting. When one is living inside of it, nothing feels simple; not even the truth.

As a wise man once said, "The best predictor of future behavior is relevant past behavior." By then, the past had already told us everything we needed to know. *Why should my son have had to carry the consequences of someone else's instability and unhealed wounds?*

After that, for a while, Kyle kept his distance from me and his dad, of course, for good reason, even though we were in the same household. He became quieter, but not for long, as Kyle and I were both at our lowest and found each other. This was nothing new but to be from me, his mom, was something that neither of us could bear. We soon became as close as we always were. It did not undo the damage, but it reminded that love, when it is real, does not disappear. It endures.

MOTHER'S REFLECTION:
Love That Refused to Leave

Kyle was broken, but not alone and I was broken too. But we found each other again, in the quiet aftermath of betrayal. That is what real love does, it crawls through the wreckage, reaches out, and says, "I'm still here." I could not undo the damage, but I could show him that my love was not conditional, not temporary, not shaken by the storm. It was the one thing that remained, and it still does.

59

DOCTOR VISIT

KYLE OPENED UP TO me about his anxiety when he was fourteen. I conveyed that he needed to stop smoking pot ASAP regardless of whether he thought it was helping him or not. He was way too young, and I believe he got the idea of a prescription drug from a peer.

Kyle wanted to see a medical doctor, so I took him, along with Kyle's dad. This doctor just wanted to dismiss his anxiety and put him on Adderall because he was told by a friend about it. This doctor did not want to do a physical exam or ask in-depth questions. He wanted to write out a prescription lickety-split and then charge us an arm and a leg. He did not want to dig deeper to find out the real cause of Kyle's pain but like many others, wanted to subdue him with more substance.

Kyle did not have ADHD! Why would he be put on this powerful drug if he did not have ADHD? They simply do not care and want to get that quick fix for their overpriced visits. I was not going to allow that.

I asked the doctor questions on the pros and cons of this medication and why he thought it was proper to prescribe my son Adderall when it was a damn near lethal drug for kids his age, especially if a child was doing other substances on the side. He could not or would not answer. I told him no way was my son going to be one of his guinea pigs. I voiced my concerns, privately and directly. I did not feel we were being heard or helped. So, we walked away and sought care elsewhere.

My son did not need medication. Kyle did not need to be numb, he needed understanding. He needed both of his parents showing up, asking tough questions, supporting his healing. He needed his dad to work with me, not against me, to get him on the right path again.

Eventually, I found a counselor who saw Kyle. He worked with both me and Kyle, individually and together. We started to untangle some of what Kyle was carrying.

In tenth grade, Kyle told me his schoolwork was becoming impossible to concentrate on. He blamed anxiety. I gently raised the possibility that substance use might be making things worse, not better. I reassured him that if medication was needed, we would find someone who would treat the whole person, not just the symptom. That is what I wanted for my son and that is what he deserved.

I tried everything I could. I pushed for answers. I researched doctors, sought second opinions, even reached out to media platforms when nothing else worked. When Kyle and I were dropped unexpectedly dropped from his dad's insurance, the system turned even colder. No rehab would take Kyle without a policy. Every door felt closed.

We both kept trying, though. Kyle wanted to heal. He wanted to change. He told me so. But he was weighed down by emotional burdens, generational cycles, and voices that did not always want what was best for him.

When I discovered his family history, addiction, depression, silent struggles passed down over generations, I promised him we could break that chain. He did not have to live inside the pain of his ancestors. We could start over. We could heal.

MOTHER'S REFLECTION:
Healing Is Not a Prescription

Kyle did not need a pill he needed support. He needed someone to ask the challenging questions, to see past the symptoms and into the soul of a boy trying to stay afloat. I watched the system try to label him, numb him, dismiss him. But I refused. Because healing is not found in a bottle, it is found in the bond between a mother and her son, in the fight to be heard, and in the promise that we could break the cycle and we tried. Oh, how we tried.

60

WHAT I KNEW

I TOLD KYLE I WOULD be there for him, always. I reminded him that we both loved him, and that even if we were not always together, he would not have to face this alone. But he had to let me walk beside him.

My energy was focused on rebuilding and restoring the Kyle I knew bright, thoughtful, full of life. The boy who once soared through school now struggled to retain what he had just read. I watched his memory fade in real time. The shift was undeniable.

He had once dreamed big. But now, anxiety and sadness filled the spaces where joy had lived.

I saw how substances crept in. I spoke up. I went to counseling with him. I asked the tough questions, even when others turned away or dismissed my concerns. Often, I felt alone in the fight.

I knew trauma, concussions, and instability had worn him down. He told me how scared he was. So was I. We were both just trying to survive. I saw him reach for escape, but substances only deepened the pain.

Kyle valued his independence. He did not always share the depth of his pain with me, Still, he gave me pieces, fragments of his inner life that showed me the weight he carried. After his passing, I found handwritten notes tucked into one of the Bibles, I had given him. They were not a suicide note, but they were confessions: things he could not say to certain people, especially his father. They confirmed what I had known all along, he was fighting a war inside.

We talked about recovery. He told me he was trying. He wanted change. He dreamed of a life away from chaos. I believed him. I still do.

I will never forget how hard he tried.

MOTHER'S REFLECTION:
When Doors Closed

It is one thing to fight for Kyle's healing. It is another to watch access vanish the moment coverage does. I learned quickly: systems do not bend for love. But I did not stop knocking.

61

TRIP TO DAYTONA

WHEN ONE OF KYLE'S closest friends moved to Daytona, Florida for a brief time, I saw an opportunity to give Kyle an experience that would not only allow him to support his friend but also give him a chance to enjoy a change of scenery. I encouraged him to go down and help them settle in, to relax for a few days, and make the transition easier. When it was time for Kyle to return, I flew him back home, knowing that these moments of connection and support were important for both him and his friend.

The following summer, Kyle decided he wanted to visit a long-distance friend. Kyle was excited about the idea but also hoped to bring another good friend along. Unfortunately, his friend's mother said they could not afford the trip, and I understood how disappointing that must have been for both of them. I did not want finances to be a barrier to their happiness, so I made the decision to fly both Kyle and his friend down to Daytona for a week; a much-needed vacation away to see the friend they missed so much. Seeing them enjoy themselves, experiencing a new place, and creating memories together made every bit of effort and money worth it.

That is how much I love my son. His happiness has always been my priority, and I would do anything for him and his friends who treated him well. I knew that childhood and teenage years were fleeting, and

I wanted to make sure that Kyle had a life filled with joy, experiences, and a sense of security, especially when so many of his friends were facing difficult circumstances.

Some of Kyle's friends were growing up in environments filled with hardship. I made it my mission to steer Kyle in a different direction, to show him there was a world beyond the mistakes and pain of the adults around him. His friends, too, deserved to experience happiness without the weight of their parents' struggles overshadowing them.

I could not control the choices the other adults made, but I could control what kind of space I created for Kyle and his friends. I could make sure they were safe, happy, and surrounded by positive experiences while under my supervision. That was always my goal to give them moments of joy, adventures that shaped their childhood, and memories they could hold onto even in the midst of uncertainty.

Looking back, I know that every trip, every dinner invitation, every effort to bring them together in happiness was worth it. Those smiles, the laughter, the feeling of safety and belonging, I hope they carry that with them, even as they grow and face the challenges of adulthood. What mattered to me most was ensuring that, for at least a little while, they could just be kids, free to dream, to explore, and to feel loved.

MOTHER'S REFLECTION:
A Gift He Could Give His Friend

I could not rewrite the stories of every child around Kyle, but I could offer them a chapter filled with light. A trip, a dinner, a moment of laughter, these were my way of saying, "You matter." Kyle's joy was my compass, and his friends' smiles were my reward. I hope they remember that someone saw them, someone cared, and someone believed they deserved happiness. Because they did. He did. I did.

62

YELLOWSTONE

I **PLANNED A FAMILY VACATION** for the three of us prior to moving my mom in with us, in early summer, right after Kyle got out of school. His dad decided he did not want to join in on the annual family vacations any longer. His depression and emotional challenges were worsening, and he apparently had other things on his mind, so Kyle and I decided to go alone. We always included my husband in everything we did, but he was reluctant to include himself, which did not make much sense. I made sure he and my brother put forth some effort to watch over our mom while we were gone; I was trusting they would.

We went to Yellowstone National Park. After the flight, we had to rent a car and drive quite a long way around and around the mountains. Yes, I was nervous, but God was giving me strength to do it without my husband and besides Kyle, with his driving permit, was able to help by driving some as well.

We rented bikes and rode throughout the park, exploring all the beautiful geysers and overlooks. It was so breathtaking yet peaceful. Honestly, we both had a tough time adjusting to Yellowstone because we literally could not get cell service anywhere and the rooms did not have television or phones. I know we were in the mountains, but I felt so isolated without being able to communicate with my mother back home and make sure that my husband and brother were watching over her and our pets. There was not even a pool at the hotel, something we were not used to.

Although Kyle was okay with a bit of ruggedness, I certainly was not. I absolutely enjoyed my bonding time with my amazing son. Just like it was when he was younger. We shared some good memories, and he shared with me what he thought he might want to do when he got out of school.

He mentioned teaching or engineering of some kind. I told him he could do both, or anything else he set his mind to. The world was his and there were so many opportunities waiting for him. He needed to explore anything and everything. I would help him achieve those goals if he kept his focus on what was important.

He still wanted to move away, just as he did when he was younger, and feeling unseen. (Something I will always regret not doing.) But I did what I thought I needed to do to keep him safe, at the time, that meant keeping the family unit together. I believe now that Kyle was trying to tell me in his own way about his dad. I truly did not know the depth of Kyle's longing to move away from the ones that plagued him until a few years later and this is where we began planning our permanent move to the ocean.

After a couple of days of biking and driving around the mountains, dodging buffalo and moose on the roads (who evidently had the right-of-way), and spotting a black bear about a hundred yards away, along with other sightseers who pulled over to get a glimpse with their camcorder, Kyle and I saw all that we could see. We were bored so we opted to check out of the hotel and drive down the mountain to Big Sky, Montana.

That was our favorite part of the vacation. We spent two more days at a beautiful log cabin hotel with a pool. We went zip lining and took a river rafting trip on one of the most beautiful rivers I had ever seen, the Gallatin River. Then we headed home.

I will forever cherish that one-on-one time with my son and being able to share and learn so much from him, and vice versa. The people in his life who missed out on those opportunities that I was privileged with, I hope will forever regret it.

Our trip to Yellowstone was a moment of transition and bonding between me and my son, set against the backdrop of our family navigating change. Planning a vacation to Yellowstone without the man of the family showed the challenges of our evolving family dynamics, particularly in light of my husband's endless health struggles. The mix of nerves and isolation I felt during the trip, made worse by the lack of communication with home, clashed a bit somewhat with the beauty and excitement of exploring the park.

A deep connection was formed during our moments spent biking and discussing Kyle's dreams and revealed not just my intense love but also my desire to support my son's aspirations. Yet it came with a somewhat bittersweet realization that Kyle's yearning to move away was tied to deeper feelings about our family situation.

The shift to Big Sky, with its comfort and fun activities, was a turning point in our journey together. A reminder that even in challenging times, opportunities for connection and growth can emerge, leaving lasting memories that I will forever hold close to my heart.

MOTHER'S REFLECTION:
Big Sky Bonding

Yellowstone stripped away distractions, no phones, no screens, no noise. Just me and Kyle, winding through geysers and mountain ranges, finding each other again. I was nervous, yes. But I was also brave and so was he. In the quiet, he shared dreams. In the stillness, I saw the ache he carried. In Big Sky, we found peaceful joy again. That trip was not just a vacation, it was a reckoning, a renewal, and a reminder that our love did not need a cell tower.

63

STORM CHASING

AFTER YELLOWSTONE, I MOVED my mother in with us as her Parkinson's worsened. Kyle was fifteen. Mom had been in and out of nursing homes and rehab units, but they were clearly neglecting her needs. I opted to move her in with me to take better care of her. Shortly after, I got news that she had terminal lung cancer. This was extremely hard on Kyle as well, but I also needed to take care of my beautiful mother as she had done for me for many years. I pointed out to Kyle that he would be able to bond even more with his Momo and learn things about her childhood. This is what we do for the ones we love. We became so much closer in those last few months. When other family members saw it as a burden, I knew it was a blessing and will never regret having the opportunity to take care of her and be with her in her last moments of life.

In late spring, Mom was sitting on the couch when Kyle got home from school. We knew a storm was coming. We were outside reading the clouds and watching them slowly circulate as the sky took on an ominous look. A weather alert came on the television. There was a tornado heading right towards us, coming in from the south. It seemed to go around us at the last minute and headed toward Pleasant Hill. Mom yelled at us to come inside. Kyle and I were getting anxious. This was an eager anxiety; we were not at all scared but excited. I made sure mom was comfortable and told her not to worry. He ran inside, looked at me with this big grin and spoke, "Let's go mom!" "Hurry or we'll miss it!" "Love you Momo!"

"Mom, Kyle and I will be back in a little while," I said.

She shouted, "You're not taking my grandbaby out there!"

"We'll be okay. We won't be gone long…. Love you!"

Kyle and I jumped in the car, headed out as fast as I could go without exceeding the speed limit or getting stopped by a police officer, but not wanting the twister to get too far ahead of us. He was watching the clouds and directing me where to go and saying, "Faster Mom, faster!"

I could not, and would not, go any faster as we were trailing it just fine and far enough behind to not be in harm's way and besides, I was not about to get caught or wreck. We drove for a few miles watching the funnel clouds above us as the rain started to fall and then hail came down. He was laughing and at the same time I think he was as apprehensive as I was, but we loved the weather, and this was our chance to chase a real live tornado.

Just to let you know, Kyle was close to being sixteen at this point, not a small child but almost an adult, and I made sure I did not put my son in harm's way. We had nearly reached Pleasant Hill as the tornado had not touched down yet but was right above and a few miles in front of us as we were traveling. We finally came to a police blockade. They ordered us to turn around and go back home, the tornado was set to touch down any second. They would not let us go any farther. We had to turn around and go back.

We were so full of adrenaline that we stopped by Dairy Queen on the way home and got some ice cream and a chocolate shake to take home to Momo so she would not be mad. That was our first ever storm chasing adventure. It was an adventure to say the least. I felt a bit guilty afterward, allowing my son to go, but I was going to go either way. We were unharmed. We never tried it again though. After that, we decided to read the clouds from the safety of our backyard.

MOTHER'S REFLECTION:
Chasing More Than Storms

We were not just chasing a tornado; we were chasing time. Chasing joy in our common ground. Chasing the kind of memory that lives longer than any funnel cloud. Kyle's grin, his excitement, his trust in me to drive us toward something wild and beautiful, that is what I hold onto. We did not outrun danger. We outran doubt. In the car, with the sky swirling above us, I saw my son's spirit in full flight and full of wonder.

64

MOMO'S PASSING

MY MOTHER WAS ONLY with us a few months prior to her transition. Her doctor said she only had about six months, and she only lasted four. I needed to take care of her myself as she did me for many years. I was struggling to drive back and forth multiple times a day to check on her and make sure she was eating and had her medicine as well as toileting and bathing. My priority was my son, but he also knew that his Momo had to be taken care of properly since my brother and sister-in-law who lived across the street, chose to relocate during this time. Kyle and I struggled with the emotional weight of them leaving and taking my nieces, Kyle's close cousins away from him and my mom's grandbabies away from her, which led her to decline much faster than anticipated. So, I moved her, her furniture, and everything she owned in with us. She cried for her grandbabies every day, longing for their presence, but her cries went unanswered. Her family and loved ones refused to pay a visit.

Kyle and I had a lot of powerful and meaningful talks, including a deep-seated talk about his Momo. I needed him to know that Momo was passing onto a better place and that she and Popo would be together again. I wanted him to be prepared, and I also needed him to truly know of her profound love for her only grandson. She also knew how much he loved her. I knew not to expect too much from him knowing he was still a young teen. It was so hard on him, but he was a brave soul, a true testament to his strength. I just wanted him and his cousins to spend time with her knowing it would not be long.

As my mother was passing away, I yelled for my husband to support me, to hold my hand, to hug me, to call 911, to do anything that might ease the unbearable pain of the moment. I struggled to understand his response in that heartbreaking moment. He simply sat on the couch, as lifeless as my mother herself. The room felt suffocating, filled with silence where there should have been compassion and urgency. He could not even say goodbye to her or tell her that he loved her. He sat there, an empty vessel, devoid of the emotions that any decent human being would show in such a heartbreaking moment.

Two weeks later, he came to me, accompanied by his cousin, to apologize. He claimed that he did not know what to do at the time, but I knew better. I believed there were clear things he could have done, what many loved ones might do instinctively in that moment. But he did not. His absence in that moment of crisis left a void I could not ignore. A loved one's passing away meant nothing to him. That moment was not just about the loss of my mother; it was about the realization that the person I trusted to stand by me in my darkest hours chose to remain. The absence of love and care spoke louder than any words he could have offered in his belated apology.

Kyle's Momo, my mom, passed away December 2, 2014. While she was extremely ill with lung cancer and Parkinson's, Kyle never once ceased to show his Momo how much he loved her but seeing her in the state she was in did indeed worry him. Even though her illness and passing were exceedingly difficult on him, I knew he would get through it.

After she passed Kyle tried so hard to be strong. I asked him to help carry his Momo to her final resting place. He needed to do this for her, and he respectfully did. I cannot tell you how deeply it affected him, but I remembered how losing my grandma at an early age affected me, so I allowed him to feel whatever he needed to feel. He was angry for a while, taking his pain out on me, and of course fled to the people he needed to stay away from. Again, as I tried to steer him away and get him into counseling, certain influences seemed to suggest that numbing the pain was easier than confronting it head-on.

I did not tell Kyle how his dad reacted, not acknowledging and in complete stillness, when his mother-in-law, who was more of a mother to him than his real mom, was passing away. He could not have handled it and would have gone after his dad. I was not about to burden my son even more than he already was.

It was one of the most emotionally disorienting moments I had ever experienced, not only his detachment, but the quiet absence of others when I needed them most, but my son was there for me regardless of what he was going through, and knew we needed to console each other. Kyle made me incredibly proud, which was nothing new.

Kyle saw the weight I carried, even if he could not name it. From caring for my mother through terminal cancer to the quiet sacrifices I made. Her passing was a struggle... and a privilege. I got to give back to the woman who raised me, and I hoped Kyle understood that same depth of love.

MOTHER'S REFLECTION:
The Boy Who Carried Her Home

Kyle did not just love his Momo, he cherished her. He was her light, her laughter, her comfort in those final months. Even as her body weakened, his devotion never did. He showed up with support and warmth when others walked away. He whispered "I love you" when her tears called out for family that never came. When the time came to say goodbye, Kyle did not flinch. He carried her to rest with the same tenderness she once gave him in her arms as a baby. That is who he was: the boy who stood tall for the woman who gave him every gentle thing. I pray he always felt how proud she was.

65

SIXTEENTH BIRTHDAY TRAUMA

NOW COMES KYLE'S MILESTONE birthday, the day he got his first car. Before my mom passed, she made me promise to ensure all her grandbabies were taken care of and received a car for their sixteenth birthday. I agreed wholeheartedly. Kyle was doing reasonably well in school, not exceptional, but he was putting in effort, and I believed my son deserved this. My parents had given me a car for my sixteenth birthday, so I wanted to provide the same for my son.

The excitement of surprising Kyle was overwhelming. He wanted to be part of the decision-making process, though. He had a clear idea of what he wanted. For weeks, Kyle and I scoured different dealerships, exploring various cars. Unfortunately, his dad was not involved in the search with us. Eventually, Kyle found the perfect fit, a top-of-the-line Acura. It was not new, but a gorgeous black Acura in impeccable condition. I had it detailed, fitted with new tires, and minor issues were addressed. We both eagerly awaited his big day.

Kyle's incredibly special day arrived, a time traditionally set at 2:00 p.m., the moment of his birth, for his birthday celebration. We, and the rest of the family, including both grandparents, cousins, stepmom, uncle, and aunts, raised our glasses with his favorite Welch's sparkling grape juice, celebrating my King Kyle. Then he would unwrap his gifts, capturing the entire event on video for him to relive later. However, this time, no one showed up.

Regrettably, juggling work and responsibilities, without the support I needed, I could not manage to send out invitations even though I still made a spread of delicious food for everyone. I made the mistake of entrusting Kyle's dad, a full month prior, mind you, with the task of informing everyone about the 2:00 party at our house. But to my dismay, no one arrived. Why? Because, inexplicably, Kyle's dad had lied to me for weeks, telling me that he had reminded everyone repeatedly throughout the month about the upcoming event, telling me, "Stop worrying Deanna, I told you I reminded everyone already, even yesterday."

Only later, on my son's special day, he confessed that he had not done so, callously admitting when I took him aside in the hall and away from my son and asked him where everyone was, his answer was, "I didn't invite anyone."

Responsibility, in my eyes, falls directly on him, as well as on the family members who professed their love for Kyle yet chose to shatter his special day, subjecting my son to more heartbreak. His Momo had passed prior to this special day and his cousins and uncle, and aunt had not been invited either. I had to tell the painful news to Kyle, my voice quivering with tears. I have photos of his day that show the extreme pain in his face while his dad is smiling and laughing, seemingly unaware of Kyle's emotional state.

Suppressing his emotions, with a lump in his throat Kyle accepted his new car along with the specially crafted Acura birthday cake that I had specially made and the custom-crafted mahogany hot rod I had specially designed just for him, only for it to be stolen later down the road. He received another violent video game from his dad that I was against him having in the first place.

Kyle managed to hold his composure throughout the day, masking his hurt as we dined at Margaritas because no one showed up at the house. His aunt, who belatedly showed up without an apology, pushed him over the edge. He later cried himself sick, and I comforted him, expressing apologies for his dad's and the family's thoughtless actions. I would have given anything to take Kyle's heartache away. This event was heart-wrenching for Kyle, but by then, he was no stranger to feeling emotionally or physically distant from the Wiley side of the family. This time, my son was caught in the middle of their cruelty. It felt like the lack of empathy from some of them had deeply hurt him, and by extension, me.

Days blurred together in apologies, mine alone, as I carried the weight of what others could not. or would not, take responsibility for. Kyle deserved better, and I wanted him to know someone, unfortunately only Mama saw his pain. To this day, they never took ownership of not showing up. *How could a child not be broken by the indifference of those meant to love him most?* Kyle had a beautiful soul. How could anyone overlook the chance to celebrate a boy like Kyle, especially when his heart held so much light, and this special day called for only love and presence?

That side of the family rarely embraced birthdays or holidays with the kind of joy or enthusiasm Kyle had come to know from my side. While our gatherings were filled with warmth, and togetherness, theirs often felt subdued and distant. Kyle radiated life, he brought energy into every celebration, and it saddened me to see how little that seemed to matter to some. Over time, he began to ask why certain relatives seemed to withdraw from shared memories and family traditions. The emotional weight affected Kyle deeply. As certain behaviors became harder to ignore, my empathy wore thin. What felt most painful was the sense of indifference surrounding Kyle's special day, a day meant to celebrate the bright, kind soul he awas.

I want parents to recognize that every word and action influences their child, whether acknowledged or not. I am not even certain that my husband's family as well as others understood this yet seemed to dismiss its significance regarding Kyle's emotions. I had no answers for Kyle about their behavior, but I would never let their desolation define him. They gave up countless cherished moments with him. It is something I may never understand. *What can you say to someone who has lost their sense of right and wrong, and does not even notice it is gone?*

Kyle's sixteenth milestone birthday stood as a pivotal event for him on his special day and was very important to my late mother as well as me. Its impact endured until his passing. He often brought it up during his final years, a haunting memory that refused to fade. I sensed the profound trauma it caused him, just as it did me, and it is not forgettable. But the question remained: *How could I possibly make up for the emptiness left and the distant disregard from family?* I knew they would not make amends, yet I struggled to find a solution. Kyle had already been through so much pain and grief, more than a child should. He sure did not deserve this. Turning sixteen is a singular occasion in a teenager's life.

The continuation of ruining a significant moment in Kyle's life, from birthdays, holidays to vacations became more frequent, turning something that should have been moments of joy into something dark and painful. I tried desperately to shield Kyle from the wreckage, hoping he could salvage some happiness from those moments. The older he got, the harder it became to hide. Some of the behavior surrounding our family became increasingly difficult for either of us to overlook. *Who, in their right mind would intentionally hurt their child and not flinch?*

MOTHER'S REFLECTION:
What He Deserved

Kyle did not just want a car, he wanted to be seen and to be celebrated. To feel like his life mattered to the people who claimed to love him. When they did not show up, something inside him cracked. I saw it in his eyes, in the way he held back tears in front of his dad, in the way he tried to smile through the ache. That day was not just a missed party; it was a message. One that said, "You're not worth the effort." But he was. He always was. I will never stop saying it, even if I was the only one who did.

66

HAWAII

AFTER MY MOTHER PASSED away, Kyle and I were left feeling lost. My husband began struggling with a significant psychological decline after receiving multiple diagnoses. I found myself asking, "What *in the hell has happened to our family?*" Kyle was terrified of losing his home and his family, and I was just as scared.

Before my mom passed, she left me a small amount of money and told me to take Kyle to Hawaii. She knew it had always been my dream since he was a little boy. Years earlier, when my father passed, she had wanted to buy me a car. I did not need one, we already had a new car, but because she bought my brother one, she thought I should have one too. We were always treated equally. Instead, I told her I would rather take Kyle to Hawaii one day.

So, before she passed on, she reminded me that when the time came, it would be the perfect chance to take Kyle and my husband. After I lost my mom, I decided it was time for what I knew would be our last family vacation, especially as my husband continued to spiral into his psychosis.

My husband did not want to go. Forget about me, but it seemed like he only wanted to spend time with Kyle during moments that revolved around unhealthy habits. Kyle could not wait for the trip, and neither could I.

My God in heaven, how is it possible that someone could have so little desire to create wonderful, healthy memories with their child?

I had gone to Hawaii when I was thirteen. My parents took my brother and me for a two-week Christmas and New Year vacation, visiting three different islands. I had been in heaven. I swore to myself that one day, I would take my own kids and finally, I got my chance.

I booked first-class tickets all the way, and just like my childhood trip, we visited three islands over the holidays. It was breathtaking.

Kyle tried to enjoy himself, but at times, he seemed withdrawn, weighed down. I think he was struggling with wanting to be with his friends and feeling out of place. It is heartbreaking to think he felt that way, but he was a teenager, growing up and naturally pulling away from his parents. I understood. I had felt the same at his age. Still, he took surfing lessons and, like everything else he tried, he excelled. We went on a whale-watching dinner cruise, a more majestic experience than I could have imagined.

The morning of the cruise, I woke up as usual, bright-eyed, full of energy, ready to take on the day. That morning, Kyle was awake, but he seemed quiet, withdrawn in a way that made my heart ache. There was a heaviness in his spirit that I could not quite pin, though I worried it might have been sadness; maybe even the physical and emotional toll of trying to push through something silently. I had hoped this trip might help him catch his breath, reconnect with himself, and soak in the calming beauty of the ocean and the tropical breeze. My son needed that. We both did.

I asked them both to get ready so we could enjoy the day, begging for Kyle to eat a good breakfast with me. It was early morning, and neither one of them liked getting up early. I had so much energy and decided I was not letting that ruin my day in paradise. I told them I would go have breakfast and then hit the beach, when they were ready, they could join me, or I would meet them at the dinner cruise.

Then my husband became distant again, saying he did not want to go at all. I was not going to force him. In fact, I preferred he did not come, given his attitude.

I told him straight out that I was done with this oppressive energy, the constant tension and unpredictable energy that surrounded both Kyle and me. I had had enough. If he was going to mope through the rest of the vacation instead of enjoying time with his family, then he might as well call his mother and take an early flight home. Eventually, Kyle and his dad met up with me, and we attended the dinner cruise.

It was a stunning evening, the most spectacular yet. We watched the sunset over the Pacific Ocean as humpback whales jumped and dove out of the water. Some even came close enough to rock the boat slightly, playful, and friendly, used to their human observers. That moment will stay with me forever.

One evening, as we strolled along Waikiki, the night was nothing short of magical. The warm air, the city lights, the hum of the ocean, it was all perfect. We wandered through the souvenir shops, and taking in the sights, we glanced over at Trump Tower and saw Dog the Bounty Hunter and his wife Beth having dinner on the patio.

From a distance, we waved and called out, "Hey Dog, Beth...we love you!"

To our delight, they waved back and shouted, "Have a beautiful time in Hawaii!"

Kyle was ecstatic. He loved moments like these, and we had spent countless hours watching *Dog the Bounty Hunter* together on TV.

We took the trip over Christmas, a holiday trip meant to be a time of togetherness and joy. But my husband had not brought a single penny to spend. Not one.

On Christmas Day, I purchased a beautiful silver cross necklace for Kyle from a local jewelry store. He adored it, picking it out himself. It was a small moment of happiness amidst the weight of everything else but even the precious symbol of his faith eventually had been stolen. My husband, however, did not get him a single thing, not even a Merry Christmas. He joined us on the trip but made no contributions, which had become a painful pattern simply going along for the free ride.

Our last day arrived, and we decided to take a short drive around the rainforest on Maui before heading to the airport. What was meant to be a scenic detour turned into a three-hour ordeal, round and round the mountain we went. My husband slipped into another fog, another episode, another state of dissociation or withdrawal, I did not even know what to call them anymore. It was difficult to describe exactly what was happening to him.

This was not unfamiliar. His episodes had occurred before, but they were becoming more frequent, and much harder to manage.

As we drove, Kyle and I both needed to use the restroom. We asked my husband several times to stop at the nearest pull-off, but he ignored us, saying nothing, just driving. We spotted fruit stands along the way, their vendors slicing fresh pineapple, papaya, and mango. Each time we pointed one out, "Hey Dad, there's a stand! Please stop!" he kept driving, lost in his own world. Kyle grew more desperate to stop, and so did I.

After repeated pleas and frustration, Kyle actually having to curse at his dad to snap out of it, and nearly three hours, he finally snapped out of it long enough to stop at a fruit stand. We got out, stretched our legs, breathed in the rainforest air. Bamboo covered every inch of the landscape along the winding road, it was breathtaking. But then we noticed the time. We were dangerously close to missing our flight, all because of our three-hour detour. Rushing to the airport, we barely made our flight home.

Hawaii had been beautiful, a true paradise. But even in paradise, there were battles to face and we had endured so much. Even amidst the magic there was always some sort of drama to deal with where my husband was concerned. No vacation was ever completely peaceful, and somehow, moments of joy between Kyle and me were often overshadowed, perhaps, from an inability to connect with those moments himself.

MOTHER'S REFLECTION:
Silence and Sunset

Hawaii was breathtaking, but it was Kyle who made it beautiful. Even when the skies were clear, the storms inside our family followed us. Yet, Kyle still smiled at whales, still waved at Dog and Beth, still holding onto the joy he could find. That silver cross he picked out was not just a gift, it was a symbol of his faith, his hope, his heart. I wish the world had protected that better. But I saw it. I cherished it and I will never forget the boy who found light even when the shadows tried to steal it.

67

INTRODUCED TO HIS FIRST SUPPLIER

I FELT **KYLE SLIPPING AWAY** even when I tried to hold him close. Kyle was trying to find his way in the world as many are at that age, and my husband did not appreciate this challenge of authority. Someone had to lead the family and my husband's refusal for years made me an authority figure. I did not want this! I was just trying to keep things sane and stable. This caused my son to look elsewhere for belonging if he could not find it from his dad.

When Kyle reconnected with a boy in junior high, he asked if he could go over to his house to hang out. Earlier, when the boys had first met, I had seen enough to know that his parents were drinkers and smokers. I did not want my son in that environment. They thought nothing of indulging in front of their child, but I did. So, when they were younger, Kyle's friend always came to our house to play. My intuitions were right on as usual.

One night, Kyle confided in me that his friend's parents were openly using substance while the boys were there, I was furious.

That evening, after picking Kyle up from his friend's house, I brought his friend home with us to hang out. Later, his dad came to get him, and I saw an opportunity to address the issue. I told my husband that he needed to speak to the man. It was unacceptable to be drinking and getting high in front of our son, let alone his own. My husband took him for a drive and confronted him directly. To my disbelief, he admitted to it without hesitation. He apologized, assuring my husband it would not happen again.

Even with his promise, I knew I could not allow Kyle to go back to their house. The boys either hung out at our home, or they met up in the park, where his friend began offering Kyle substance, casually handing them over as if it were no big deal. It was shocking. To me, this behavior was completely foreign, so far removed from the way I raised my son. But to his friend, this was normal. This was his upbringing, his reality. He did not know anything different, and I can only assume he thought this was the way things were supposed to be.

It was heartbreaking to see the difference between the two households. It was clear just how much a parent's choices shape a child's world. Now, I had to make sure Kyle understood that just because something was normal for someone else did not mean it had to be normal for him.

I knew this when his main sidekick came back into Kyle's life in junior high. It had been a while since the two boys had seen each other, but they were going into the eighth grade, so it was bound to happen eventually. My son called me on the way home from school one day just after the final bell rang to tell me who he had seen in one of his classes. Kyle was so excited to see an old friend again and their friendship picked right up where it had left off. Something in the back of my mind made me worry though and I wished I had listened to it. *What could I have done differently?* I think most good parents would ask themselves the same question.

This boy had changed quite a bit from his childhood self. He seemed to be running from one hardship to another at break-neck speed. And of course, Kyle, being the friend he was, came along for the ride. At first, I thought nothing of it. He was still just as sweet and introverted as he was before. I thought it was just teens being teens, but things changed when Kyle himself changed. He was a fragment of the sweet kid he was. He was angry and apathetic on good days, and on bad days it was worse. I could not pinpoint what the exact root of the problem was, until his friend brought the problem to my doorstep.

One day, this boy mentioned an older brother. This was only the second time I had ever heard of this brother, so I assumed he was a stepsibling or an adoptive brother figure. Of course, the boy seemed to idolize him. To him, this brother was the epitome of what he thought, a cool adult should be and when I say adult, I mean young adult, yet he spent time with people considerably younger. My son was one of those people due to his association with his friend.

I had heard whispers from mothers in the area that there was a young man in the area that fit this person's description, and that he was involved in illegal activities. At first, I did not act on this. I had no basis for this claim other than a few whispers and some speculation. Plus, the more I tried to voice my concerns to Kyle, he would either retaliate or brush it off as if it were nothing to worry about. But with Kyle's changing behavior, those worries only amplified.

My fears of this mysterious brother would only be confirmed when I came face to face with him in person a few years later and learned that this kid was not actually related to Kyle's friend.

At this point, Kyle was beginning to drive and had gotten into a fender bender, a few short months after getting his first car, without me knowing. *How you ask?* He had an anxiety attack that was caused by an outright fabrication told to him by his relative. This sent my son into such anxiety that he did not go to school that day, instead going to this kid's house where he was given alcohol. A neighbor offered to give him a ride home as Kyle's car was being pulled from behind on a flatbed trailer.

I was on high alert when I saw them pull into my driveway. I did not have a face to the name yet, but I knew almost instantly that this was the person involved in illegal activities. Shifty and shady would be two good words to describe him then. I, out of fear, threatened to call the cops when he got in my face while I was reaching out to hug my son and make sure he was not hurt.

This person called me a vulgar name for no reason other than he was under the influence of something, but as luck would have it, a police car turned the corner. The young man's first reaction was to run, confirming all the whispers and suspicions. To this day, he hides his wrongdoing.

I believe this individual ruined Kyle's future and likely, had a profoundly damaging influence on others who were drawn into the same world. Kyle's dad and others may have chosen to believe his false narratives, but I did not. It broke my heart to see people, including my husband, accept that version of events while dismissing the truth.

He told people that Kyle did not have any family and put it on social media quickly after he passed and refused to allow me to join it, knowing his true motive. His lie about Kyle's family came from someone admitting that he was a reformed Christian.

Kyle had a huge family on both sides. My side was close-knit and full of life and energy and social gatherings. The other side was completely opposite. This young man admitted to me that he had a difficult upbringing with a mentally ill mom and absent father and assumed that Kyle had the same. I am deeply sorry for his upbringing that no child should ever endure still not excuse to hurt another.

Most substance abusers or addicts will tell you they had a difficult childhood to avoid their ownership in their downfall. In fact, many come from exceptionally good homes and families.

Substance does NOT discriminate in any way. Rich or poor, happy, or sad, ill, or healthy…it does not matter. When the wrong person, an evil person, comes along to sway an innocent child, if they can, then it is absolute heartache after that. It seemed like this young man was hurting and wanted others to hurt too. I saw myself, how he pulled Kyle, and others, into that world of pain, all while professing his Christianity.

Despite Kyle's happiness and heartache in his childhood, he sometimes pretended to be someone he was not to appease the wrong people. Kyle was not a ruthless, tough, unloving rebel like those who seemingly lured him into the world of substance and corruption. Yet, at times, pretended to be so just to fit in with the wrong crowd. His old friends had gone on with their lives and he felt stuck. He felt he would never get normalcy in his life again. This unfortunately put people into his life that were not conducive to a healthy future, and they only brought on more chaos. It is sad to think that this person told me if Kyle had drugs, he always had friends.

When his initial supplier suggested that having drugs or alcohol would also mean having a friend, I strongly disagreed. Such a notion is baseless and certainly not the hallmark of genuine friendship. This individual was far from the kind of friend any responsible parent would wish for their child. I believe he lacks the integrity he claims to have and has unjustly shamed me without understanding the full picture. Some of Kyle's friends were not loyal although most of them were. Regardless, my son always had a ton of friends even before substance took over. We all only need one or two genuine friends in our life anyway.

My son had an alcohol intolerance, a fact known only to Kyle, me, his doctor, and unfortunately, his dad, who not only disregarded it but, from my perspective, and encouraged drinking with his son. Alcohol, being a toxin and a depressant, combined with any substance like marijuana, created a dangerous mix, making detoxification incredibly challenging for Kyle. This placed immense strain on his organs, including his brain, and disrupted his blood sugar balance. It is so frustrating that people fail to grasp these risks or even care. Despite my efforts to raise awareness with my husband, I was met with ridicule and isolation. Kyle believed his "friends" would judge him if he abstained and did not understand that certain ones were not authentic anyway. But loyal friends would not change their opinion based on his choices. He remained the same fun-loving person regardless.

I have seen how people coping with addiction may deflect or avoid responsibility, like the older peer who introduced Kyle to substance when he was just fourteen years young, enabling him and others while struggling with his own instability. Despite what happened, I have never received an apology for the time he lashed out at me while under the influence or for the influence I believe he had on Kyle and others. He has yet to apologize for supplying my son and trying to entice him and other young ones.

At my son's farewell gathering, words suggested he wanted to be seen as reformed and committed to family and healing and wanting to deter others. Yet, in a conversation, asked me to stay silent and not mention his involvement. That contradiction stayed with me. *What does it mean when someone speaks of redemption in front of a grieving crowd, yet later asks to stay silent and not mention their role to anyone?* He obviously does not know me or any mom who lost their child. How dare he ask me to keep quiet. Not a chance!

This behavior exemplified how destructive forces mask themselves and can hurt those around them. I tirelessly warned Kyle about this individual, despite his dad's opposition and subsequent anger towards me for trying to protect my own son from this negative influence. I find myself having to forgive this person daily, recognizing that his actions were likely clouded by his own struggles. In defiance, he has yet to truly own up to the harm he caused.

I will continue to wait patiently, perhaps indefinitely, for him to acknowledge the repercussions of his actions and words.

This is what the demon does. It masquerades in public and looks to devour anyone in its path. I tried desperately to convince Kyle of this as his dad would lash out at me for trying to get him away from whatever light this kid claimed to carry, that led others into darkness.

I did an exercise that another parent from my grief support group told me about. We were instructed to write down all our burdens; our worries, our pain, our anger. After writing everything down, I nailed it to a crafted wooden cross I had at home. In that moment, I knew that Almighty God would not let the guilty go unpunished, and I had to let it go and give it to Him.

To me, this act symbolized that I had truly surrendered it all to God. I trusted that He would heal me, not just from my anger but perhaps even from the deep hurt I carried. It was, without question, the second hardest thing I have ever done, right after saying a final goodbye to my beautiful boy.

Over time, I have come to realize that forgiveness is not always something I will receive from those who have wronged me and my son.

But when I placed my whole trust in God's power, I may find a small fraction of relief in knowing that the apology I longed for, especially if it was not sincere, was never mine to carry. Whether they speak words of remorse or remain silent, it means little if their heart is not moved by the spirit of God.

At this point, I am choosing to let the burden of truth rest on them. I will continue to love them in full, but I no longer need their words to justify my healing. That is between me and God.

Looking back, it seemed he may not have grasped the weight of what he was doing, whether because of his own inner struggles or a simple lack of awareness. God sees and knows all and now so does my son.

MOTHER'S REFLECTION:
To the One Who Helped Break Him

You knew Kyle's heart. You saw his light but still, you handed him darkness.

You may have been hurting. You may have felt unseen. But that does not excuse what you did. You introduced a boy, my boy, to a world he was never meant to enter. You watched him unravel and called it friendship. You stood in front of a grieving mother and asked her to stay silent. That silence will never come.

You helped dim a light that was meant to shine. While you may hide behind redemption, I will not hide behind grief. I forgive you because I must. But I will never forget and neither will God. Neither will Kyle.

You wanted to be seen as reformed. Then own what you did. Speak truth. Not just in front of a crowd, but in the quiet where it matters most.

68

OUR NEW BEST FRIEND

WHEN KYLE WAS ELEVEN or twelve one of his friends' parents came to me and said she had a friend who was getting a divorce and needed to find a loving home for their Golden Retriever. He came over to meet Kyle one evening and we fell instantly in love. His name was Kojak. He was an older male with a heart of gold. This was perfect. Kyle could have his Golden again, without the hassle of training. We could basically enjoy the easy temperament of the breed without the work of training. We jumped at the chance to take care of him and give him a new home and much love that he desperately needed and deserved. I believed Kyle was old enough at this point, to be more responsible for feeding, walking, and exercising a dog.

Kojak was a dream, truly man's best friend to all of us. Except on occasion when we left a loaf of bread on the counter, and he quickly found and devoured it. We would come home and all that was left was an empty wrapper lying on the kitchen floor. I could not figure out what was happening.

We decided to set up the camcorder in the kitchen and solve the mystery. Kojak was caught red-handed. Honestly, all we could do was laugh hysterically. No way was I going to get mad at such a wonderful companion for my son. I quickly learned to hide the bread in the refrigerator.

We had Kojak for many years, a steady presence in our world that was constantly shifting. But just before Kyle's seventeenth birthday, his dad decided he had enough of playing the role of family man. The need for money, freedom, and personal desires, in my opinion, seemed to outweigh any commitment to us. So, without warning, without explanation, he disappeared, as if the family were nothing more than an inconvenience. This was not some figure of speech or dramatic exaggeration. This was our reality. He left like a man running to the store for milk who never came back, even leaving behind most of his clothes and possessions.

Kyle, longing for his dad's attention, eventually agreed to live with him, against my better judgement, drawn in by promises that, heartbreakingly, were never fulfilled. From what I saw, his dad permitted nearly anything, even when it was harmful, so long as it aligned with his own wants or needs. There seemed to be little concern for consequences, for Kyle's emotional or physical well-being, or for the toll that kind of freedom might take. Whether intentional or not, those choices created fractures in our relationship, and I as well as my son, felt the weight of it every day.

I needed to somehow figure out a way to take care of Kojak, my Yorkie Daisy Mae, the cats: Crash II, Rusty, Dancer, and the lizard Buddy. It was exceedingly difficult.

Kojak was now on medicine daily for his arthritis as he was getting old and not as active as he used to be. Two of my cats were getting old as well and one was not eating and losing weight and very fragile. Another one was bulimic and had intestinal problems. My Daisy Mae had Addison's Disease and had also been put on medicine a few years prior. She was going downhill to the point I had to rush her to the hospital on occasion but came on more often as she relapsed.

My fur babies were indeed our family. My kids. It was overwhelming to care for them all, but I had to be there for the family I had left at home. This strained Kyle. He loved all his animals but was not able to take proper care of them and knew that I could not do it alone. Kyle was becoming aware of what his dad had factually done to all of us, including our pets. In so many moments, I could see Kyle struggling, his anger and distress growing as he tried to reconcile the dad, he wished he had with the one he saw before him.

Kyle loved the animals so much but as he got older and more unhappy, he just did not seem to put in effort at all even though I know deep down he did love them and cared about what happened to them. Using substances seemed to numb Kyle's ability to feel or find motivation. He struggled to care for himself, and support from his dad was not something we could rely on. None of it felt like Kyle's fault, he was aware that he could not manage the responsibilities left to him. So, I did my best to take care of them for my son, for as long as I was able.

When my husband left, it felt like we were discarded, left with no support, no plan, and no regard for how we would survive. We received nothing to help us move forward. As a full-time mother, I was scraping by on less than five hundred dollars a month, barely covering food and fuel for our little family. Our monthly expenses were over three thousand. I pleaded for help, not just for myself, but for Kyle and the animals we both loved. But the silence on the other end made it clear: we were on our own.

Sometimes we must put our fur babies down, so they do not suffer any longer. I did not want to. It was a road that I did not want to take. I would rather they find a home, with people who would love them as much as I did. I wanted my furry children to have happy final days even if they were not going to be with me.

I sought out shelters and rescue groups to take them and no one would because they were either too full or because they would not take sick animals. I was told they would not be able to be put up for adoption and they would ultimately have to be euthanized after being imprisoned in a cage. I could not find homes for them and did not want them to spend the rest of their traumatized lives in a cage I tried many times to contact my husband via my mother-in-law and even asking her to help with the animals and give me money to buy food and medication for them, but never saw a penny, ever.

One evening, while Kyle was with me, his father said something that shook me to my core. At the moment, if felt like our well-being did not matter to him, He had made it painfully clear. Kyle later shared that he had been told I had harmed our pets. That could not have been further from the truth. Those animals were our family. Kyle and I loved them with everything we had. I have never, and will never, harm an animal. Caring for them and all animals is one of the callings of my life and always has been.

When their health declined, I had to make heartbreaking decisions, alone, facing medical realities I could not change and financial obstacles I could not overcome. Support was not offered, despite my pleas. I still cannot fathom what would drive a parent to create distance between a mother and her son through stories that caused such deep confusion and pain. The position we were left in was beyond cruel.

That moment caused agony I can hardly put into words. Kyle heard the words himself, spoken over the speakerphone, and I saw the light in him dim just a little more. Hearing that kind of disregard from someone he once trusted made his oppression even more deep. For me, it was a turning point, a moment that confirmed just how far removed his dad had become from the reality of our lives, and how unreachable he now seemed, no matter how much we needed him to show up.

I had no choice but to let them go, to surrender them to the Lord with more grief than I thought one heart could carry. I searched for help from every corner, but no one stepped forward, not even the person I believed should have. At the same time, I watched Kyle sink deeper into sadness, not realizing how much this pain was dimming his drive to keep going. He later confided in me that he had talked to his dad, hoping for something, anything, to help. But there was nothing offered in return.

He told me verbatim, "Mom, dad is too involved with his whore to care about any of us."

Kyle's entire family was falling apart. Watching the grip addiction took on my husband was heartbreaking, but watching the shadow fall over our son was nearly unbearable.

My husband made choices that left a lasting impact on both of our lives, ones I never thought we would have to face. Those decisions, which felt rooted in absence and broken trust, set in motion a storm we had no choice but to endure on our own. For Kyle, the betrayal ran even deeper and was drawn into a web of false promises and harmful behaviors. *What kind of wounds are left on a child when their well-being is dismissed, time and again, and who decides they should have to carry that weight?*

In the end, we were left to gather the fragments of a life we had not agreed to lose. I know that my fur babies are in a better place, just as Kyle is, but I want them all here! I see Kyle now running in an ever-so-green pasture with Kojak, who he loved dearly. They are all together and happy beyond what we could ever imagine.

MOTHER'S REFLECTION:
Where Loyalty Still Lives

Kojak did not know betrayal. Daisy Mae never withheld love. The others never asked for more than presence.

They were the teachers of truth, the kind that cannot be faked, forgotten, or talked away. In the turmoil that grew around Kyle, these beautiful animals stood as a quiet reminder of what constancy looks like. What loyalty sounds like. What love feels like.

When the noise got louder, when the pain came in waves, they did not leave. They did not lash out. They did not blame. They just stayed and they loved him through it.

Their silence held him. Their eyes forgave what the world refused to.

I often think about how Kyle treated them with tenderness even when he could not give that to himself. They reflected the best in him, the parts I never lost sight of, even when others did.

So, if you are asking where love still lives… it lives in pawprints, in whiskers, in soft fur curled beside a boy whose heart was bigger than his grief. It lives in every moment he showed up for something that loved him without condition.

69

We Were Meant to Do Better

WHEN KYLE WAS YOUNGER, I often sensed that his dad may have viewed both of us as added responsibilities that might hinder his true pursuits. My perspective could not have been more different. Kyle was my everything, a true blessing after a difficult journey to bring him into the world. The struggles of losing three earlier pregnancies and being told I could not conceive made Kyle's arrival, without a doubt, even more miraculous.

Every time I looked at my son, I saw divine grace reflected in his existence. I will always remain profoundly grateful to Almighty God for the gift of being Kyle's mother after years of longing. I am still deeply and forever grief-stricken by my son's untimely passing, particularly given his status as a true miracle with a unique purpose.

While the notion that a child needs their dad holds a degree of truth. A father's presence alone is not what shapes a child, it is constancy, safety, love, and selflessness. I have come to realize that being a dad in name is not the same as being a father in heart.

I could not get my husband to understand that we were never meant to raise Kyle the way his parents raised him or the way my parents raised me. We were not supposed to mold him through their choices, their fears, or their pain. He was not just a miracle baby, he was our baby, born out of our love, a love I thought was strong enough to build a life on.

We were supposed to raise Kyle differently, better in every way. Every generation is meant to grow, to break old cycles, to heal what the past. That was supposed to be our purpose, to love Kyle enough to give him something new, something whole, something better. Not just to repeat what we were given, but to reach for something greater.

Maybe he was afraid to challenge what he knew. Some people hold onto the past because it feels safer than imagining something different. Maybe he did not see the harm the way I did, or maybe he could not feel the weight of those patterns pressing down on our family the way I could. Or maybe he just did not want to fight for something new, some people choose comfort over growth, even when growth would lead to something better.

But I saw it, I wanted more and that speaks to my heart, my vision, and my strength that I had for our son. I stood in the gap between the past and the future, determined to build something better for Kyle. That was everything to me and should have been for Kyle's dad.

I initially believed our marriage was a mutual partnership to raise our family together. That was my dream and my reason for committing to my husband, yet I ended up shouldering much of the responsibility. I had hoped my husband's values and intentions were the same as mine, but unfortunately his priorities differed greatly. I chose to deeply believe he wanted the best for our son and for our family to thrive. Surely, he did. I would hope that most men do. However, his actions fell short of those ideals, leaving me to question my own judgment and blaming myself every day for not seeing it for what I did not see.

MOTHER'S REFLECTION:
The Blueprint We Were Meant to Rewrite

We were not meant to repeat what broke us.

Kyle was a chance to start fresh, to raise love without fear, to rewrite the story we were given. I saw that. I wanted that. I fought for that. But not everyone is ready to let go of old patterns. Some stand still, even when the future calls them forward.

I carried the hope. I held the line, and I will never stop believing we could have done better, because Kyle deserved it. Every child does.

70

WHAT WAS MISSING

WHAT DOES A SON *do when the one he hopes will teach him* never reaches out?

A mother can only take her son so far before he begins looking to his father for guidance. There comes a point in every boy's life when he needs a male role model, someone to help define his sense of manhood. I sensed that my husband struggled to step into that role, perhaps because he had not been shown consistent or compassionate leadership in his own upbringing. Often, he deferred that responsibility to a relative whose harsh views and controlling behavior seemed to override gentler voices.

Kyle's sensitivity, his quiet brilliance, characteristics that made him so special became white noise to his dad; blending into the background of his life. I did not want that to happen with Kyle. If I tried to speak to my husband about it, I seemed to be white noise as well.

In all the moments when Kyle needed consolation and mentorship, he was nowhere in sight. He missed Kyle's beautiful childhood and teenage years so much because he was so preoccupied with other seemingly more important things. Nothing could have been more important than spending time with Kyle or me, his wife, helping me raise our beloved boy together. I kept hoping he would see the value of spending real time with his son. I prayed for a turning point.

If Kyle had had a strong, stay male mentor, someone who lived out the values he craved, I believe with my whole heart that he would still be here today. He needed that kind of presence. He longed for it. He cried out for it in many ways, and too often, there was that one person who was not listening.

Kyle was on his own trying to learn what being a real man entailed. In many ways, he surpassed the examples that were before him, these things stood apart. Being a true man with Godly character but still struggled to uphold this while others pressured him and tried to steer him from it. He struggled to hold onto what he knew was right. Kyle did his best to reconcile what he saw in his dad's life with the kind of life he wanted but the contradictions cut deep.

I never spoke openly about everything I saw, only to a select few, but I often find myself wondering: *What happens to a family when emotional maturity is missing where it is most needed?*

When Kyle was sixteen, right before everything came to light, his dad admitted to both of us to not believing in God, telling us both that he never did believe and for years, only pretended to. This revelation profoundly impacted Kyle and me. The contradiction shattered Kyle, whose faith was real and rooted. Kyle told me he sensed inconsistencies for a long time, because his actions and words rarely matched, but this left Kyle with a foundation. I believe Kyle understood far more than I realized at the time.

I reflected on Ephesians and other scriptures that speak to a father's role, to provide guidance, protect, and teach with love and spiritual integrity. Unfortunately, the choices Kyle's dad made over time stood in contrast. Some involved betrayal. Others, spiritual or financial recklessness. All of them sent a message to both Kyle and I that he nor I mattered, and this slowly broke him.

And then came the part I struggle most to speak about. Kyle confided in me that another male relative, the same one entrusted with influence, had deeply harmed him. Not just emotionally, but physically; repeatedly, while his dad sat by, watched and did nothing. These were my son's words, not mine.

He shared his memories with such pain and detail that I knew, without question, they were real. He told me that he was not allowed to contact me or friends to help. That his phone was taken. That he felt trapped. He was mistreated by one relative and ignored by another, and that silence... the silence of someone who should have intervened, cut the deepest.

In one heartbreaking moment, Kyle told me he had even pulled a knife to protect himself. He was terrified, alone, and had no way to reach out. I still grieve the idea of my boy begging to call and being denied. No child should ever feel that kind of fear in a place where they are told they are safe. And no parent should have to live with knowing their child was silenced in their pain.

While I cannot definitively prove my suspicions, I have collected information from Kyle's friends as well as my mother-in-law who told me that my son was telling me the truth. I feel like the choices they made were not just about Kyle, they meant something deeper, something personal. I have often wondered if the pain my beautiful boy endured was, in part, a reflection and retaliation of unresolved tensions and aimed at me.

Later, those same individuals tried to bring him back into their world, with empty gestures and shared hobbies, as though basketball could erase the damage. *But how does a child trust again when the hands reaching out for him are the same hands that once let him fall?*

Kyle did not know how to hold that contradiction. He tried. He wanted to. But when care is blended with control, and when support is tied to silence, even love feels like a threat.

What broke my son was not just the trauma. It was the confusion. The minimizing. The gaslighting. The absence of anyone who would say, "This was not your fault." I did tell him it was not his fault and never was. The others should have been saying the same thing.

Kyle lived in that silence far too long. And I watched as the weight of it chipped away at the light inside him.

I stood between the past and what should have been the future, doing everything I could to offer Kyle something better. I had hoped his father would stand there with me. I once believed our marriage was a promise to raise our son together, with shared values and a mutual commitment to love. But somewhere along the way, that dream crumbled.

And in the end, I was left to hold what remained of it all, for myself, for our son, and for the love that brought him into the world. Kyle was our miracle. He deserved better. And I will carry that truth for the rest of my life.

MOTHER'S REFLECTION:
Read Between the Lines

Some things I have written in this chapter are softened, not because the truth was not sharp, but because the law does not always make room for the rawness of a mother's grief. I have removed names. I have reshaped sentences. But the truth? The truth sits untouched beneath every word.

What my son endured cannot be fully captured in what I am allowed to say, but I was there. I heard his voice. I saw the bruises, I held him when he trembled in fear and tears, in heartache. I remember the words he could barely speak without shedding a tear and the absence of protection that should have come. That absence is louder than any line I have written.

71

HONOR AND HEARTACHE

We ARE TAUGHT TO honor our father and mother. But that does not mean submitting to abuse or neglect. There is a line; one that no parent should cross, and one, children should not ever have to navigate on their own.

Children are still growing. Their hearts and minds are fragile, and they rely on us, their parents, to guide them with care and wisdom. Looking back, I wonder if staying in that environment, one that did not feel safe for either of us, was my way of hoping things might change. Maybe I should have taken him far away. His father made his own choices, choices that hurt deeply.

He will never admit it, but the truth is, he walked away. He left us without a home, not just emotionally, but physically. No shelter. No support. No presence. That kind of abandonment leaves scars that do not easily fade...if ever.

I say this not from a place of bitterness, but of faith. I follow Jesus Christ with all my heart, and I believe in a God who is loving and just, a God who would never ask a child to honor a parent whose actions were harmful and unkind. God does not ask us to follow someone who refuses to lead with love. That is *not* what this commandment is meant to convey.

To truly be honored, a parent must live in a way that earns respect.

A parent does not demand it, while acting in ways that damages the only child they were called to protect. Kyle saw it. He knew it was so wrong on so many levels. Their treatment of him demanded obedience without merit. They did not command it, so they did not get it. I pray no child ever believes they must follow in those footsteps. I hope and pray no loving parent expects them to.

MOTHER'S REFLECTION:
Honor Must Be Earned

Honor is not demanded, it is demonstrated. Kyle was asked to respect what did not protect him, to obey what did not guide him. That is not God's will, it is man's distortion. True honor begins with presence, with safety, with love that does not fracture the spirit of a child. I pray no one confuses silence with virtue ever again. Kyle knew the difference. So, do I.

72

A HOUSE WITHOUT BOUNDARIES

AT SEVENTEEN, KYLE MADE the decision to live with his dad and grandmother, hoping to rebuild a bond that had always felt absent. The lax attitude toward responsibility in the home gave him more freedom, freedom to skip school, to experiment with substance and avoid structure. Still, despite these circumstances, Kyle held on to the hope that living with his dad might finally bring them closer.

But the reality, the actual situation was undeniable and told a different story. Kyle soon realized that his dad struggled to be the stable, guiding presence he had longed for. His grandma, while present in her home, did not provide the kind of structure or emotional support Kyle needed either. She and her son had never shared a model of nurturance, and that gap carried through to Kyle. In a home without boundaries or accountability, it spiraled into utter confusion, leaving Kyle with little support to grow, heal or succeed.

From the sidelines, I pleaded with my mother-in-law to have my husband bring Kyle home, where I could offer the support, encouragement and care he desperately needed; he still needed someone to make sure he ate right and stayed healthy and clean and continued his education. At the time, I did not know our family was on the brink of losing everything including our house due to financial circumstances I had not been told about, decisions that broke our marriage and our security. It felt clear to me; Kyle's needs were not the priority in that house.

One evening, his dad picked him up from a friend's house because he did not have a car at the time. Kyle told me he thought they were going back to grandma's but instead his dad, who Kyle believed had been drinking, began driving around aimlessly visiting liquor store after liquor store. According to Kyle, they ended up in a liquor store in Bonner Springs where his dad told him that he was going to meet up with his girlfriend (we were married at the time). Kyle had not wanted to meet his dad's girlfriend, so they had turned back, but the situation seemed to be more dangerous. He told me that he tried to get his dad to stop the car, but he would not listen. Kyle did not want his dad to know he was communicating with me, so he texted from the back seat, saying he was scared, and I needed to get him.

He said, "Dad is acting weird, Mom. Can you come get me?"

I could sense the pattern repeating itself, instability, unpredictability, fear. I jumped in my car and drove out to find him, following the vague directions Kyle managed to text while his dad kept altering the route and stopping at another liquor store near the house.

Finally, Kyle texted again, saying he was near his grandmother's house and felt safe enough for me not to come. He told me he did not want his dad and me to argue and said he thought dad would just pass out on the couch. Still, I knew this pattern of recklessness could not continue.

Kyle told me that his grandmother had gone to the liquor store for him and his dad. He said she let him drink at home and did not stop him from having a party. There were not any rules, not the kind a teenager still needs. It felt like anything went, and that kind of freedom, at his age, was just dangerous, and to me, painted a tragic picture.

In hindsight, I wish I had intervened more forcefully. I wish I had called the authorities that night on my husband. What I did not understand was how deep the cycle of dysfunction had gone on. What I witnessed and heard felt like a legacy of patterns that ran deep and left marks on Kyle that time alone could not erase.

MOTHER'S REFLECTION:

Freedom Without Safety Is Not Love

Kyle was given freedom, but not the kind that protects, nurtures, or guides. He was handed pandemonium, and it was called choice, but a teenager does not need permission to spiral. He needs someone to say, "I see you. I will not let you fall." I tried. He knew I was there. From the sidelines, I tried. I will never stop wishing I had been allowed to do more.

73

TATS

AFTER KYLE PASSED, ONE of his closest friends wanted to get a tattoo in his honor, the date, engraved in Roman numerals. Knowing this made me feel wonderful, I knew she loved my son deeply. It was not just ink. It was loyalty. Loss. A silent promise never to forget. A permanent tribute to the bond they shared.

A colleague's grandson, an incredibly talented professional tattoo artist, agreed to design a piece I had envisioned for my forearm. I was always against tattoos and had raised Kyle to avoid them, but after seeing his tattoo, I wanted to honor him in any way I could, daily, just as I still do. Kyle would flip if he saw mom with a tat, but I wanted this tattoo for him. I wanted people to be able to see it and ask, "What is the story behind it?" Not all, but most tattoos usually have a story attached to them and I wanted it to be a starting point to where I can talk about what a beautiful son I had and tell his story. But the artistic work is so expensive, and I simply can't afford it.

I remember the day Kyle came home after hanging out with friends. I was cleaning the house and doing laundry. I asked him to take off his dirty white T-shirt because I was about to wash whites.

He said, "No, Mom, that's okay." I asked him again, nicely, reminding him that he had plenty of clean shirts in his room, and I did not want him walking around in a dirty one. Again, he refused.

I looked at him and immediately knew he was hiding something. He was afraid to tell me. That hurt. Yes, I was against tattoos, but he should never have been afraid to share anything with me. It is not like I ever yelled at him; I never did. And then something clicked. I suddenly knew what it was.

I softly said, "Kyle, please take off your dirty shirt now."

When he did, I saw a beautiful piece of art, a tattoo of a scorpion stretched from the top of his chest, leading toward the side of his neck. It was big, for sure. But it was breathtaking. My son was so thin that I knew it must have hurt him.

I said, "Oh my God, Kyle, it is beautiful. It really is."

Then I asked, "Did it hurt?"

He smiled and said, "No, Mom, it really didn't."

I know it hurt; it must have.

Among his tattoos, this one stood out. It represented his birth sign, as he was born in November, a true Scorpio. Kyle had always been drawn to anything celestial, fascinated by the skies, the stars, and the vast universe beyond. His tattoos reflected his spirit, his deep connection to the cosmic and the unseen wonders of the world.

After that, he got a stunning KC Royals tattoo with his initials seamlessly embedded in the design, along with a couple of other tattoos. He was proud of them. And, honestly, at that point, I did not mind that he had gotten them. They were beautiful tattoos, nothing evil, nothing ungodly. Just incredible works of art, engraved on a beautiful and perfect canvas, my son Kyle.

MOTHER'S REFLECTION:
Ink That Speaks

I used to believe tattoos were a mistake. A stain; maybe even sinful. Something to regret.

Then I saw Kyle's scorpion, etched in bravery and pain, in birthright and spirit. It was not rebellion. It was revelation. A mark of who he was and what he carried.

Now I dream of my own tattoo. Not to match him, but to carry him. To start conversations that deserve to be had. To say: "My son lived. He loved. He mattered."

Because sometimes, the most permanent things are not scars. They are stories. They are testimonies. They are tributes.

74

WORLD SERIES

EVERY YEAR, WHEN FATHER'S Day rolled around, Kyle and I would ask his dad what he wanted. His answer was always the same, a KC Royals muscle shirt. Baseball was part of our lives. Even when Kyle was just an infant, we went to games, and his dad never missed watching it on TV. I liked baseball too, but only live, never on the screen. Kyle and I only loved it in its rawest form, at the stadium, under the lights, where there is so much energy, walking around, and joining the activities. Also, where we could pig out on hot dogs, cotton candy, and funnel cake. Some of my favorite memories, even when Kyle was just an infant, was bundle him up and headed to the ballpark.

When the Royals made it to the World Series, the excitement in Kansas City was contagious. At work, my supervisor handed out Royals T-shirts and a few giant chocolate chip cookies at our monthly meeting. One cookie was left over, so she gave it to me. Then something unexpected came, she told us that she and her husband had season tickets but was headed to Vegas to join him at a convention, so she offered them to me. No charge.

My first thought was Kyle.

Although I would have loved to go with Kyle, I figured it would be a great father-son moment. A once in a lifetime chance to see a series game. So, I called Kyle, and told him the good news, and said I would bring a T-shirt and cookie over for him and when I got the tickets, I would let him know.

Then I called his dad.

I told him about the tickets, thinking he would be excited. "It's a great chance for you and Kyle," I said.

His response caught me off guard. He said, "I do not like baseball." He shouted.

I hesitated. "Since when? We've gone to games for years. Every Father's Day, you have always asked Kyle for a Royals muscle shirt."

"I never liked baseball," with his voice raised.

After trying to convince him to go with his son, I brushed it off and reminded him I would drop off the cookie and shirt and bring the tickets when I had them.

That evening, I drove to my mother-in-law's house. As I parked along the curb to park, he was pulling in the driveway. Before I could step out, he was already yelling. "What are you doing here?"

I reminded him I was dropping off the gifts. "I do not want them!" he yelled.

"They are for Kyle, not you," I said.

Before I could say anything else, he grabbed them out of my hands, tossing them onto his passenger seat. Then, stepping out of his car, I asked him if he had been working late. He muttered, "I was at a bar."

"Why were you at a bar?" I asked.

"I was watching the Royals game."

My stomach tightened. I said, "You told me just hours ago you didn't like baseball."

Then, before I could react, I was struck in the nose. Pain rushed in as I grabbed my nose, which started to bleed profusely. "You didn't have to do that!" I screamed, running to my car. Arrived home, I cleaned up, took pictures, and cried through it.

The next day, Kyle called, thanking me for the T-shirt and cookie. I told him his dad was not taking him to the game, but he could bring a friend. His voice grew quiet, heavy with disappointment. Another healthier chance misses with dad.

I encouraged Kyle to ask a friend, go, and have a great time. Kyle did go and he took a friend and told me he had an amazing time. It should have been a father-son memory. Another rare moment that could have meant something.

But me? I never saw motherhood as a sacrifice. Loving Kyle was easy. I never missed a chance. Showing up for him was never hard.

MOTHER'S REFLECTION:
Showing Up

Some people think parenting is about a sacrifice. I never did. I believed it was about showing up, without conditions, without ego, without excuses.

He needed his dad in his corner. Someone who saw him, thought of him first, and never hesitated to make him feel included. It could have been a memory. Kyle did not get a father who showed up for that. It was not about baseball. It was about belonging.

That night reminded me of all the times I said yes for my son, to T-shirts, to chocolate chip cookies or ice cream, to pain, to presence. Because showing up was never hard, not when it was for him.

I did not need a World Series ticket to prove my love for him. I needed him to know he was worth cheering for.

75

WHEN SUPPORT
DISAPPEARED

MY HUSBAND MADE A choice, a devastating, deliberate choice. He did not want to be married. He did not want to be a father. He did not want to be a family. He discarded us; just like that. He walked away, leaving Kyle and me behind like we were nothing. He stopped paying the mortgage, the utilities, the groceries. seemed, to me, redirected into his personal habits and compulsions. That was his priority, not his son, not his wife, not the life we had built together. Because in his mind, every single penny that belonged to our family unit was meant to fuel a gambling habit alone.

For a short time, Kyle tried living with his dad. At first, he had an apartment down the street, that his mom supplied but that did not last. Soon, he moved back in with his mother, contributing nothing, not rent, bills, not even sharing the expense of food. He told others he was still supporting our home, but from what I saw, and heard from his mother, she was covering the apartment.

To me, it felt like a performance, one meant to preserve an image rather than reflect reality. I watched people continue to believe in him, unaware of what was really happening behind the scenes. It was all a facade. He was not paying for anything. From my perspective, he was presenting a version of himself that did not match what was happening behind the scenes.

Despite making a massive salary plus bonuses, he told others he could not afford Kyle's school lunches. More money siphoned for himself, while his son went without. Kyle told me later how hard it was, not always getting the same food as the other kids, the ones whose parents cared enough to pay. He said he was so embarrassed and humiliated. I had no idea. I did not know how deep the wreckage went until Kyle told me what his dad had done.

I did not realize, at the time, how the choices he made, one after another, left us increasingly desperate. *Was it carelessness, or something more deliberate?* I did not know then how each decision seemed to pull us deeper into struggle.

Kyle lost weight. He was not eating right. He was not taking care of himself. He was not even taking vitamins. I needed him home. I needed to nourish him, to heal him, to rebuild what had been broken. But the damage had already been done. And in the end, it was Kyle, not his dear old dad, who suffered for his dad's sins.

Even before his dad left, Kyle struggled with the boundaries I set to keep him safe and healthy. He did not like the rules, so when the opportunity came, he chose to live with his dad, where there were no rules at all. He allowed unruly behavior because he modeled it himself. Kyle did not have a male role model to learn from, so he followed his dad's lead into destruction.

I was begging my husband for money for bills and food. One night Kyle came to me with a small twenty-five-dollar gift card, money his dad said he got from work, meant for pet food. Kyle missed me. He told me his dad was not cooking, cleaning, or even buying toilet paper. I gave him a couple of rolls and told him to hide them. If his dad wanted him to go without, then he could go without too. *How does a father look into his son's eyes and still choose absence over care? Is neglect passive or is silence its own kind of cruelty?*

I asked Kyle why he thought living with his dad was a promising idea if he was not being cared for. He had no answer. But I knew the truth. Every boy longs for a father. A man who shows up, who teaches, who protects. It often felt like Kyle's dad was building sandcastles when what Kyle needed was a foundation of stone. He showed up for the fun, the tides, the easy laughter, but the structure never held when life got heavy.

"Mom," Kyle said to me, "I have to take what I can get."

That broke me.

While I was still in our home, before the bank took it, I asked Kyle to move back in. He said he would, but only if I did not have so many rules. But my rules were not harsh. They were the rules of any loving parent: get a good night's sleep, eat well, go to school, stay away from harmful people and substances, walk the dog, and stay on the right path. I was not going to let my son spiral into destruction. I was trying to prepare him for life, to help him become a man who could stand on his own.

The motto at Grandma's house was, "Do whatever you want, whenever you want." But life does not work that way. We all live by rules, at home, at school, at work. I was trying to teach Kyle that, but my voice was drowned out by a louder, more tempting call of chaos.

It baffled me that Kyle followed others when he had been taught better. But I realized he was being manipulated. His dad's lies and lawless behavior confused him. Kyle thought if his dad could get away with immoral behavior, maybe he could too. But it only led him further from the light.

The mind games people played with Kyle showed him a life that made me cringe. I knew it would only lead to pain and destruction. I was left alone, ostracized, shunned, and eventually homeless, because I refused to enable my husband's destructive behavior. I tried to save my son, and for that, we were both punished severely.

I do not share this to hurt anyone. I share it because no parent should ever be afraid to stand up for their child. Parental alienation is real! It is cruel! And it destroys the one who matters most, the child. The beautiful, innocent child of two people that once loved each other enough to create and bring that child into the world. The child who just wants a family and a stable home.

Our children depend on us. We fail them when we ignore their needs or put our own desires first. I hold no anger toward my husband anymore, only sadness. He seemed lost, carrying pain that, in my experience, spilled over into our family's life. So, stop and think before you damage your precious child.

I would have lived under a bridge if that is what it took to make my son whole again. And maybe I did, in a way. But I never stopped fighting for him. I never stopped loving him. And I never will but I was going to do it all alone.

MOTHER'S REFLECTION:
When Love Is All That Is Left

There is a kind of grief no one prepares you for, the grief that comes when the people who were supposed to stay end up walking away and the ones who remain are left picking up the pieces in silence.

Kyle did not need perfection, just presence and consistency. He needed a father who protected instead of disappeared. What he got instead was a lesson no child should learn: that absence can look a lot like betrayal.

I could not save our family, our marriage but I stood in the torn corners and waited. I stayed. Even when everything else vanished, I held the line because sometimes love is not enough to fix things, but it is still enough to prove I never gave up.

76

CONCUSSION

KYLE TOLD ME ONE day that his depression and substance abuse, which led to more anxiety, might have been elevated by a concussion he suffered three years prior due to an almost deadly car accident he'd been in with a few of his friends.

He said he was riding in the back seat when their car was side swiped by another car, and they veered off the road. Kyle was knocked unconscious and taken to the emergency room at Research Medical Center. He had a concussion and needed stitches near one of his eyes. The other kids in the car were also hurt but thank God everyone survived.

Kyle later shared that his dad was aware of the accident and injuries but did not contact me. I learned that other individuals close to the situation, including my mother-in-law, extended family, and acquaintances, were also aware but never reached out to me. *What makes a person in their right mind think that it was the proper thing to not contact Kyle's mom to let her know that her son almost perished?* It felt like a devastating oversight, one that I still cannot explain.

When someone on Facebook told me about the accident and that Kyle was in the ER, I did not hesitate, hung up the phone and sped to the hospital, desperate to get there as quickly as possible. When I arrived, they told me he had just been discharged. My heart was racing, and when he finally called, I was frantic, overwhelmed with worry and confusion. *Why had not anyone informed me sooner?* He said he did not want me to worry. Why do kids not understand that worrying is a part of being a parent? I needed to know where my son was, how he was. It is impossible not to care, impossible not to want to be there to sit beside him and hold his hand and to tell him how much I love him and need him. *Why do they not realize just how much that matters?*

Later, Kyle told me he feared that his head injury may have worsened his depression. The thing was, he was fully aware of what was happening to him and wanted it to go away but he just did not know how and was trying to fix it in a way that did not help.

MOTHER'S REFLECTION:
More Than Just a Headache

When a concussion heals on the outside, it does not always mean that it is healed on the inside. Something shifted and Kyle knew it.

Kyle did not make excuses. He was trying to understand the changes in himself, the fog, the sadness, the edge that never seemed to fade. He said it out loud, even when he could barely face it. That is not weakness. That is bravery.

If I had known sooner, I would have fought sooner and shown up sooner because for Kyle trying to climb out of invisible pain, my love was not just medicine, it was witness.

77

STRANGE VOICE

I CALLED TO SPEAK WITH my son one morning as I drove to work. It was early, but I thought he would be up. A strange voice answered the phone. A man. It did not sound like my husband at all. I hesitated for a second and then said, "Kyle?"

He said, "This is Kyle."

"No, it is not. Let me talk to my son."

"This is his brother."

"I didn't know I had two babies after fourteen hours of labor and delivery."

"I'm his brother from another mother."

"Let me speak to my son, please!"

"Kyle is fine, Kyle will be fine." Click.

The phone went dead. So, at this point I was panicking yet again, not knowing who I was speaking to. Was my son in trouble? Was he being hurt? Was this a game of his? I cannot tell you what it does to a mom to know everyone around your child is on substance and messing with their minds and mine. I did not know what to think, especially since my son was spiraling and I felt I did not have the support or help I needed from those around him.

I thought the worst. I did not know where he was or who he was with. I called my mother-in-law and had to leave a message. *(She often screened her calls, and I was left uncertain if she ever heard my messages or simply did not respond. At the time, it felt like my concern for Kyle's well-being was left unanswered.)* I called my son back with no answer. My thought then was to call the cops. Then I stopped and hung up the phone, thinking What would my husband do? What would my son do if I called the cops, and he was fine? He would lash out at me and so would my husband especially when I considered calling the police for a wellness check on Kyle. I never knew what he might do, and that uncertainty kept me silent more than once. No more.

My husband always thought I exaggerated. He would dismiss my fears or label them unfairly, calling me irrational. But I knew I was not. I was simply a good, loving mom on a mission to save her son. My son would be upset at me and not talk to me sometimes but not for very long. Did I want this? No, of course not. I called my mother-in-law back. Still no answer. I left a message asking her to call Kyle and let me know that he was okay so I would not worry.

A couple of hours later I called again, and Kyle answered, saying "I'm up now."

He told me that his best friend answered the phone earlier. I was upset that he left me hanging instead of speaking appropriately to me and letting me know who he was in the first place and that Kyle was fine.

This is the game these young kids play. It is not a joke. Substance abuse and depression are *NOT* a joke. I took my son's issues and his life very seriously, but it seemed I was the only one. Kyle said he was fine, and I did not need to worry. Well of course I am going to worry. That is what a good, attentive, loving mom does. After his bouts in the past with law enforcement, hospital stays, car accidents, and near-death experiences, of course I was going to worry. He knew this but always reassured me and told me he loved me no matter what.

I share this as a reminder that our inward pain is not always outwardly obvious. I knew of my son's sadness and the reasons behind it. His dad and a few others were aware of his pain, but I was the only one that acknowledged it and begged for help from anyone that would listen to me. No one would listen, not his family or his friends in any way. Only his mama was willing to acknowledge his cries.

At times, those around him would say things like, "We love you. Here Kyle, take another pill to relax you." "Maybe you should take a Xanax." "Here is a shot of a fireball." "Drink some Twisted Tea, you will feel better." What the hell were these people thinking? They were not thinking at all, especially someone I had believed would have shown more maturity or foresight. Some, it seemed, were not thinking even a little bit about my son and his well-being.

I pray their actions and words will sink in once they have children of their own one day. I am not speaking of everyone. They were all going through their own battles as Kyle would share so much with me that their struggles were also weighing on him.

People around him that I spoke with later said they did not see the signs and that he seemed happy. *How could you not see the signs?* Their minds were also clouded with substance, but what was his grandma's excuse for ignoring her grandson crying for help? I struggled to understand how some family members seemed to look away while Kyle was hurting. I could not find any justification that made sense, and in those moments, it felt unconscionable.

Kyle was looking for a way out, I knew he was, and they just kept pulling him back in, handing him increased distractions. Each one got increasingly dangerous because of my son's near-death experience with fentanyl. This opioid is typically prescribed to cancer patients and those recovering from surgery for pain management although it has been misused as an illegal recreational drug.

Someone gave Kyle the drug that nearly took his life. I was later told it may have involved someone he was close to, but I never received clarity, just fragments of blame passed between people but I do not know for sure, none of it bringing clarity, only more heartbreak.

What I do know is that he overdosed at a friend's house, and it shattered something in both of us. Kyle told me he flatlined and was revived after seven minutes, but no one informed me. I was furious and determined more than ever to get him away from them.

As a mom, this breaks me. We were always so remarkably close. ALWAYS! Even though he would be absent when he was high, I knew, and he knew deep down, that our connection was unshakable.

MOTHER'S REFLECTION:
What They Did Not Hear

I knew Kyle's voice. I knew its laughter, its doubt, its sadness. I knew when it was missing, when others heard joy, but I heard the quietness underneath.

People said they did not see the signs. But I did. I listened when he was not speaking. I paid attention when others were distracted. I begged for help when no one else would.

That does not make me perfect. It just makes me a mom.

78

Shattered Bonds of Betrayal

I WILL NEVER UNDERSTAND WHY a parent would choose not to be present for their own child. Not for a second did I believe my husband wanted our son to be independent to build his character. His refusal to spend time with Kyle unless one of his mistresses or someone else was around deeply affected Kyle.

This woman had come into my son's life without truly knowing him, and from my perspective, it felt like she was trying to rebuild herself at the expense of an already fragile situation. In her quest for happiness, she targeted even strangers, hoping, perhaps, that attaching herself to a married man and stepping into the cracks of a broken family would help heal something in herself. But the result was pain, for Kyle, and for me.

Kyle often would confide in me about how his dad would bring his mistress along during their very few and far between times together, trying to portray them as a couple instead of emphasizing that he was still married. If you think this messed with my son's head, you are right.

While I expressed to Kyle that his dad's behavior was wrong on many levels, I felt powerless to influence his dad's troubling choices. When he introduced her as his wife to a couple of friends, even though we were still married, it felt like a profound denial of reality. Kyle was told by his dad and cousin that we were divorced; one of many false narratives. When he later discovered that his dad had been lying about the divorce for years, it sent him into a more relentless descent into despair. This revelation made Kyle question what else his dad might have been dishonest about, intensifying his feelings of betrayal and utter confusion.

When Kyle needed his dad during the weekend, he felt a deep need to spend time with him and seek much-needed advice. After listening to Kyle explain why he needed to be with his dad, which was particularly important to Kyle, I encouraged him to simply call his dad and let him know how much he needed him that day. Kyle had a weight on his shoulder and felt that dad may be able to help lift it. Kyle still had faith that his dad would be there, so I encouraged him to reach out. When Kyle did connect with his dad and asked to spend the day together, Kyle told me his dad responded without hesitation, "No, it's a no-kid weekend. We're going to spend it in bed."

In that moment, it became painfully clear that he prioritized useless adult companionship over meaningful moments with his son. It broke my heart to realize that our loving son could only spend time with his dad when it was convenient for him.

Flashback to the time when Kyle and his dad used to have "Men's night out" on Fridays after my dad passed away. Kyle was only six years old. After just a few short weeks, Kyle came to me in tears after a night out with dad, begging not to spend more Fridays alone with his dad, and said all his dad would do was take him to a movie, avoiding any real interactions with him and not even wanting to talk to his own son. Kyle felt bored and lonely, preferring to be with me or his friends instead. I asked my husband why the nights out always had to be a movie; why not miniature golf, bowling, go carts, a playground etc.? He had no answer, which was the typical response, so Kyle stopped going out with daddy.

I also recall a specific morning when Kyle desperately needed to talk to his dad before school started. He had already gotten to school, and when Kyle called, his dad seemed preoccupied and would not speak to his son on the phone which sparked an argument between us. I believe my son needed his dad that morning specifically to get him through a rough day ahead and I needed my husband to understand his son's pain and longing for connection, but he seemed completely oblivious. This was not what I or any good mom would envision for their son.

Kyle craved a father who would be present and supportive, but instead, he often felt overlooked, especially when the moments did not serve a performance or the image others might see. Sometimes it seemed like time with Kyle only happened when it reflected well in front of friends or those close to his dad. Only then did his dad show any interest in spending time with him.

During one of the times his dad acted on impulse, he wanted to spend time with Kyle, in my opinion, (and I do know him better than anyone on the planet) to project the image of a good father. However, he seemed unaware or unwilling to acknowledge that Kyle had not forgotten the past. He remembered the false narratives along with the hurt caused by feeling dismissed. In his false reality, everything he had said or had done to Kyle and our family seemed acceptable, but it was far from acceptable.

One weekend, when the mistress was out of town and Kyle's dad was alone with his own thoughts and no one to lean on, he decided to take Kyle to a concert in Kansas. My son told me everything that should never have happened. He said his dad asked him to sneak alcohol inside the venue, hiding bottles of Fireball in his clothing so his dad could drink. By doing so, Kyle bore the consequences of his father's choices. Like when Kyle was sent to detention, for actions that were not his fault. Kyle was the one left carrying the fallout.

Just a day later, Kyle recounted to me that his dad did not want to be alone and ended up getting drunk at the concert and could barely walk to the car. He told me he ended up driving his dad home and staying with him as he passed out on the couch.

Kyle shared more stories, too. That his dad and the woman he had introduced to Kyle often drank excessively, even in front of friends. Some of those friends later confirmed that to me, and Kyle felt humiliated.

Kyle once videotaped them acting belligerently at a pool hall and showed it to me.

"Why is dad being so stupid?" he said.

Those were Kyle's words. My heart ached hearing them. All I could say was that sometimes people are so lost inside their own pain, they cannot see beyond themselves, but that does not excuse bringing others down with them. Still no reason to subject my son to this behavior. It was the only explanation that made sense, given everything Kyle, his friends, and even his grandmother had shared with me.

It was hard to understand how someone could knowingly pursue a married man, especially while his family was unraveling. To me, it did not feel normal. It felt like another layer of betrayal.

I once asked my son if he remembered being traumatized by something else besides the obvious pain inflicted by evil cops, his dad, and other family members. This incident, of course, was enough to have caused him to lash out in substance and pain.

He denied it until about five years ago, when he finally shared that his dad's girlfriend had made him uncomfortable, he said she made a pass at him. Kyle said he tried to tell his dad but was brushed off.

I encouraged Kyle to speak up again. I was firm when I told Kyle he needed to try again to tell his dad what she had done.

He looked at me and said, "He won't care." And he was right.

My husband told me, in his own words, that he had picked up a woman in a bar called her a "whore" and was using her. *I remember thinking: if he were in his right mind, how could he possibly believe this was the kind of example his son needed?*

Kyle said, "It freaked me out!"

Of course it freaked him out. He did not like how they acted, drinking heavily, saying things that made him feel out of place. *Sure, Kyle drank when he should have not but what child wants to see their parent in a different state of mind?*

Kyle knew some of his friends thought it was cool to drink with his dad. But others? They saw something else, something that did not sit right. They did not say much, but Kyle said he could feel it. Kyle told me he hated it, but he did not know what else to do because it was the only time that his dad would spend time with him, either when alcohol was involved, or when the girlfriend was not around.

On many occasions, Kyle shared with me how the presence of the mistress made him feel. He described her as having a certain demeanor that made him extremely uncomfortable. He expressed that she would pretend to be his mom, despite him already having a devoted mom.

How does a woman justify stepping into a child's shattered life with deception in one hand and a drink in the other? And what does it say about her, to think that's love?

It felt wicked, so far from anything a healthy mind or heart would choose. Kyle knew it too and he assured me of this. He never wanted her in that role.

This individual was completely unfamiliar with my son and husband, and from where I stood, she seemed to be a stranger to love and what it truly meant. Kyle conveyed to me his feeling of uneasiness and his reluctance to be around her, yet he felt compelled to appease his dad.

How can one truly love someone else when they have never learned how to love themselves? It is so heartbreaking to think that in their pain, they became their own worst enemy?

She kept crossing lines I never imagined, and his dad kept trying, it seemed, to dismantle what little family we had left. Whatever they were trying to destroy, it was not just me that was fractured, it was Kyle's sense of safety, of his belonging. In the end, it was Kyle who bore the deepest break.

Even after my beloved son passed, she continued to find ways to insert herself into my life, maybe because of her insecurity. Whether it was to provoke me or gather information, I do not know. But it felt invasive. It spoke to something that did not feel secure or whole. It was like being watched through a keyhole by someone who refused to knock, someone who needed to know everything about me, but could not face me directly. My door has always been open to whoever wants to walk through it including her. *If she had not been afraid, would she have been able to handle the truth about the man she clung to, the truth I was more than ready to tell, the truth she seemed to want to avoid? Or was it easier to pretend than to confront what she might already know?*

Jesus did not die for us so that we could continue treating people the way people treated him. So, I realized that, even though this person did not deserve my forgiveness or even remotely care about whether I forgave or not, this gave me the strength to do what I really did not want to do at the time.

Kyle even told me that his dad at one point asked him to move with him to another apartment because he did not want to live with this mistress any longer. Kyle declined the invitation, knowing even then what it meant for his emotional and physical well-being.

I tell this to the reader because I want to emphasize the negative impact on Kyle and highlight the importance of every parent as role in their child's life. It is crucial for a boy to have a positive father figure, just as it is important for a girl to have a positive mother figure. Actions and words from parents profoundly affect the well-being of their innocent children. Kids should be the top priority for every parent, and both moms and dads should come together, not apart, to provide the best possible upbringing for their children, whether married or not. Get over themselves and focus on what is best for their kids. I cannot imagine not putting my child first above everything else.

Parents should want their children to have everything that they did not have growing up. Without their parents' support, kids feel lost.

My son was adrift and incredibly sad because his dad split without notice, any honest justification, nor support, prioritizing his own desires over his son's well-being. Even though his dad, to this day, has not acknowledged the emotional impact of his absence, Kyle was left to live in an environment that felt unstable, with someone in a demented state, someone who struggled to provide the clarity, consistency, and care he needed and all of this was the result of being sidelined by the most important male figure in his life. This is why I stressed to Kyle the importance of a deeper relationship with Almighty God to help get Kyle through his struggles.

MOTHER'S REFLECTION:
When Love Is Not Enough

I loved Kyle with every ounce of my soul. And I believed love could shield him. Heal him. Carry him past the confusion and betrayal that swirled around him.

But some wounds do not respond to love alone. They need protection, clarity, truth, and a steady presence that does not disappear when life gets heavy.

That is what Kyle was missing. Not affection, but foundation. Not just love, but leadership.

Even now, I still ask myself: how could someone look at Kyle, and not choose to fight for him?

79

THE GRASS IS NOT ALWAYS GREENER

OUR HOUSE WAS THE place to be. In his younger years, every kid in the neighborhood wanted to be at Kyle's. He had it all, a loving home, and an attentive mother who catered to him and his friends. He was blessed with many toys and the boys loved to come over and play with his things and spend time with him because he was so full of life. He had a lot of toys that other boys did not have, and he was very protective of them. He never broke any of them and when a friend misused something of his, he would get sad. I would tell him that some kids just did not respect things that did not belong to them.

He sometimes got upset that he was not living in the other subdivisions closer to his friends so he could ride his bike over to their house. They either lived in the richer subdivisions or in the country, too far away to be able to walk or ride the bike. He wanted us to move closer to his friends. I told him to be happy with everything he had because they in turn wanted other things he had. Is that not the way it always is? We want what someone else has? We always think someone has it better? The grass is always a shade greener behind the picket fence.

This was simply not true in Kyle's case. He did have it better than many of his friends. He just was not aware of it. I made sure of it. He was my only baby. My miracle baby was put on a pedestal. Kyle was never neglected by me. He never lacked love and affection and nurturing and teaching from mom. Where our family might have lacked, I was determined to provide for him in other ways. I am well aware that things were far from perfect (what is?), but I did the best I could to make Kyle's home the happiest possible, and for many years, it was. Memories of those moments often get me through my day.

I miss getting up early in the morning and talking to Kyle as I made him a good breakfast. We had some genuinely good talks about our plans for the day. Even though I always talked to him when he was out on his own, I could not always help him plan his day. I miss taking him to school, going to all his activities and sports practices.

I always made sure something was cooking when he would get home from school. If not, we would get one of his favorite takeout dinners which was French dips at Arby's and Jose Peppers, usually on a Friday night. I miss him coming in and smelling what mom was cooking and being excited about having dinner with me.

I miss his energy. There were so many times we had up to ten or more boys running through our house talking about girls or wrestling with each other or playing games and talking about life. It is so difficult when your kids leave to spread their wings. Suddenly, my son did not need me as much anymore, or so he thought.

He was my priority over everything else. It was so extremely hard to let go and let him be on his own knowing that his dad would not help take care of him and keep him safe. That proved to be true when Kyle was left yet again at his grandma's house without thought, without insurance, or a penny to live on. We both were struggling at that point, while his dad was exploring, without either of us, what he thought was greener territory.

My job was to give my son roots and allow him to grow and develop wings to fly on his own, but I cannot convey how hard it was on me emotionally to free him and just be on the sidelines if he needed me. I hated not being able to always be there physically as I was when he was at our home.

The home that Kyle grew up in seems like a glowing palace in comparison to where I live now. The pit that I live in is such a sad place. It is small and cramped, even if it is just me, and always dark. It has been since my boy passed. My son had an aura that seemed to brighten even the dingiest of rooms.

When my child left this world, the whole dynamic of my life changed. Coming back here every day after work is like reliving his passing all over again. It is hard to explain. But even after six years, I am still expecting him to be there, lounging on the couch saying, "What took you so long Mom? What's for dinner?"

I am fighting vigorously to keep my own self above water and strong while trying to find the right words to author his story, along with working multiple jobs, going to church, a new life of daily (sometimes weekly) grief and support groups, which I know will be lifelong, trying to spend quiet time with the Lord, and volunteering. I am overloaded as usual, but I think that keeps me going. In a sense, it is a purposeful autopilot. Just knowing that I have something to do, something to contribute, and trying to do my best to fulfill the promise that I made to my son. I feel like I need to be someplace different. Far away from here. Of course, I do and so did Kyle.

MOTHER'S REFLECTION:
The Light That Made It Home

They say the grass is greener on the other side. But for Kyle, the green was here. In our kitchen. At the table. In his laughter and the rhythm of his footsteps coming through the door.

He did not always see it then. That is how it is sometimes, with kids, with life. But I saw it and I made it as vibrant as best I could.

I do not live in that place anymore. Not just the house, but the life we knew inside it. Now, it is quiet and dim. But the glow Kyle carried has not left me. It lives in memory and in every story. In every word I write.

Because he was my light, and wherever I end up, I will carry that glow with me in the shape of my son.

80

A BOND TOO HEAVY TO CARRY

I DO NOT RECALL EXACTLY how Kyle met his first girlfriend, perhaps through school or mutual friends. I honestly do not remember her from Ray-Pec. She was a stranger to me, just another name I had heard, until suddenly, she was not. She appeared one day, seemingly out of nowhere.

It was a Sunday afternoon, just after church, when I drove to his new apartment complex, the back seat of my car loaded with a care package, groceries, little comforts, things I knew would make him smile. He was not home, so I prepared to leave, but just as I was pulling out of the parking lot, I saw his car turning into it. I felt such relief watching him step out of his car with a young woman at his side. Both, beautiful, polished, exactly as I had imagined.

I pulled to the curb, turning off the car to catch up for a bit. This was the girlfriend I had been concerned about from a few stories I had heard. At that moment, though, she was perfectly pleasant, introducing herself with warmth, telling me she had heard a lot about me.

I smiled, answering, "It is so nice to finally meet you! You're gorgeous. Kyle had wanted to introduce us sooner."

She offered a polite response, before walking away, leaving me alone with my son.

We chatted for a while, catching up on small things. Since he had company, I told him I would bring the care package by later, or he could stop by the house when he had time. I kissed his cheek and reminded him, as I always did, how much I loved him, to be safe, and I would talk to him soon.

Not long after, he came by to pick up the care package, along with some extra groceries I had set aside. While he was there, he helped me with a little project, a bamboo table and chair set I had found while volunteering. I loved the set, although it was old and worn, and needed to be spruced up; some fresh paint and new cushions. I told Kyle I wanted to revive it using tropical fabric I had bought, imagining it in our future home when we finally made the move to Florida.

He picked up Arby's French dip and Swiss sandwiches, one of his longtime favorites, for lunch, and we ate as we worked, struggling to remove the old cushions and paint the chairs. We talked for a couple of hours, but even then, I could feel him pulling away, tethered to something unseen. Whether it was her influence, guilt, manipulation, or even fear, something kept him from fully engaging. His phone sat in his hand, lighting up and pinging repeatedly.

I gently asked him to put it away, just for a little while, so we could enjoy our rare time together without distraction. He hesitated but eventually slipped it into his pocket, trying to be present. Then, another text came, and just like that, he said he needed to go.

I knew, without knowing, what had happened, and who it was. The timing was too perfect. It felt like he was being pressured to leave. The hold that was on him, from my perspective, was suffocating and controlling, and I struggled to understand why. *If she loved him, genuinely loved him, would she not let him breathe?* Would she not allow him this small, precious window of time with his mother?

She was a nice girl at first and oh so beautiful with two small children, but she seemed to me to be greatly troubled. There was nothing wrong with her being a young mom, I had tried for years to be a young mom, although it did not happen until I was thirty-two. My niece is a beautiful young mom as well.

I think my son's pain fueled her. If they had met later in life, maybe they would have been good together, but they both had to work on themselves first, not each other. I knew if I voiced those opinions too soon, it would only make them closer, as is usually the case with young love.

I am sure his dad believed he would eventually get over the relationship, but I was concerned about the negative impact she may have been having on Kyle. From where I stood, he did not just tolerate the relationship, he welcomed it, blind to the danger I believed it posed. I prayed fervently and had many people across the world join me in intercessory prayer for Kyle's healing and recovery from the influence he was experiencing.

While Kyle may have believed she loved him, I had my doubts. *How could anyone not love him? Can you call it love when someone tries to control, confuse, and diminish the very person who trusts them most?* Kyle had a heart full of light and love for everyone, and what he got in return felt like shadow.

My son told me she tried to pressure him into taking pills, and one of his friends later said they had seen her encouraging him to take them. I was not there, but the story haunted me. Whether it happened exactly that way or not, the fear in Kyle's voice was real, and that is what stayed with me.

"Mom, I broke up with her." He sounded so sad and just plain tired.

I felt a long-needed exhale and a huge sigh of relief that everything was looking up. Thank you, Almighty God!

Oh, how I wanted to snap my fingers and take the anguish away from him.

I did inform him, "Make sure this is the last time, Kyle."

"I know, I know Mom."

I told them both, "Every time you get back together it will get worse because you are not giving each other space, you are not learning from your mistakes, so you are bringing in the same old baggage and it is bound to get worse instead of better."

"I know, Mom. Trust me, you aren't the only one that has said that.

"Ok then, just stay away from her and bless her."

"I miss the kids though."

"Yes, I am sure you do, and it is going to be hard, but Kyle they are not your kids. I know she tried to make them yours, and you love them, but they have a daddy, and I hear he is a good daddy. You said so yourself. One day you will have beautiful babies of your own."

"He is a good daddy, Mom but I miss them."

I sympathized with him. Kyle did try his best with her kids and formed a strong and protective bond with them. He would have been a great father if he had ever been given the chance to have his own children or any child for that matter, but you cannot replace a relationship that still exists. *Is it possible to rewrite a family by force, one that is rooted in love and history, by pretending the past never mattered?*

That is what it felt like: as if I could be replaced, as if Kyle could be replaced, as if love was something you could swap out like furniture. But the damage? That was real. I sighed, "Well Bubber, all you can do is pray for them, think about them and maybe ask about their wellbeing every now and then, but they will be fine but that is not a reason to continue this toxic relationship with her."

"I know, I know Mom, but she was my first girlfriend."

"I get it Kyle, I really do. I had my first boyfriend once. We never forget our first love, but she is not the one that God want you to be with, Kyle. Please try to understand."

I saw the look on his face; it was a little defeated and grieved. I knew it was not what he wanted to hear. The thing with first love is that it is always the brightest yet also leaves you with the worst burns when it is over. It would take a while for that burn of Kyle's to heal and would leave a scar as well due to the prolonged end of the relationship.

"She keeps trying to get me to take pills, Mom," he told me. "Says it will make me feel better."

I was a protective mom, but never so fragile I could not tell Kyle what I thought, even when he did not agree. It was for his own greater good that I offered my voice when I felt it was needed.

I pleaded with him, "Please just stay away from her, Bubber. See what pills can do to people? How substance can distort reality or cloud judgment, especially when someone is struggling to detox. Every thought, every choice is totally irrational. Please, let Mama help you. I am begging you to stop and get away from her and others doing the wrong things. You will feel better. You will want to pursue your dreams again."

There were moments I think he heard me, truly heard me, but whatever hold she had on him was stronger than reason, stronger than love. This did not feel like my son anymore, not the way I knew him.

Kyle could not see past what he was going through. First love is hard to release. It is so difficult to open your heart again after devastation unless you have grown cold, or cruel, or are simply numb.

One weekend, Kyle drove her out of town for an appointment. He told me that while they were away, she was texting another guy off and on. Kyle was distraught, and they argued. The police were called, not because of anything he did, but because they were concerned for his emotional safety. He did let me know he was not arrested; they kept him briefly to ensure he was okay emotionally. I had to call my mother-in-law to reach my husband, who was unreachable, so he could drive down and bring Kyle home. I could not make the trip myself in the car I had.

The next day, Kyle called me and apologized, mostly for worrying me sick. He promised he would do better.

I never wanted my son to apologize to me. I hated it actually but respected it. If he had hurt someone else or made a mistake, I wanted him to make it right with them, but me? That was never what I needed. He was my beautiful boy, already perfect enough in my eyes. There was nothing to make amends for. No apology required, and certainly non desired.

I spent countless hours and days reminding Kyle that he was just bent, not broken. His situation, and the agony of the breakup, could be mended. I had a tough time trying to convince him.

After this, I knew that if she stayed in his life, the year ahead would be rocky, and it would get worse until the situation reached a breaking point I had feared for a long time.

My dad had a story for every situation, bad or good. Whether he crafted them from imagination, he was great at that, or inherited wisdom from his parents, I cannot say for sure. What I do know is that his wisdom helped me through some exceedingly grim times so I too, wanted to share his wisdom with Kyle.

He once told me to imagine a beautiful garden that had been neglected for a long time. Weeds. Wilted flowers. At first, it seems beyond repair. But then he said:

"You can't revive the old garden. But you can use the soil, the tools, and the seeds to create a brand new one."

I believe this meant even if something falls apart, the potential for new growth is always there. You take what is rich, what helped you before, and you plant something new. Build something better. That is what I tried to share with Kyle.

That is why I believed moving away to start fresh could be a powerful choice. It was an opportunity to cultivate a new life, a paradigm shift using resources from the past to begin again. Kyle needed a radical change from his environment, his relationships, as well as his belief system to redefine his way of thinking. Kyle loved that story, mostly because it came from Popo, who he loved so dearly.

"You are going to be okay, Kyle. I promise. Please hear me when I tell you this. I am going to make sure of it. Trust me, son. I have never let you down, and I never will."

But I did. The transition was not progressing quickly enough. I promised to take his pain away; to protect my only child from people whose actions made me question whether his wellbeing was truly being protected. But I was outmatched. I was fighting too many forces alone. And I was overwhelmed.

MOTHER'S REFLECTION:
Not All Love Heals

It was not just that I did not trust her, it was that I watched my son fade. I saw light dim where there used to be laughter. I saw a boy who once danced through the kitchen now tethered to someone else's demands. And maybe she did not see it. Maybe she did not mean it. But it happened.

Some say first love is sweet. But I do not think sweetness should leave bruises. I know my son loved her, and I know he adored her children, and I will never dismiss that. But I also know the pain he carried, the doubts he whispered, the pills he resisted, the breakdowns he survived. You cannot call it love if it drains the very thing it claims to hold.

Kyle was made of light. But in this bond, all he got back was shadow.

81

HEADED FOR THE OCEAN

I SPOKE WITH KYLE IN May 2018 and told him I was going to take a week off and go to Florida to explore places to live. I had told him I wanted to move to Florida in the next year or so and he needed to think about going with me. I could not make him go but I knew he would, and I knew that this would be the best thing for him.

"It will be good for you Bubber," I said. He at once replied, without hesitation, "I'm going with you!"

I did not ask questions but simply said, "Get ready" and felt the biggest sigh of relief that I was going to get to take my son away from the shady people in his life so he could get back on track without interference from them. My dream had come true. I was wishing and praying for years that he would come around and move with me. I told him to get his ducks in a row, and it would take some time, but we would try to move within the next year if all went as planned.

I did not have an exact timeline; I was writing and working and communicating with him throughout his off-and-on relationship with his ex-girlfriend. I gave him advice when he asked for it and tried my best to keep my mouth shut when he did not. But sometimes as a good mom, I needed to step in and give my two cents' worth.

One day he asked if he could come over and talk. "Absolutely!" I jumped at the chance to spend time with my son and talk face to face instead of through that dreaded text messaging. My door was always open for anyone that wanted to walk through it. "You never have to ask Bubber, your home is here with mom, not at Grandma's."

Grandma's house was just a place he used to crash, like other people's couches he occasionally slept on. He did not have a choice after what happened to both of us. Until he could get his life together and move out on his own, he used his grandmother's address for mailing purposes only, not as a permanent home. He did everything he could not to be there. Of course, she made the delusional excuse that it was his home. Of course, it was not. My mother-in-law struggled with several conditions, dementia among them, that she kept hidden for years. But I knew. I saw things others did not, and, from my experience, there were many moments when she seemed unaware of her actions.

Kyle did not want to be there, and it seemed clear his dad did not either. Soon after, he entered a relationship with a female who, from my perspective, appeared to offer him a sense of shelter and support among other things. We were still married, which made the circumstances even more painful to witness.

Sometimes, it felt as though my husband and his mother were moving through life in their own version of reality, where accountability blurred and truth shifted depending on the moment.

Kyle did share with me his many pains and secrets that I know he had not shared with anyone else, including his dad. *How many times can a son reach out before he stops expecting to be heard?* Kyle already knew the answer. He had tried for years to have a real conversation with his dad. It never came.

He knew I loved and accepted him unconditionally even though I did not agree on his transitory lifestyle, I loved him through it anyway. Yes, he did get a stern talking to once in a great while... absolutely he did, but Kyle and I never once had an argument. Not one time in his almost twenty-two years did we ever raise our voices to one another. We did, however, debate about certain things as he would, as most teenagers do, earnestly try to make me believe that he knew better than mom on certain things. Sometimes he did and would set me straight on a few things and vice versa.

A good parent will do just that. I was not going to ignore unruly behavior and reward it. But I would praise his good behavior for sure. He received both praise and grace from me without enabling him.

One of the other evenings Kyle came to visit, I made him one of his favorite dishes, salmon patties, fried potatoes, and macaroni and cheese. I made him a carrot cake from scratch because he preferred my homemade cake over one from a box. I had not been able to do that since we were all together several years ago in our home.

Kyle looked so good. He was sad but dressed nicely, bright-eyed and talked oh so sweet. It made me happy to see that he put in so much effort to see me as I did him. It was obvious he had been doing well for a while.

He gave me a big hug and a kiss. As we ate, we continued our conversation. He still came to me and trusted me with his heart. It meant everything to me when he opened up to me, just like he used to, before certain influences began pulling him away from the life he knew.

He asked me when I thought I was going to Florida, and I told him I was shooting for the following year but that I really needed him to go with me. I really wanted him to, which is the main reason I was going in the first place, to give my son and me a fresh start. This would give him time to get things in order. I could tell he was putting serious thought into it and knew that would be the best thing for him.

This is when we discussed our plans to move. He was going to go ahead and work with a concrete company (mentioned in later chapter), in hopes that he would be able to get a job out in Florida with his experience to back him up.

I insisted he get into recovery as soon as possible. It had been long overdue. I was trying to find him good facilities and counseling but since we were both abruptly dropped from my husband's health insurance (along with many other things), it was exceedingly difficult to get Kyle somewhere other than on a waiting list.

He had the legal right to keep Kyle on his health insurance until the age of twenty-six. He could have helped with something that could have changed Kyle's life for the better but chose not to. It seemed that none of the facilities cared about helping someone in desperate need unless they could get something in return. My heart ached for my son. I did so much research, and I just could not afford insurance at that time after my husband's abandonment, which is why I went without. *It was not because I did not care. It was because the system offered no grace, and I had to choose between surviving or giving up. I chose to fight for my son's life.*

I was told he could be put on a waiting list. Okay, so let us put him on the waiting list and pray he gets in soon and dad changes his mind about helping. Every door I knocked on felt bolted shut. People spoke in policies, not compassion. And while the system insisted it was overburdened, I knew it was my son who was being left behind. I was frantic trying to get things in order and get him out of dodge.

I asked Kyle, "Wouldn't it be awesome if we could write a book together about how God delivered you from all your pain?"

I told him to ruminate over it as it might give him some incentive to strive for a better future. We continued our day together as it should always be.

MOTHER'S REFLECTION:
Chasing the Ocean

We were headed for the ocean, me and my son, chasing a future that might have been softer than the past. I can still hear his voice: "I'm going with you!" Those words were a lifeline, a promise, a shared dream between us.

Florida was not just a place. It was hope. A fresh start. A second chance. I believed if we could just get there, maybe the tides would shift. Maybe the darkness would lift. Kyle believed it too.

We never made it together. But the journey, the planning, the talks, the carrot cake, and quiet hugs, they were real. They mattered. And even now, when I think about the coastline we did not reach, I remember what we were building: a new beginning shaped by love, not circumstance.

He was ready and so was I. Some journeys are measured not in miles but in meaning.

82

BEAUTIFUL BOY

KYLE INVITED ME BACK a few years ago to see the movie, *Beautiful Boy*, a biographical film about a father and son struggling through addiction. This was his idea. I had not even seen the previews or heard of it since I never watch TV, except to get a glimpse of the daily forecast, plus I work all the time. So, I went into this movie very blind.

During the movie, I realized Kyle was trying to tell me something. I tried to hold back tears several times. I know the story had an impact on my son. I would turn my head to him occasionally and see his glossy eyes tear up, but he tried to be tough. I could feel his pain and remorse for what was happening to us, and himself. After the movie was over and everyone was leaving the cinema, we sat still for a while until the crowd died down. He held my hand, turned to me slightly and said, "Mom I'm sorry. I love you."

I hate being so emotional in front of Kyle but could not help it at that moment. I simply said, "I know Bubber, I know you are sorry. It is not your fault. You are not to blame. It is going to be okay. You are going to be okay Kyle. We are going to be just fine. I love you so much. Give mama a hug."

He hugged me and as we were walking out, he unexpectedly put his arm around my shoulder just as his dad did sometimes, to let everyone know that I belonged to him, I was his wife. Same with my son. I belonged to him. I was his mom and no one else could claim me.

As I lay in bed that night, replaying the evening, I realized how much that small gesture from Kyle meant, and it brought a few bittersweet tears. The movie was more than just a film, it was Kyle's way of reaching out, of acknowledging everything we had been through together. It was not just about addiction; it was about the profound love, regret, and the quiet understanding that no matter where life had taken my beautiful boy, I had never stopped being his anchor. In that moment, I knew that despite all the struggles, despite the pain and uncertainty, our mother/son unit remained unbroken. No matter what lay ahead, I would always be here, his mother, his safe place, his unwavering love.

MOTHER'S REFLECTION:
More Than a Movie

That night was not about a movie; it was about a message. Kyle did not need to explain it. I felt it in the silence, in the way he held my hand, in the way he said, "I'm sorry."

He was telling me he understood. That he saw the pain, the love, the fight we had both been carrying. In that moment, I knew he still saw me as his anchor. His safe place.

"Beautiful Boy" was not just a title. It was a truth I had always known. That night, he reminded me that no matter how far he had gone, he was still mine.

83

THE GUN

HIS TWENTIETH BIRTHDAY ARRIVED. I met him for lunch at Red Lobster. I told him to pig out on as many crab legs as he wanted. We had a wonderful time. After lunch he drove his car and followed me to Academy sports where I bought a Carhartt coat for him with some gloves and a stocking cap for his birthday. We spent an hour there trying on various coats and talking. He finally decided on the one he wanted.

As we were leaving, he needed to grab a few bags of groceries from my trunk, groceries I had bought to make sure he had something nourishing at home. I had seen too many signs, too many times, that no one else was stepping up in the ways he needed.

Every quarter of the year, I would get a care package together for him consisting of all his favorite foods, meat, honey buns, mini-tacos, mac-n-cheese, Babybel cheese, salmon, Gatorade, V-8 (tropical blend, his favorite) bottled water, vitamins, probiotics and numerous other things that he loved, along with a shirt and pants or shorts, socks, toothpaste, toothbrushes, mouthwash, and soap to make sure he was taken care of. I always gave him a gift certificate to Kohl's so he could get some jeans or whatever he needed beyond what I already was giving him. This gave me peace of mind to make sure Kyle had as much as he needed to take care of his health and decent clothes to wear.

At his final farewell, I overheard someone quietly suggest that I never gave Kyle care packages. *Did his person not think that I could hear her speak out of line and dishonor him along with his grieving mother?* I knew the truth, and so did others who heard it. In that moment, it felt like a direct wound, not to me, but to the memory of a young man who was deeply loved.

He tried to keep the things I gave him hidden from certain people knowing everything would be taken in a flash. This broke my heart. Oh yes, indeed, I most certainly did carry the weight of my son's needs his whole life, faithfully and quietly. I made sure my son had everything he needed, food, clothes, car repairs, school supplies, insurance. I still have the receipts and photos to prove it. I did what a good mama does, especially when it felt like no one else was stepping up to help him

Anyway, he was getting the things out of the trunk and putting them inside his car. I made an angel food birthday cake for him, as I always did every year, and wrote "Happy 20th Birthday Poo Doo" on it. After he loaded up his car, he gave me a hug and a kiss.

As he was standing up against the trunk of his car, he looked at me and said "Mom, maybe this is who I really am."

My beautiful boy felt defeated. Drowning without a lifeboat in sight. He looked so sad, so lost. I could not help but wonder, who put those horrible words into his head? His dad? His ex? His grandmother? Someone else? I knew my son and that was not his voice. It never had been. I instilled security, wisdom, talent, courage, and spiritual truth into my son, so I know darn well he did not think this of himself. Someone was trying to convince him of being less than. *What kind of evil would convince him of this?*

I said, "Nope, drugs are not who you are Kyle, and shame on the person who told you that. It is just what you are doing right now. You are a beautiful child of God, a beautiful child of mine who has made some mistakes, just like everyone else, but will start making better choices the older and wiser you get."

We all make them, some worse than others. When we know better, we do better...right? That is how it should be anyway. Famous words from Maya Angelou that always stuck with me among much of her poetic wisdom.

I told him, "I know that you are on the road to recovery and that is all that matters. Just keep your head up and look forward please. With a lot of patience, willpower, and determination everything will work out, I promise. This is not the worst thing nor is it the last thing. You will get better, Bubber. God did not bring you into this world to let you destroy your life nor did I. Please believe me when I tell you that you are here for a reason and a purpose."

This is where he told me that he bought a gun. My jaw dropped.

He quickly reassured me, saying, "Mom do not get mad, I know how to use a gun. Remember we went through the safety classes together in Scouts?"

I did not get mad but started to shake a little and I did tell him he had no business having one.

I asked him, "Why do you feel the need for one?"

Kyle said he wanted it for protection since he was on his own now. There was nothing else that I could do or say to change his mind. He bought the gun legally the year prior despite me telling him that he did not need it. He said that he did not carry it on him all the time, and he kept it at a friend's grandpa's house, and this man lived an hour or so away in the country. He said that he and his friends would go to his grandpas on occasion and shoot at targets. He did assure me that he did NOT use animals as those targets.

As we were talking about the gun that he had bought, he said he had to have it where he lived yet he said he kept it elsewhere. This did not make sense. *Did he have two?* I stood still and stared at him for a moment. Thinking to myself again, this is not who I raised. I asked him nicely to get rid of it. I told him again; he did not need it. He knew self-defense and could handle his own, easily breaking bones if needed. He debated with me, telling me how everyone has one now, especially at the apartment complex where he lives.

He asked, "What am I supposed to do if someone pulls a gun on me?"

I had no answers except to tell him to pray to God for strength and to use what he learned in self-defense classes.

This is when he decided to tell me that a guy at the complex walked up behind him when he was coming home one night and pulled a gun at him, and he did not have his gun on him. That is why he felt he needed it. My son did not feel safe. Trying not to panic, so as not to upset Kyle, I got a lump in my throat. As I started to tear up from the fear I had for my boy, I told him that he needed to get out of there. The ultimate fear of my baby being hurt permanently was running through my mind as so many have hurt him already.

He had come over to my place a few weeks prior and told me that he wanted to move out of Grandma's, a home that, in my experience, had grown increasingly tense and emotionally unhealthy. Kyle asked me to help him find a place.

He specifically said, "I do not need anything big, something like what you have."

I told him, "I will talk to the landlord and see if he has anything available."

I eventually found a nice apartment in a nice, safe area that he may be able to afford and was going to help him with deposits and whatever else he needed but when I told him about it, he said he had found something already and signed the lease. If he had informed me about it before he signed, I would have told him that it was, in fact, in a very unsafe area. His dad and his grandma both knew how dangerous the area was. *Why did his dad or grandma not convey this to him? Why did they not try to talk him out of it and help him find a better place to live?* He assured me he would be ok.

He was going to get hurt. He needed to move.

He said to me, "I just got my own apartment."

He had only been there for a couple of months. I continuously begged him to just move.

He told me they wanted a thousand dollars to break the lease.

I said, "It does not matter Bubber, I will pay the fee to break the lease and get you into a better place, I will pay to get you moved to some place safer." He refused. Again, this was his hard head and wanting to be independent like me. Kyle felt even a difficult apartment was better than staying in an environment where he did not feel seen or supported. That is how heavy it had become; how much he wanted out.

Kyle did not want me to come over, he knew it was not safe for me. I wanted so badly to clean his apartment and make sure his refrigerator and cabinets had food for him and his friends. I wanted so badly to continue what I had always done for him and that was to take care of him and keep him safe. He did not want that, until of course he wanted and needed it. It was difficult watching my son strive to be independent, but I deeply admired his determination. He was doing his best. He wanted to show his dad that he was better than him in every way and he absolutely was.

Next thing I know a few months later, Kyle told me that someone broke into his apartment and stole the majority of everything that he had including his guitar, jewelry, and things that I had given him and many items that he had worked so hard for. I was suspicious of certain people, and to this day believe that it was someone that he knew well and was messing with his head. He put too much trust in others that were clearly not trustworthy. Some of the people that he spent time together with were authentic, but some had no good intentions toward him. Amazing how later, I am told by his girlfriend and many others that she had most of his things in her storage unit and refused to let him have them. My suspicions were confirmed.

I saw it with my own eyes, the last house they lived in had a dumpster in the driveway, and inside were his furniture and bags of his things. I was not able or allowed to retrieve them. My son did nothing but love and serve others. He did not deserve the pain he endured, not from her, and not from anyone.

MOTHER'S REFLECTION:
The Burden He Carried

It was not the gun that haunted me. It was what drove him to believe he needed one.

A boy who once ran barefoot through the sprinkler now stood at the trunk of his car, looking older than he should and sadder than I could bear. This spoke of protection, danger, and independence. But I saw something deeper: the silent burden of feeling alone.

I did everything I could, grocery bags, care packages, angel food birthday cakes, but nothing I carried could lighten what he had already strapped to his heart.

I watched him try to survive in a world that should have lifted him, not hardened him. That chapter, that day, became proof that love is fierce, but sometimes love alone is not enough.

84

MENTOR

I WILL TELL YOU THAT the agony I saw in my son was something no mother should ever see. It was a deep, unrelenting pain that seemed to seep into his very being and all I wanted to do was take it from him and take the pain on myself. Over the years, I made it a point to confront Kyle about his struggles, just to make sure he was safe, asking him if someone had touched him sexually and inappropriately. For a while, I thought something along this line was the cause of some of his pain. To my relief, his consistent answer was always "No." Thank God.

That was until the summer when he was twenty-one right before his transition to Heaven. He told me that he was working as a camp counselor for children and young teens with autism, a role he embraced with open arms.

He loved kids and had a natural affinity for helping others. I always saw my son as a mentor and big brother too many. I envisioned it and it became reality as he got older.

I have said this before Kyle had the natural ability to feel the emotions and attitudes of those around him. He was drawn to helping others, knowing he could make a difference in their lives. One of Kyle's friends told me how he loved to help these kids at camp, and he was so good with them, dedicated in his role. But the risk of being an empath lies in the vulnerability to being easily taken advantage of which I may have stated before.

Kyle confided in me about a night he woke up to one of the campers crossing a boundary that felt physical and deeply upsetting. He said it upset him greatly because he sincerely enjoyed what he was there for, and he put so much effort into helping them and mentoring them, but in return one of them had now tried to hurt him. When speaking to me about it, I first thought he was joking, simply because of the way he related the story, but then his voice trembled and escalated as he continued to tell me what happened. I realized he was serious. I calmed him down and told him to tell the people in charge immediately. It caused him great pain to know that he poured out his heart and soul and was trying to help someone only to be hurt once again.

After that experience, he made the decision to leave the camp at once, feeling he could not return to a place where his good intentions were met with such betrayal. It seemed every time my son tried to do good in his life, it would backfire on him. It's not fun being someone with a heightened ability to sense and absorb the emotions and feelings of others.

At times, other moments were a huge blessing to be able to connect with many people on an emotional level, but it is emotionally exhausting as well. Even though it was such a heavy burden on Kyle, even when the world felt so overwhelming, my beautiful boy was able to help and love so many people in his brief period. Most people do not leave the profound impact that he did.

MOTHER'S REFLECTION:
The Campfire Went Out

He went to camp to shine, like a flame in the woods, guiding others who wandered in darkness. But the light flickered when pain crept in through a trusted place. And when he left, I could tell something quiet in him had dimmed.

Still, Kyle never stopped mentoring. Even in his final months, his compassion remained intact. Not every wound heals in time, but every kindness he gave still burns bright.

85

WORE OUT

HE HAD EVERYTHING GOING for him and then he did not and then he did. It was on and off the wagon a few times before he finally agreed to get into rehab and move away with me. He just started a new job that he was so excited about, and looking forward to the move. He had tons of love and family and friends, but they were not good for him, and he finally realized how detrimental they all were to his growth and future. I understood his trepidation about falling into his old patterns from time to time. His fear was that he would relapse once we got into our new home. All I could say to him was that I would continue to pray for him and others all over the world were as well. I promised him I would be there to hold him up when he felt like he was falling.

I confirmed with him that recovery was a process, and to be more gracious with himself and really think about all the benefits, such as how he would feel once he got through the withdrawals. The high energy he would have, the greater clarity, the more ambition he would have to pursue his dreams. Whatever it was it would be a difficult road but far easier than the one he was on then.

We had a good long talk. We talked about everything. We talked about his job and what he really was thinking of doing with his life. I told him to slow down and take his time. If he went slower, the world would open for him, and he would discover more about who he was supposed to be and what he was supposed to do. I never understood why he needed to live so fast.

"Why are you in such a hurry to grow up Kyle?"

"I do not know, Mom."

He responded as if the thought had never occurred to him. I am sure I tried to live fast as well when I was his age. I think many teenagers and young adults do and do not even realize that they need to slow down. One day you are going to look back on your life and realize how fast it flew by. I laughed to myself, thinking almost prophetically,

"There is only one way to stop time, so why give it a reason to speed up? Make it last as long as it can."

Instead, I said, "Well then slow down, please. You have so many more years ahead of you." If only he and I knew.

He drove up to the Redbox and got us a movie. We folded out the couch into the sleeper sofa and watched the movie and overindulged on homemade Rice Krispy treats while we talked.

I realized the intense depth of my son's despair when my young, adult child curled up on the couch, seeking solace by asking me to scratch his back, reminiscent of when he was younger and feeling distraught over being let down by his dad and feeling unseen or unimportant, dealing with a bully at school, or simply having a rough day, needing reassurance that everything would be all right.

As he drifted off to sleep, I gently scratched his back, just as I had so many times before. When stress kept him awake, the familiar comfort of Mom's touch was the only thing that could ease his anxiety. And once again, it worked. Watching the tension fade, knowing I could still bring him peace, filled me with a warmth that is hard to describe. There is no greater feeling than still being needed and wanted by my sweet boy.

A little side note to teenagers and young adults; no matter how old you are, you will always be your mama's baby so deal with it and enjoy it while she is still here to help you and support you in any way possible.

I did not really expect him to stay the night, but he was so exhausted and drained emotionally from the breakup of his girlfriend, and I am sure, living his life too damn fast, as it was wearing him out. Overall, I say it was a perfect night with just the two of us as it used to be.

I tried to be as quiet as I could the next morning to let him sleep in. I made him breakfast. I think the smell of bacon woke him up. Waffles, eggs, and bacon were what he needed to get his day started.

I made him one of my green protein shakes which he was reluctant to drink but I assured him it was delicious, since I made it with cucumber, kiwi, pea protein powder, and a bit of agave nectar and almonds. He needed to get that protein and fiber in him that he was obviously lacking and needed a healthy energizer and focus to boot.

I kept him stocked on bentonite clay to help him rid the toxins from his body and it helped when he was going through withdrawals. I also made sure he had oatmeal for his eczema. I had given him nightly oatmeal baths when he was younger to help soothe his extremely dry skin, which turned out to be eczema. He was not eating properly. From what I witnessed, day after day, Kyle was largely left to fend for himself. Meals, comfort, care, those things that speak love, I do not ever recall seeing them offered with consistency from those closest to him, except me. Yet he was expected to do everything for everyone, and it was wearing him out.

Changing the subject from one to the next, we started talking about his job that he was trying to get. He said he had an interview in Atchison, Kansas but it did not turn out well. I told him that it was not meant to be, and he probably needed something closer.

Our conversations when he got older were not always long, but this one was a bit longer than usual and I could tell that he seemed so upbeat, and things were going to look up from there. I needed to get to work for a few hours but told him he could stay and rest a bit longer and hang out with his lizard, Buddy, and Rusty, his cat.

I had a sense that he just needed to be still for a while and was starving for much needed sleep as he could not sleep at his grandma's house; what he would describe as a dark, lonely place. He told me it felt heavy and empty. There were absolutely no signs of faith, no signs of light of any kind, just silence and shadow. She did not even display my son's beautiful school photos that she was given every year. Not one single photo of her son, my husband, or her daughter. Not one symbol of Christ; only the darkness of complete despair throughout the entire house.

He told me he felt as though there were bad spirits there and he felt so uneasy being there. These words rang true for the many times I was there as well, which is why I never understood how his dad could leave Kyle there, alone and without support. From what I saw, he seemed eager to distance himself from that place. And if he had truly considered what Kyle needed, his safety, his future, I believe things would have unfolded differently.

Kyle was always pushing himself physically and emotionally. It was starting to show, as young as he was, I could see it in his beautiful, hazel eyes and his face was aging. While it seemed, things were moving positively in the right direction for both of us, I was worried.

He said he needed to get some things taken care of that day. I asked him to call me later to let me know how he was doing but I guess he got busy and forgot but hooked up with me the next day, which was fine as long as I could hear from him and know that he was safe.

MOTHER'S REFLECTION:
The Stillness He Craved

He never stayed long. But when he did, I made the couch into a nest, the kitchen into a refuge, the morning into something warm. Bacon, waffles, kiwi shakes, quiet symbols of the care he could count on.

That night was just us. No storm. No shadows. Just one son looking to slow the world down long enough to remember who he was.

It may have seemed ordinary. But it was sacred. Because in those hours, the weight he carried did not win.

86

A BIT OF NORMALCY

MY SON WOULD WATCH his dad pick on his guitar every now and then, not actually playing a song all the way through. We always wanted to hear a song through its entirety, so Santa Claus brought him a guitar when he was small. Kyle would play it endlessly, not actually knowing what he was doing but watching daddy. Then Kyle decided, as he got older, that he might want to learn to play for real. Of course, I gave my son every opportunity to learn about new and exciting pastimes and was especially hoping that he would be good at an art medium like music. So, I enrolled him in private lessons. He enjoyed it and was, of course, natural at it like everything he did. After almost a year of bass guitar lessons and practicing at home, Kyle eventually got interested in other things and put his passion for the guitar aside. I knew he would pick it up again at some point and he did.

Kyle called me one day in 2018 and told me he was getting his life together and wanted to start playing electric guitar again. He asked me if I would help him find a nice one because he had outgrown the first one, I bought him years before when he was first starting out. I, of course, told him I would look for the nicest one I could find but that his dad knew more about picking out electric guitars than I did. Before I could purchase one, he bought one himself. He was excited and called me immediately to tell me he had gotten a new one and sent me a photo. Kyle said he was going to practice every day until he got good enough to get a job in a club. I was deeply moved, as always, and relieved that he was finally settling into something that he truly loved.

He said, "Mom, I'm gonna write you a song. I've been working on it a little bit every day."

This brought tears to my eyes. I could not express how happy I was at that moment. I always knew how much my son loved me, and this was just another reminder of his devoted love for his mom and proof of our bond. Kyle wanted so badly to focus on this, and he just wanted to live his life in peace without interference from the ones in opposition. My boy was not allowed to finish the goal he started.

I took Kyle out to a ski area near Hillsdale Lake one summer about six years ago, thinking he may enjoy skiing since he had not been able to do it in a while. This was yet another activity he was a natural at, and it would help get him away from the company that plagued him. After his dad left us both, and quickly moved on to another family without flinching, it felt like he and his girlfriend were doing everything they could to pull Kyle away from me. Whether it was jealousy or something else, I will never fully understand. But the harder they tried, the closer Kyle and I became. Their efforts to divide us only deepened our bond.

We would try to go out weekly and have a picnic lunch on occasion, relaxing a bit after he did a few rounds on the lake. I did not ski but would watch in silent awe and marvel at his perseverance and talent while taking photos and videos capturing several moments of one of many natural gifts my son instilled. There were so many times when we would just enjoy being the two of us even though, sometimes, I secretly wished for all three of us, as the whole family we once were. Our bond remained as yielding as the serene water.

As I sat on solid ground, admiring my young man's skill, the water seemed to mirror a bit of serenity. We seemed to find solace in each other's company. Kyle could share things with me and I with him, that no one else would really understand or relate to. He told me of his fears and aspirations. He enjoyed debating with me on a few things. I would explain things the way that he would understand, which at times was difficult.

I just wanted to get him back to where he once was. Back to the vibrant spirit that once defined him, a spirit brimming with vitality, love for sports, and a zest for physical activity while doing my best to instill in him the healthy, clean fun he used to have. I let him know that he could still get that back and be healthy and happy again without interference from others that tried to keep him stagnant. The activities he dabbled in kept him from searching for something that would grip his enthusiasm, even though he desperately tried, yet every effort seemed short-lived, unable to satisfy his true aspirations.

He had carried out skiing in Scouts and was of course, like everything else, it seemed almost innate. He just needed to learn which sports he liked the best and stick with them. He pretty much dove into every sport there was but would get bored easily. There just did not seem to be any one thing that would keep his interest for very long. He wanted something to share with his dad, something meaningful. But from my experience, his dad missed too many of the moments that mattered most to Kyle. Whether out of distraction or distance, the absence left a mark that can never be undone.

Oh, how Kyle's dad had forsaken countless irreplaceable occasions, choosing to be absent when his presence was paramount. I will say it repeatedly. He will never have the chance again, but that is his cross to bear.

The time spent with Kyle in those days is a testament to the power of our connection. Despite the hardships we both faced, alone and together, it reminds me that the simplest moments can exert the greatest impact.

The memories of those summer afternoons remind me of how strong we were together, mother and son, weathering every storm and ready for whatever the future held.

MOTHER'S REFLECTION:
The Water Listens

Those afternoons on the lake were more than distraction. They were reminders that even when life pulled at our edges, we could still float, just the two of us. The rhythm of skis, strings, and silence stitched something sacred between us. I did not need a full crowd, a perfect family, or a plan for tomorrow. I just needed that boy, and the water that let us rest a while.

That lake heard things no one else did. In its stillness, I felt the closeness that only water, and love, can hold.

87

MESSAGES TO HEAVEN

I ALWAYS MADE SURE I called Kyle in the morning and evening. If he did not answer, I would leave a message, or text him or Facebook him before I fell asleep to say "Goodnight" and "I love you." I would leave words of encouragement or advice and sometimes an affirmation.

I hated that dreaded text messaging. It is so impersonal and yes, one can take a simple sentence and perceive it negatively or anyway they want. I honestly did my best to be careful that Kyle took my messages the way they were intended. I knew when he was under the influence or when he was with bad company that he would be on the offense. On other days he would appreciate my words of encouragement and advice. I could not control his perception, but I was going to continue the lines of communication with my son regardless.

I continued to call or leave a text daily for Kyle after he had passed, letting him know how much I loved him and missed him. I knew he would not text back but something inside me told me to just keep doing what I always did and maybe I would get a sign from him somehow, someway. I had created this habit for so long that it was hard to break, nor did I want to. At the time, Kyle said he was on a family phone plan through his dad's mistress. But then the service was cut off; her decision, from what I was told. It left Kyle without a phone, without a lifeline. After a few months, I received a reply.

A young woman texted me back and told me she was sorry, but she had Kyle's number now. I felt betrayed and grief-stricken. My little connection to him was broken when I realized that the voice I would hear when I called would be hers.

She was so sweet when I explained to her that I was continuing to relay messages to my son even though he had passed. This girl was so understanding and told me that she lost her boyfriend to the same thing, ironically just a couple of weeks prior, and I could continue to message Kyle as much as I needed to, and she would not intrude, or I could message her if I ever wanted to talk. We were connected in our heartbreak. While in our grief, it was nice to know that this person respects my process and is in my corner.

I still message my son every morning and every night on Facebook.

"Good morning, Bubber. Go fishing with Momo and Popo today, have a beautiful day in Paradise. I love you, Poo Doo."

"I miss you to the moon and back Kyle, I can't wait to see you again."

I leave him different messages and talk to him as if he were here with me now. I tell him about my days, good and bad. In the morning, I let him know of my plans for the day and when I get in bed at night, I tell him what I carried out that day. This does not make me crazy; it makes me a great mom. A mom in mourning. A mom that will forever miss and long to be with her son again. A mom that wants so desperately to talk to him and hear him answer back.

Kyle would make sure I knew what was going on with him as much as possible. All moms want to be included in their child's life whether they are at home or out on their own is irrelevant. I am sure there were many things he kept secret from me and that is okay. Personal privacy is an important and healthy thing. If something needs to be revealed, it will be in its own time. As much as I wanted to know everything going on in his life, I also knew that I should not know certain things. I never shared everything with my parents. I know that he did not share them with me for fear of scaring me or hurting me. I know this to be fact.

What people do not understand is that my son was trying so hard to be independent and strong like his mom, not codependent and weak.

He was trying so hard not to be like his dad. He was always wrestling with his dad's predispositions, even if he loved him. I just wanted him to be his own person and live his life to the fullest. He did not have to be like either of his parents.

Kyle was out in society wanting and needing to make it on his own. Be his own man. When our kids are out there trying to find themselves, they are obviously not with us twenty-four/seven as we would like. That defeats the purpose of being an independent member of society. Others choose to believe that we did not see each other or talk to one another. This was so far from the truth. Those are lies from the enemy. The ones that thought they knew him better and thought they knew his comings and goings, did not know at all or did not want to realize that they did not have complete control over him as they wanted or thought.

Kyle was my everything. I made sure I kept tabs on him and was always looking out for his best interests and safety regardless of what others thought. I kept my distance where I could, but Kyle knew I was there when I was needed.

My son loved and cared for me deeply. I was his mother, a role no one else could ever take. Some may have tried, but they could never hold a candle to the devotion, attentiveness, and unwavering commitment I gave him. He already had a nurturing, loving mom who did not enable him or steer him down the wrong path. I was not perfect, no parent is, but being his mother was my purpose, my life's greatest calling. And to this day, nothing and no one has ever stood in the way of me being the best mom I could be.

Some days I wonder if he reads my messages. If a breeze carries them to him, or they reach him in some quiet way. But I send them anyway. Because grief is not silence, it is the sound of love that refuses to stop speaking.

MOTHER'S REFLECTION:
Love Does Not Log Off

I used to wait for the "read" notification. A ping. A reply.

Now I send my words into the quiet and trust they travel farther than cell towers reach. Good morning rituals, Facebook posts. Bedtime texts. Whispered prayers.

Maybe Kyle hears them. Maybe he already knows. But I send them anyway because love does not log off. And mothers never stop talking to their sons. I will never stop, Kyle.

88

FINDING HIS NICHE

I WISH I HAD KNOWN more of the man that my son was becoming. I just felt I needed to know more. I do know that he wanted to help others. He loved children and loved helping the homeless and those who were less fortunate than him. Deep down he knew he was a very blessed child in many ways and others wanted what he had. I have had people tell me how Kyle saved their life. He also talked others out of a slump or suicide. This was one of the many gifts God bestowed on him. I just wish he would have pursued them.

I thought for sure he would go back to school and become a teacher, not necessarily in a school but a mentor or counselor for children and teens, maybe even in social work with foster children, as he always wanted us to foster a little boy or girl when he was younger. He longed to be a big brother. I was not positive, but I could see it in my son even though he was a hard labor worker and enjoyed it, he also had a gift that he needed to share with others.

He worked at Sonic temporarily. That was fine. He was still young, and it was money well earned. He got a job roofing that scared me to death. But he started to get into sales, and I imagine he was exceptionally good at it as everything he did. He told me he would go door to door and try to upsell. I felt so much better about that then he told me it was not challenging enough. Then the dreaded tree trimming. Oh Lord help me!

Why was Kyle doing all these hard, manual labor and extremely dangerous jobs when he did not have to? I did not know what scared me the most, the fear of him getting hurt on the job or the fear of him getting hurt by the people that surrounded him. Regardless, I was on edge constantly, worrying about my son.

I tried to be as optimistic as possible and assure Kyle that something would come up and he needed to pray about it. My son did, indeed, pray but mostly like me, he had a tough time praying for himself. Most of us go through a few jobs until we find the right one. Many people are lucky enough to land the perfect job right away and others may search for many years.

He said he was going to go back to school online as soon as he got over his breakup. I was so happy. This was a move in the right direction. One that would help him better himself. It was an admirable goal to work towards.

I conveyed to him that school and work would help him heal. I assured him that the right woman was waiting for him, although he did not, at that point in his life, need a woman in it to deter him from his goals.

I come from a family of hard labor workers. His Popo, my dad, my mom, my brother, as well as other family members were extremely hard workers. I really did not want my son to work physically hard and hurt his body but that is what he wanted to do. He told me that he had no intention of sitting behind a desk and pushing papers. He also knew that he needed to work for God's glory and not for man and this sometimes proved difficult for him as it does with all of us at times, but he persevered.

Kyle was working at an auto body shop at one point, doing detail work, and told me he was also learning how to fix dents and other exterior repairs. When he mentioned it, I immediately thought of our old neighbor who did that kind of work for a living. I suggested Kyle talk to him, ask some questions, and get advice, some much-needed guidance, on how to do well in the job and build his skills.

For a while, Kyle was doing great. He really enjoyed the work and was excited about learning more. Then, one day, he called me, sounding completely defeated. He told me he had to quit. His boss had ordered him to do a repair on a customer's car, something he had not been trained to do. Kyle explained to him that he was not comfortable doing the job because he did not want to risk messing up someone's car. But instead of understanding, the boss gave him an ultimatum; do the job or leave. So, Kyle walked away. Way to be empowered, Kyle!

It crushed him. Just another let down from someone in his life that he looked up to. Another person who did not value him or treat him with respect. But I knew, without a doubt, that he had done the right thing. He refused to risk damaging someone's car, and he refused to be forced into something he was not trained for.

His boss clearly did not appreciate Kyle's integrity and had no concern for whether Kyle got in trouble or not. He had no choice but to move on. I reminded him he could always go back to school to learn more about bodywork and detailing, expand his skills, and build a solid career in the field. But at that moment, he just was not ready to go back to school. He needed time to figure out what his next step would be.

In the summer of 2019, he said he had started his job pouring concrete and even sent me videos that he took showing me different job sites. He was so excited. He said that he was going to get great benefits and be able to join the union. His boss told him that he would be able to work anywhere he wanted and not just stay in Kansas City if he chose to move elsewhere, even getting a job when we moved to Florida.

I continue to elaborate on our decision to move because we were both feeling a healthy sense of anticipation and excitement about experiencing an unfamiliar environment, meeting new people, and embracing new surroundings. The desire for change was so strong in both of us, and we felt it was necessary for our personal growth.

MOTHER'S REFLECTION:
The Work He Did

He worked harder than he had to. Roofing, concrete, tree trimming, auto detailing, anything to build something with his own hands. Some jobs scared me. Others just broke my heart.

But what matters most now is not what paid him. It is what shaped him. Kyle worked with integrity, even when it cost him. And whether he knew it or not, every effort, every early morning and aching muscle, was building something bigger: his character, his courage, his legacy.

Kyle did not work for applause. He worked to be better. He worked for God and that was enough.

89

NOT AGAIN

As far as he let me know, everything was going positively in his life until I got a call from him one day. I was at work at the time. I excused myself and went outside. He sounded coherent but there was also urgency in his voice that he needed to talk to me. We were having a friendly conversation, talking about everything he was thinking, until he flipped a switch, and I heard her in the background.

"Hang up the phone, Kyle!"

"I love you Mom, I gotta go!"

I interrupted before he could hang up. "No, no, no, Bub. Do not hang up yet!"

Shock ran through me. My heart sank to the pit of my feet when I heard the voice. She was there. He was back together with her. I had a gut-wrenching feeling in the pit of my stomach. I heard her saying things in the background that were not true. I was flabbergasted at how fast he turned on me over the phone. It did not end well with me in tears.

Again, I heard, "Hang up the phone Kyle!"

"I love you Mom," Click.

He wanted to finish talking to me, but she hung up the phone as he was in mid-sentence. She seemed, to me, to cast what seemed like a spell over him, as I begged him to get away before he was brainwashed.

Trauma bonded, that is what came to mind when I saw how deeply

Kyle clung to her. *Is that not what trauma bonding looks like?* When someone holds on to the very person who has caused them pain, unable to break free, even when it hurts? That is what I witnessed in Kyle's attachment. When I think about the emotional toll of his dad's unpredictable episodes, I cannot help but wonder if it all tangled together, trauma, loyalty, and the echoes of PTSD.

I used to call it 'dangling the carrot.' That's what it felt like. Just like Kyle's girlfriend, his dad would show kindness, make promises, validate him, just enough to give us hope that maybe, just maybe, he would change. But then he would disappear again, ghosting us and the words he had spoken. The unpredictability wore us down. It left Kyle and me anxious, disappointed, and desperate for something steady. When he returned, acting like the man we needed, the cycle would start all over again. *Is that not how trauma bonds form?* Like me, Kyle wanted so badly to believe they meant well, that they truly had his best interest at heart.

Back when I stated that Kyle and I both were empaths; I do not mean we are psychic (mind readers). It means we feel so deeply for another person and sometimes can read that person well enough to know their pain or inner turmoil that we take it on ourselves. *Is that not that what covert manipulation does to someone like Kyle, so tender, so empathic?* He absorbed everyone else's pain like it was his own, and in doing so, he put his own healing on hold. Whether it was a personality disorder or just deeply broken behavior, the result was the same: he was exploited by someone who saw his kindness as a tool. We were both programmed before we knew what hit us.

I wanted nothing more than for Kyle to find happiness, to have love, companionship, and the kind of relationship that lifted him up instead of weighing him down. I truly had nothing against this young woman as a person. My urgency to distance Kyle from her had nothing to do with jealousy or control. It had everything to do with the emotional patterns I saw unfolding, and how much I cared about his future.

When they were together, something in him changed. It felt like she had a hold on him that he could not shake. The emotional highs and lows, the love-bombing, the confusion, the mind games, reminded me of what I had lived through with my husband. If she had loved him, even a little, I believe she would have let him go. Because when we genuinely love someone, we want what is best for them, even if it means stepping back. Loving from afar, as agonizing as it is, sometimes becomes the most selfless act. I told her that once, during a phone call. I hoped she had understood.

It was not healthy, and I could not ignore the impact it was having on him. As his mother, my concern was never about keeping him from a relationship, it was about making sure he was not caught in one that chipped away at him instead of building him up. I pray that this beautiful young woman would want the same for her children one day.

Kyle was capable of so much, and I refused to let anyone pull him off track. One day, I knew he would meet the woman of his dreams, the one God intended for him. She would truly support him, challenge him in all the right ways, and love him the way he deserved. But this was not that person. How could I possibly sit back and watch him unravel under the weight of a relationship that felt more harmful than healing?

I was sickened to my core and scared out of my mind after that. My mind was constantly overwhelmed with worry for my son. *What was being said to him? How was he being manipulated? How could I save him?* My mind was frantic trying to figure out what to do.

A couple of his friends told me that they tried to get her away from him. I tried once again to call his grandma with only a response that would leave anyone utterly confused.

"Wanda, I need your help. Kyle is back with her. Wanda, she will hurt him again. Please try and talk to him for me. Please. I'm desperate. She will continue to hurt him! She will ruin his chances for a better life. He is supposed to be moving to Florida with me to get away from her. You know this. Please help me save his life, Wanda, please!"

"Deanna, I do not care what he does or who he does it with." Click.

In complete monotone, this was the same response I received when asking her to help me with her own son, my husband, and his addictions.

The tears of fear began to roll down my cheeks and eventually washed away every bit of makeup. I called her back.

"Wanda, get ahold of my husband please. I need his help in talking to Kyle. Please, Wanda, this is urgent. Why do you not understand how important this is?"

"Deanna I can't."

"You mean you won't?"

"That's right, I won't."

"Wanda, this is NOT about you or me or your son, this is about my beautiful son's life...his future!"

Click. She hung up again, dismissing a need for help, help that could have made a difference for her grandson.

I could not call his dad as he was, and is still incognito due to extreme, life-altering decisions. There was no way! I had no idea where he was. It felt like no one, neither her nor his family, was honestly thinking about what would happen to my beloved boy. I was the only one carrying that fear, that urgency.

Mother's Reflection:
The Bond That Broke Us

I used to think love was enough. That if I loved Kyle fiercely, he would be safe. But trauma does not play by those rules. It twists love into loyalty, pain into dependence.

I watched my son cling to people who hurt him, not because he did not know better, but because he hoped they would change. I knew that hope. I had lived it too.

Trauma bonding is not weakness. It is survival. Kyle was trying to survive in a world that kept pulling him under.

I could not save him from every storm. But I never stopped reaching for him. Never stopped believing he deserved peace.

90

MY SURPRISE

EVERY MORNING, I WOULD text Kyle first thing and then I would wait a couple of hours to call him. Every night I would text and call him. If he would just let me know that he was somehow doing okay and keeping afloat, I would have understood if he did not answer me right away. Kyle always knew how much mama loved him and caring about his well-being was all that mattered to me.

He called to wish me a happy birthday and tell me that he loved me. I wanted him to go with me on the Going Ape obstacle course and zip line in Swope Park, and he said he wanted to but then he paused. He was with his girlfriend. She made her way back in. He was not going to spend my birthday with me because she was there. He told me that he did not think he would be able to do the obstacle course anyway. I told him if I, a fifty-four-year-old woman, could do it, then he could too. He laughed and said he would talk to me soon and we conveyed our love for one another.

He must have been able to get away from her for a while because when I arrived home completely worn out, there was a bouquet of flowers sitting on the sidewalk in front of the door with a card that simply read, "I will always love my mom" with a necklace hanging from one of the stems. He was always so full of surprises. What a beautiful thing to do as I was sad that he did not join me that day, but he did not forget to tell me and show me how much I meant to him. I was reminded that our love for one another often finds its way to us in unexpected moments.

Even when life got busy, and circumstances changed, the essence of our relationship was still intact. Kyle's thoughtful gesture reinforced what we had always shared, and reaffirmed that even when he was physically distant, he was always close at heart. It taught me that surprises can come in many forms and serve as beautiful reminders of the love that has carried us through life's ups and downs. In the end, it is these moments filled with love, thoughts of one another and connection that truly enrich our lives and keep our spirits high.

MOTHER'S REFLECTION:
When Love Found the Door

He did not show up at the zip line that day, but he showed up for me anyway.

With flowers. With a necklace. With a message that said more than any obstacle course ever could.

Kyle always found a way to remind me I was his mom, and he was my boy. Not just on birthdays, but on sidewalks and in silence.

And that is the kind of love that does not fade. It just keeps showing up when you least expect it, and always when you need it most.

91

LABOR DAY

HE SOUNDED SO SAD when I talked to him on his dad's birthday, which was on a Sunday, and I told him that no matter how busy he was, he was to call his dad and wish him a happy birthday. Not sure if he did or not. It was the right thing to do.

He had told me his dad produced yet another weak excuse to avoid seeing him on his birthday which happened to be on the day before Labor Day that year. Rather than dwell on it, he went to the lake with some friends for the weekend.

During the conversation with him on Labor Day Monday, he asked me if I was really going to move to Florida. I told him that I was eventually, but not right away. I was a bit perplexed because we had been talking about it since May and several times before that. *Did he forget? How could he not remember?* He said that he was going with me. I reminded him that we had already agreed that he was going with me months ago and I was getting things in order. I felt uneasy and nervous when I spoke to my son on Labor Day because he did not sound like himself. How could he be himself, when once again, he told me his dad had blown him off?

This made me quite nervous. I wanted him to come home and stay with me for a while but for some reason I figured he would say no. I told him to please enjoy himself while he was there and not worry about anything at that moment.

He did not tell me she was there. Speaking to him on the phone, he tended to whisper, sounding somewhat somber, maybe so she could not hear him talk to his mother. It was reminding me of the time he went to the lake with some friends when he was much younger and called me to come get him as he was homesick and missed me. I prayed with him over the phone. He said he would get in touch with me after he got back from the lake.

She had invited herself, and he let her come, maybe against his better judgment, but that was Kyle. He was kind, accommodating, always trying to keep the peace. He told me she had begged to go with him to the lake. I do not think he wanted her there, but he gave in, like he often did. It felt familiar, the way he tried to placate her. It reminded me of the dynamic he had with his dad, and the one I had with him too. That same pull, that same imbalance. *It made me wonder, what else was happening beneath the surface?*

I was told by Kyle's friends she had conned her way to go to the lake with him and several people. It felt like she was wearing him down again, his energy was depleting, his spirit sounded heavy, he seemed more withdrawn, more weighed down. When he tried to take space for himself and went into one of the bedrooms to lie down, she did not seem to allow it. That constant pressure, that inability to breathe, tormented him. I could see it in his eyes when he got back in town. I was told that several people told her to leave him alone, but she would get angry and of course not listen to them. I only heard about this from his friends after he had passed.

It still makes me angry, knowing how tightly she seemed to hold him, how much it drained him. And what hurts even more is the silence. I do not have to wonder if others saw it too because they told me after he was gone. *My question is, if they did sense and witness what was happening, why did not anyone step in to stop it, to help my son?*

It felt like everyone looked away, even when he needed them most, instead of turning a blind eye. My baby would still be here! Why does no one understand this? He would still be here where he belongs!

I could not shake the feeling that she sometimes pressured him in ways that left him emotionally cornered. It was as if she did not want him around me, or anyone else, really. I knew that feeling all too well. Over the years, I had seen how his father's struggles, his illness, his choices, seemed to create distance between Kyle and me. It felt like our bond was something he just could not tolerate, and he tried, more than once, to pull us apart.

Sometimes I wondered if it was just jealousy, rooted in something deeper, something darker. Maybe it was because I did not follow their lead, because I tried to live a Christian life that clashed with theirs. Whatever it was, it felt like they resented me for it. And that resentment did not stop with me, it reached Kyle too. The jealousy, his dad's rage, it all seemed to chip away at his self-worth. Every time I tried to build him up, it felt like someone else was tearing him down.

I wanted my son desperately to turn back to the days when he relied on the Lord and loved Him with all his heart. I knew that if he did, he would at some point make better choices, stop the speedy lifestyle, and choose not to keep the company he did, to better his life. It is heartbreaking to think about what Kyle went through in his final days. He deserved so much better than what life handed him. But despite all the challenges that came his way, Kyle remained committed to helping others and making a difference in their lives. As his mother, I am proud of the person Kyle was and the legacy that he left behind. I think his story is an inspiration to all those who knew him and those who will come to know him through these words.

I want the reader to understand the damaging power of jealousy. It is a form of hate and resentment that does nothing but debilitate, sabotage, and harm the person who is the target of that evil sin. It can lead to destruction, possessiveness, controlling behavior, and aggression. It can hinder a person's growth and progress among many other things. It is toxic and can even lead a person to take their life.

Every person should build their confidence and self-worth but not based on someone else's perception of them. Set goals for yourself and pursue your own passions. Focus on your own journey and not someone else's. Do not compare yourself to others because we are not the same nor does God intend us to be. We are all on our own journey. *If jealousy interferes with your relationships or well-being, please seek support or counseling to help you navigate through your emotions.*

It takes time and effort to overcome jealousy. Celebrate the small steppingstones and please try to be patient with yourself and others. Please do not bring someone else down because of your hate. Stop the hate! Look what it did to a beautiful person! Look what it did to my boy!

MOTHER'S REFLECTION:
What Jealousy Took

Jealousy is not just envy, it is erosion. It chips away at love, at trust, at the quiet spaces where healing might have grown.

I saw it in Kyle's eyes. In the way he whispered. In the way he tried to keep peace while losing pieces of himself.

If love had been louder than jealousy, maybe my boy would still be here. But even now, I carry his light, and I will keep speaking truth, so no other child is dimmed by someone else's darkness.

92

WANTING TO GO

I WAS TAKING SOME CLASSES which started on the first of September in 2019. I had to get through these classes and start a new job, and Kyle was also starting a job.

Kyle at one point seemed extremely adamant and told me we needed to go to Florida before Christmas. I said that I could not jump up and leave that fast because I was working on getting a job lined up out there and was looking for places to live for us that I could possibly afford.

I wanted to live in a mobile home community as close to the ocean as possible, not even caring what it looked like, as I would make it as livable as I could but when my precious son made the final decision to go with me, I thought it better to research other places to live. I thought we could get an apartment together for the first year or so until he could get on his feet and be on his own.

I could not just walk away, not like his dad had. It felt like he had vanished, leaving us to carry everything he would not. The silence, the absence, the weight of what he left behind, it was all consuming and paralyzing. Everything takes time. That was not the mature adult and disciplined thing to do. We had to make a list of everything that needed to be done and things that needed closure. It was not difficult, but it was time consuming. He tried to understand but I could tell by the sound of his voice that he was ready to go right then. Sweet baby Jesus, what were they doing to my boy!

Looking back at these conversations, I realize my son was looking for an escape from his life and the people in it, both geographically and emotionally. Kyle thought that Florida was what he needed to reset. I also believe that it was. Kansas City, his home, was turning into a ghost town for him. Everything and everyone were haunting him.

I kept reassuring him that it would all work out and that he needed to hold on a bit longer as I was trying to save a bit of money to get us started. I was saving as much as I could, selling a few things, and working triple shifts to raise money.

I thought there may be a great recovery program for him there that I could afford. I was not sure how but was going to take the chance to get my son the help he so desperately longed for. It felt like every time I tried to get Kyle the help he needed, I was met with resistance, from his father and others. Whether intentional or not, their actions made it harder for him to find stability, and even harder for me to support him. That is why we had to distance ourselves. We needed space to breathe, to heal, to hope. I was going to get him on track and do whatever it took so he could be on his own again. I have been on my own for ten years now without a dime from my husband, so I had to plan and budget carefully. He agreed.

I said, "Get excited Bubber. We are going to make a whole new life, and it will be wonderful. You know one day you will truly fall in love with the right woman and have kids of your own. Please do not hurry to make me a grandma though." He chuckled.

Kyle was slowly beginning to understand that I had more wisdom than most. He even told me once, "I think I might have to start listening to you better, Mom...LOL."

Relaying once again to my son, "Kyle, the most amazing dreams for your life have already been imagined by God, you just need to make them become a reality. Never settle for less than God's best for you Bubber; please just listen to Mom. Listen to Him. He, who is in you, will lead you in the right direction."

MOTHER'S REFLECTION:
The Escape We Were Building

Kyle was ready to go. Not just to Florida, but toward something lighter, something freer. I saw it in his voice, in his urgency, in the way he clung to the idea of starting over.

We were not running, we were rebuilding and even though the road was long and the money was tight, we were dreaming together. That was the gift.

He believed in the plan. He believed in me, and I will always believe in the life we were trying to create.

93

NAVIGATING THE DARK

THE TRUTH IS THAT my son was dying a little bit every day before his actual passing. I knew that he was trying to get better but the substance, whether it was cigarettes, alcohol, or something else, even if it had been weeks or months without, was killing not only his brain but his body, and the horrific company he was keeping was killing his spirit. Kyle was not allowed to succeed in fulfilling all the hopes and dreams I had for him or the ones that he once had for himself.

It felt like the people around him were draining his will to live a clean, healthy life. The man he looked up to most did not seem to help him rise above the pain, instead, it felt like he encouraged the very things that numbed it. And worse, he did not stand in the way when others followed that same path. One day, I believe he will have to face the weight of that emptiness, and the consequences of the despicable choices he made.

I wish for my son's story to be a blessing of hope and perseverance to other kids going through such pain and trauma in their life. I cannot really express how God can turn your life around completely if you allow him to, but it is so difficult to do when the devil tells you to numb. He tells you to run from God.

Saying, "Here my child, take this pill it will take the pain away. Drink this poison, it will make everything better."

This is not God speaking, but that is the dark side speaking over you. Everything you put in your body is a temporary fix. Numbing yourself is not going to repair the pain and heartache. Only God can do that. Kyle knew this and was trying everything he could to get right with God again. Kyle was not a bad person by any means, in fact, just the opposite. The substance that consumed him was bad. The oppression and pain that was inflicted upon him came from evil. The people that supplied him with it, not thinking about the welfare of my son, were under the same evil hold. It is in fact a demon in its many forms that comes to kill, steal and destroy a good person.

Someone once said to me that addiction is not a demon, it is a sickness. It is indeed a disease. However, any substance or person that alters another person's perspective on living a good, clean, healthy quality of life is not of God; it is not good. It is the opposite of good, which is evil. We all understand this, but we also need to understand that it can potentially be overcome if one wishes it strongly enough and genuinely allows others that know how to help them do it. Get professional help. Just allow the healing to take place, as painful as it is. You can get through it. Not over it, but through it.

Kyle wanted it strongly enough, and I was determined to help him overcome it regardless of the push and pull games others played with him. I was committed to restoring his health at any cost. Those who opposed Kyle and me were individuals who did not wish for his betterment because they did not wish better for themselves, or anyone else. These individuals are fortunate to still be alive, but they may be haunted by their own demons to this very day, and I will continue to pray for their redemption.

Only God can do a complete overhaul on your life. I tried to convey these same words to my husband for years only to be laughed at. I realize that many kids and young adults, including my son's friends, are probably laughing at these words too. So many of them think they know what is best for them and they know more than a wise adult. As someone that was once a kid and young adult, I know much wiser, older adults that do not do substance and follow the narrow path, do have more wisdom, and you need to listen to them, as they really do know better. God's commandments clearly say among other passages that we must follow His rules for our life, or it falls apart. God's way is always better, not necessarily easier, but always better and more fulfilling.

I understand that some children just do not have that male role model and authority figure in Christ to look up to which makes it much harder for them to learn the right way. I imagine the ages between thirteen and twenty-five have the most dramatic changes for most, as their brains are still developing. It is a time when teenagers and young adults feel a little lost even with a strong support system and a foundation in Christ to stand upon. I will admit, during my teenage and young adult years, I was a bit lost too, trying to fit in as best I could.

My son had a foundation in Christ and in me, but even with that, he struggled. It felt like what he needed most from the man he looked up to, healthy support, leadership, and accountability, was missing and that absence left a wound as it would in any growing boy, that I could not fill alone.

Kyle's many other friends were lost too, trying to do their best with even less. They were just lost young kids trying to read a map in a foreign language. The drugs they took was like using a thesaurus when what they really need was a dictionary. It works but only slightly because you still cannot read the map.

So yes, people will laugh at their parents at times for their advice and beliefs. They seem silly because they are not living your life. But they have lived a life. They might not have all the answers or the key to your map, but they did figure out theirs, hopefully, most of them.

I wish these were things I could tell Kyle and his other friends. Even if, I doubt that some will listen. They might not have wanted me at times to be there for my son, but I was always there no matter what was going on in my life. My son was first and foremost and that angered a few people that could not handle it. They saw me as competition. I'm his mother! Not a competitor. My son's life was not a game to be played with!

I could sense Kyle was starting to see my viewpoint in the end. Too many things were pulling him back, some who did not always lift him, a dad who seemed adrift in his own struggles, a woman whose influence felt limiting, and of course, the emotional tug-of-war with his on-and-off girlfriend.

I think Kyle wanted to save his girlfriend. Or at least he believed that he could, just as I tried to save my husband for many years. Kyle tried but was seeing just as I could not save my husband, he could not save his girlfriend if she did not want to be. His urgency to get to Florida was so that he could hit the redo button and get a new map for himself.

But reader, God only gives you one map to read. So please, please, read it slowly. Read it for as long as you possibly can. Follow it until each page is worn and they crease too easily. If you are struggling to read it, ask a fellow traveler for a dictionary not a thesaurus.

My son was wandering into unfamiliar territory, and he asked all the wrong travelers to be his companions. It became a journey of the blind leading the deaf. They helped each other but not correctly. I wish I had followed through at the time to step in when I heard that little voice whispering in my ear telling me that they were heading the wrong way. I did try, honestly, to step in but Kyle was being told horrible false narratives to deter him for the truth; so much that he came to believe at one point, temporarily, that Mom did not know what she was talking about.

I often think about that time; about the crossroads he stood at and the choices he made. As Kyle's mom, all I ever wanted was to guide him back to the right path but sometimes love and truth were drowned out by the noise of the world. Still, I never gave up hope. Even when Kyle doubted me, even when the lies became louder than my voice, I held on to the belief that one day, he would see clearly, and I never gave up hope...not once.

It is, without a doubt, a painful thing to watch someone you love stumble through the dark, but it is also a reminder of how powerful hope can be. No matter how lost he seemed, I trusted that light would find him eventually, and I stood ready to lift him up whenever he reached for it.

MOTHER'S REFLECTION:
The Map He Tried to Read

Kyle was not lost because he lacked love, he was lost because the map kept changing. The people around him redrew the lines, blurred the truth, and pointed him toward places that could not heal him.

I tried to be his compass. I tried to show him the way back to God, to peace, to himself and even when he doubted me, I never stopped believing he would find his way.

Because the map God gives us is not always easy to read, but it is always worth following. I will keep telling Kyle's story so others can find their way before the darkness takes hold.

94

THE WEIGHT OF UNSEEN WOUNDS

KYLE'S CHILDHOOD WAS, FOR the most part, a beautiful journey, yet like everyone, he faced his peaks and valleys. I often wonder if those valleys were too deep and wide for him to navigate. Our lives were marred by moments far from perfect, and I find myself replaying those memories, constantly seeking answers. What truly pushed my son to the edge after all he endured? The mulling is endless; there could have been countless factors at play. Yet, in my heart, I know who and what caused him the most distress, leaving him feeling as if there were no other way to cope with what he was going through or no other way out in the end.

Before the world introduced him to its darker side, my son was a good, honest, and happy child, innocent and full of love. However, as I reflect on those times, I remember how often my husband would slip into what I could only describe as a fugue-like state, disconnected, unreachable. Some might have called it something else, but to me, it felt like watching someone vanish behind their own eyes. In those moments, the things he did, the way he acted, left deep marks on Kyle. Some of it I still cannot bring myself to speak aloud.

There were days I wanted to run, literally run for our lives. Maybe we should have. Because even now, it feels like my husband cannot, or will not, acknowledge the pain his actions caused. He has never apologized and while I have made peace with that for myself, I still pray he will, one day face the truth, not for me, but for Kyle alone.

Trauma is an inescapable part of life; no one escapes without scars. I did my best to provide Kyle with everything he needed and wanted, yet I could not shield him completely from the pain that surrounded him. This pain drove him to seek solace in substance, like so many others who turn to drugs to escape their struggles. Ironically, while it may have eased Kyle's suffering temporarily, it inflicted a wound on my heart that will last for two lifetimes, his and mine.

But even in the darkest moments, our love remained. My love for Kyle has never wavered, not through hardship, not through loss, not through the cruel weight of regret. It is a love that exists beyond any circumstances, a love that continues to hope, continues to fight, and refuses to let go. If there is one thing I know with absolute certainty, it is that my love for my son will always endure for eternity.

MOTHER'S REFLECTION:
The Pain Beneath the Surface

Not all wounds can be seen, and not all pain comes with a warning. Kyle carried so much quietly, and I did my best to carry it with him, even when I did not always understand it.

As his mother, I stood beside him in both light and shadow. Though I could not always shield him, I never stopped trying to guide him toward healing.

Some stories cannot be rewritten, but they can be retold, with love, with truth, and with the hope that someone else will find strength in what my son could not say aloud.

95

STRUGGLE FOR REDEMPTION

KYLE WAS NOT GOING to get better until he distanced himself from the company he was keeping. I mean everyone, his first supplier, his girlfriend, and specific family members. I told Kyle that to heal and get clean, he needed to step outside of his comfort zone, take chances, and challenge himself. Without doing this, he might never experience those full blessings life had to offer.

I honestly believe in the power of provision, healing, and restoration. Everything we do not deserve can come to us if we glorify God and genuinely repent. I reminded Kyle that even though he had been saved several years ago, it was perfectly fine to ask God into his heart every single day if necessary. Everyone needs renewal. We all stumble, even after we have found salvation. This practice worked for me, and I knew God would welcome Kyle's daily prayers as a source of strength on his difficult journey.

It broke my heart to see my beautiful boy so discouraged, especially by his second cousin. That kind of hurt runs deeper when it comes from family. His cousin insisted that asking God into one's heart was a one-time event.

"Kyle only needs to do it once," he told me. But I believed, and still believe, that faith is a relationship, not a checkbox. His statement was just a doctrinal belief and not a provable fact. My son needed to understand that he could do whatever it took to grow closer to his Almighty God.

This was the battle Kyle faced, being pressured by people who claimed to speak for God yet seemed more interested in control than compassion. Their rigid James Town beliefs did not in any way reflect the Christ we knew. It felt like they wanted to mold him into something he was not and that pushed him further from the grace he was trying to hold onto.

When Kyle was younger, he spoke to God daily. All he needed was a nudge in the right direction as he began to veer off the path. I believed that God would find immense joy in knowing that Kyle was reaching out to Him every day, seeking assurance of His forever presence and love.

What kind of faith teaches a man to break a boy's spirit in the name of belief, and still call it a Godly love?

It made me wonder, how someone who professed faith could inflict such pain? The Lord and Savior I know and the Almighty God my son believed in would never do that to any of his children.

MOTHER'S REFLECTION:
Faith is Not a Formula

Kyle did not need a checklist, he needed grace. He needed to know that God's love was not a one-time transaction but a daily invitation.

I watched him reach for that love, even when others tried to box it in. I reminded him faith is not about rules, it is about relationship.

The God we knew never turned away from a child seeking Him and Kyle was seeking, even when the world tried to silence his prayers.

96

TRYING TO HELP

AN ADDICT MAY LOOK the same on the outside, but behind the eyes, something darker takes hold. They start to see only what the addiction wants, what it craves. It no longer sees a mother, a father, a wife, or a child. Just the next fix.

I know this is, I am sure, difficult for the unaware or uneducated to comprehend. I have had to educate myself on the addiction demon as it held on so tightly to both my son and husband. I have spent a great deal of time in How to Cope classes, Smart Recovery, Nar-Anon, Gam-Anon, Al-Anon. I needed to learn as much as I could, so I kept fighting, for Kyle, and even for his dad, because it felt like they were both caught in something bigger than themselves. But the difference was clear: Kyle did not want what he was battling. His dad... it seemed like he had made peace with it.

I will always wrestle with the weight of knowing I did everything I could to help my son yet still feel it was not enough. Because I loved Kyle, I kept searching for ways to reach him, asking open-ended questions, hoping he'd feel safe enough to let me in. But that was not his nature, and I had to tread carefully. I never wanted to push him so far that he shut down. More than anything, I just wanted to help my boy.

When he told me he did not want to see another counselor, I understood. Still, I reminded him there is no shame in asking for help. It is something we all should do. Life is heavy and complicated, and professional support helps keep us grounded. It keeps me steady just like daily devotionals and scripture. On the days I accidentally skip them, I feel like something is missing, like a quiet emptiness that reminds me how much I lean on hope and guidance to help me through life.

Therapy, recovery groups, and self-help have done wonders for me. They have helped me process pain, be more aware of my strength, and take the next steps. I have seen how dedicated people can be to their healing, but I have also seen others deny they need help at all. In a world as chaotic as ours, turning away from healing feels like turning away from life itself.

Through it all, I stayed beside Kyle, holding space for him, encouraging him, making sure he knew he was not alone. That is what love is to me: quiet persistence and unwavering presence. I do not know if it was enough. But I do know it mattered. Kyle Alan Wiley mattered.

Now, as I am almost to the end, and speak his story into the world, I hope what I share brings not just clarity... but peace.

MOTHER'S REFLECTION:
What Help Looks Like

Help is not always loud. Sometimes it is quiet persistence. A hand that is held. A question asked. A prayer whispered in the dark.

I tried everything I could to reach Kyle, not to fix him, but to remind him he was never alone.

And even now, I still believe that love, when offered without condition, can be the strongest kind of help there is.

97

LOST

KYLE DID NOT FEEL like he had any purpose left. He knew the drugs and alcohol did so much damage to his brain but his body as well. He hated even starting them. He told me how sorry he was for starting them and that he did not listen to me. He honestly thought he could handle it. I told him he did not ever need to apologize to me. It was not his fault and that it did not matter at that point, what mattered is that he worked as hard as he could to get healthy again and off them, not letting others alter his decision or pressure him and to never look back.

I also told Kyle that if he was serious about change and getting healthy again, he would have to go through uncomfortable and exceedingly demanding situations, but I would be there to go through it with him. I would be there while he went through the withdrawals of not only the poison in his body but the breakup of his first girlfriend. I also told him that I would do my best to contact his dad as he should go through it with his son as well. I would make sure we were both there to comfort him, hold his hand and not leave him as he fought through his pain and healing. I was never able to reach him. It felt like he kept turning away, avoiding the responsibilities that came with being a husband and a father. And through it all, Kyle's needs seemed invisible to him.

I am not afraid to tell you that Kyle and I had some deep discussions about his addiction and his attitude toward me and life in general.

Regardless of what others think or want to believe their own warped truth, my son and I shared hundreds of specials moments and as a good mom, I did have to put him in his place every now and then just as my own parents did. It was difficult for him as someone wanting to be an adult before he was ready, but he understood

He was scared to go through withdrawals. He did not want to fail. I told him the only failure would be if he did not try, and I would be there to make sure he did not fall. He would try but not only physical pain, the mental and emotional pain of withdrawals is so powerful that he would fall again and that is all right as long as he picked himself up.

"Stop trying to dodge the process, Kyle. Deflecting everything will not be conducive to your healing. Going through the fire and coming out unscathed is the only way to grow Kyle, it is the only way to succeed. I love you."

"Just go through the withdrawal Bubber. It will hurt for a while, but the withdrawal process will not kill you. I promise, Kyle, I promise you it will be okay if you just detox and go through the withdrawals. I will be there with you and for you for the entirety. I promise."

He just kept putting it off thinking he could do it on his own and did not need his mom's help. I still cry thinking about how he needed and wanted his dad, his family, and friends by his side for support, not just Mom.

He did not know who he was anymore. He hated those drugs. When he tried to go off them and get with his old group of friends, the friends that did not do any drugs, they had moved on already. They were taking their life seriously and graduating and going to college. He felt like they had forgotten him because he had left to get high and hang with another crowd. My baby was so sad. He did not want his new life. He longed for the old one. He wanted his old friends back. He wanted to go to prom and graduate school and further his education but found it difficult to get back to that. I remember him confiding in me one night telling me that he thought it was too late to go back to where he once was.

I told him, "No baby, it is never, never too late! Do not you dare give up hope! Hope is what keeps us going."

He told me he had a lot of friends, but he was not sure how many were truly real. He said that when they got together, it often turned into drinking or getting high, not always, but more often than he wanted and when it came to his girlfriend, he said it seemed like she relied on pills just to get through the day. My son just wanted normalcy. He wanted to go fishing. He mentioned getting back into Parkour, which he loved, but no one wanted to do it with him. He mentioned his BMX racing, that he once did when I would take him and his friend to the tracks out in Raytown, Missouri, and wanted to try that again, but he said none of his friends wanted to join him. That is when I told him it was a chance to make new friends with like-minded healthy, fun, safe motives, with goals and dreams. He would be able to do that once we got to our new home.

Why did he feel he needed to "go along with them" or "appease them" like he did his dad? He loved every single one of his friends so much and spoke so highly of all of them and was worried about some of them as they were going through the same thing, he was but also conveyed to me that no one had any ambition to do anything, but party and he hated it but went along with it. He saw his dad do it, so he felt out of place not to.

He said, "Mom it's all around me, I can't get away from it." I said "Yes, you can, and it is going to be oh so hard, but you must love these people, including your dad who is going through his own level of pain and toxicity, from afar to be able to get clean and start from nothing. You need to distance yourself from them. I also conveyed that no matter how much he cared about them, some of the people in his life, including his dad, may not be helping him move forward. Unless something changed, I feared they would only hold him back.

There were a lot of people I hung out with in high school, but I knew that if I wanted to progress in life, I had to stop hanging out with them. That did not mean that I did not care about them or that one day I might come together with them again during class reunions or

Facebook. I knew that if I wanted a different future, a better life than I had to move on and upward. He knew this and was trying to do just that.

Why did they not care enough to help him heal? I get that no one, addict or not, can force someone else into sobriety. True healing has to come from within. That said, people in recovery can absolutely support and inspire each other. In fact, peer support is a cornerstone of many recoveries. They could have walked beside my son, offered strength, and maybe be the reason he chose to keep going.

Instead, it felt like I was the only one fighting for him, while they turned their backs on me. Maybe they were lost in their own pain, numbing it the only way they knew how. But in doing so, they pulled Kyle deeper into the very darkness he was trying to escape, and I imagine some of them were trying to escape it as well.

I spoke of the young man, his first supplier. Kyle's dad and others chose to believe his false narratives. He told people that Kyle did not have any family and put it on Facebook. This was not true and coming from someone who claims to be a reformed Christian, the lie cut even deeper. Kyle had a huge family on both sides. My side was close knit and full of life and energy and social gatherings. The other side was completely opposite. He told me about his own painful upbringing, about a mother who struggled with mental illness and a dad who was not present. Maybe that is why he assumed Kyle's life was similar. But it was not and maybe that is why he could not see how much harm he was doing. But whatever his reasons, the influence he had on Kyle, and others, left a mark I cannot ignore. Even if he is reformed, and I am truly proud of him for that, the damage remains. Most substance users, *not all,* will tell you they had an awful childhood to deter from their ownership in their downfall. In fact, many come from a very well upbringing.

Substance does NOT discriminate in any way. Rich or poor, happy, sad, ill, or healthy, it does not matter. *What happens when a child, still tender and trusting, is led down a path of harm by someone who does not have their best in mind?* The damage does not just fade, it lingers. When he once told me about his own broken past, I thought, maybe that is why he could not see the harm he was passing on. I feel so bad for all children going through this and want to help them all although I am only one person. *But knowing what I was told, how does he now stand before others as a teacher of truth to a church or recovery group, without ever acknowledging the pain he left behind?*

Even in Kyle's happiness and heartache in his teenage years, he sometimes pretended to be someone he was not to appease the wrong people. Kyle was NOT a ruthless, tough, unloving, rebel but at times he pretended to just have friends, the wrong friends, because his old friends had gone on with their lives and he was stuck. He felt that he would never get normalcy in his life again. He once told me something that still haunts me, that when one has drugs, they always have friends.

Kyle always had a wide circle of friends, even before substance use clouded his path, maybe this person did not which is so sad. In the end, though, we all only need one or two who are truly genuine. Some people around him claimed to know him, but they did not understand the boy he was before everything changed. The one person in particular, whose influence left a lasting mark, has never acknowledged the role he played in Kyle's unraveling. No remorse. No apology. But when I saw the crowd that gathered for Kyle's farewell and his first Angelversary, releasing lanterns into the sky just for him, I knew how deeply he was loved, and how could he not be? He was the most lovable soul I have ever known. Still, the one who helped lead him astray... never showed up.

This is the main reason I needed him so desperately to move away with me. To start a whole new life. Get a complete do over. Get a whole new network of people in his life that would exalt him and would lift him up, instead of pulling him off course.

I took in a few of his friends because they needed a place to live and good food to eat and a bed to get a good night's sleep so no one could say that I was not a good mother and caregiver as I hate that Kyle felt he needed to tell stories to get others to pay attention to him and love him. He never had that problem before the substance started. EVER!!

He was popular and so full of life and happiness before the demon crept in and swallowed him.

To be honest, not all, but some of his friends came from homes marked by instability or struggle. For Kyle, that became the norm and because I did not live that kind of life, I sometimes felt like the outsider even in my own home. He wanted his friends to think his mom was no different from theirs. An ignorant person told Kyle I was the common denominator. I guess I am in a way. I did not conform to others or things that would harm me and never have. I am proud of that, and Kyle conveyed he was proud of me too.

As his mom, I did know the agony he was feeling because he confided in me and again, I felt his vibrations. I felt his pain when I looked into his beautiful hazel eyes that seemed to mesmerize me so intently.

Both his best friend and his girlfriend told me they were always by his side twenty-four/seven. But no one can be everything to everyone, not even Kyle. I knew I was not part of the world that just wanted to party with him. I wanted to share joy with him, yes, good, clean, healthy fun; not the kind that would pull him under. So, it felt like no one believed I had his best interest at heart.

MOTHER'S REFLECTION:
The One Who Knew Him Best

They said they were always by his side. But I knew the truth behind his eyes, the ache, the longing, the quiet unraveling.

I was not part of the party crowd. I was part of the healing. Even when others doubted my place in his life, Kyle never did.

He told me he was proud of me, and I will carry that pride, that bond, that truth, because I was not just his mother. I was the one who knew him best.

98

NO FEAR

MY SON AND I had many talks about his faith. Kyle did miss the church sometimes. I could not force him to go every Sunday. Sure, we did when he was little, and he loved it. but he did go with me on occasion and on Thursday night which was "Care Night," where they served dinner before worship and groups. He kept it to himself, concerned, that they would try to sway him either against me or away from his faith. The church had pool tables upstairs so we would go and play some pool beforehand, which seemed to ease his mind a bit. He told me that he did not think he fit in anymore.

I said "Who does? We are all here to try to fit in."

He felt like he would be shunned. By whom? His friends, cousins or the people at church or his dad? None of those people mattered. The one that he needed to get close to again was his one and only God and be true to himself. I do admit that we are all sinners, even the special ones that do not think they are capable of sin are worse off than anyone.

"We fall every day, Kyle. All of us." I swear like a sailor sometimes. Not intentionally of course, but it happens. Church is where we can go and know the people there will hold us up when we fall. They do not care if you cry and break down. They meet you where you are, at that moment. You do not ever have to pretend. Those are the people you want to surround yourself with."

I had my pastors from church reach out to Kyle several times and invite him to a group of young adult men going through the same thing he was. I do not think that he ever attended as he was being pulled in so many directions. They reached out to my husband as well to no avail.

The truth is that Kyle's second cousin was so forceful in his beliefs, so rigid in how he thought a Christian should act, that it overwhelmed Kyle. What should have been a place of peace became a place of pressure and after that, he was apprehensive about going back to church. I did not blame him. Churches are not supposed to be like that. Christians are not supposed to be like that; brainwashing people is not what our Lord and Savior is about. He is not about hurting children or messing with their minds. This is why Kyle did not go back even though he still believed and loved God. When someone in the family hurt Kyle, and his dad did not intervene, or at least, it felt that way to me, something in Kyle broke. I would not want to go back either.

I know that Kyle was becoming stronger in his relationship with the Lord. It was a slow process. Although he did not allow others to know it, especially his dad. Did he become so close to God that he wanted to be with him? I am tormented trying to guess what was going through his mind at the time. Only that he was trying desperately to get away from the two people that were there the day he left. One person in his life struggled with daily challenges, something she shared with me herself. Another in a demented state, now gone, who brought her own strife into our lives. Together, it was a storm surrounding Kyle that he should never have had to weather. This behavior created an emotional, relentless toll on my son.

Did he think that he would be better off with the Lord instead of here on Earth with his family and friends? Do not most of us as believers think and want that for ourselves at times? Was he courageous enough to take that chance? For some people fear means to run from. That there is danger ahead. I taught Kyle never to run from fear but to face it because I knew how strong he truly was.

I told my son, "Kyle the more your faith in God, the less fear and the more courageous you are going to be. God is always with you son.

When you face your fear, you may just learn that the fear that plagues you is not as dangerous as you think and that it is taking up way too much of your time and energy." I am saying this to myself as well, as on occasion I tend to forget.

There is a passage in the Bible that says to not be entrenched in fear. I never preached because I too, am drawing closer to God and learning every day, I have no right to preach but did indeed search for proper scripture to fit his needs at the time. We must learn somehow, and he was reluctant to go to church at times so I would pass on what I learned.

"A person who takes their life is very weak." I've heard that enough from naive people and it is far from the truth. A person that takes their life has more strength in them than we will ever comprehend. It takes every ounce of energy and power in a person to do such a profound unthinkable act of taking their own life and leaving the people that love them. Kyle must have had more strength than Goliath to pull the trigger on himself and cause himself so much pain just to leave this world.

He so desperately wanted to get away from certain people, but I know for a fact, this was *not* premeditated or wanted by him. I also think that he was so far gone at the time that he could not think about what it was going to do to the people he left behind, especially me, his mom. I think that it is partially my fault because I taught him what I was taught growing up, that God and Heaven is real, beautiful, and peaceful, and we will be there one day but only in his timing, not ours. My intentions were to help Kyle persevere through the challenging stumbling blocks he faced here on earth. I am grappling with this issue as I speak.

I taught Kyle to love and respect God; to have faith that God would guide him through every test he endured. The trauma he endured and then substance he dove into to mask the pain did not mean that his love and respect for God was null and void, because it simply was not. Did I instill in my son so much courage that he felt strong enough to take his own life?

No one who has passed away from suicide is weak. I am tired of hearing ignorant remarks claiming that suicide is selfish. Those who say so have no understanding of the immense pain and the titanic strength to leave this world and the people that wish them to stay.

For the many people that fear death, my son knew there was a more peaceful, beautiful place after death. That dreaded day, Kyle did not leave room for a partial rescue. No chance of waking into a broken body or a broken life. Kyle made one hundred percent sure there would be no survival, not in a state that would feel like hell on earth, so maybe he had an instantaneous peace even though the pain in that last moment was beyond unfathomable for him. To me, this took every ounce of courage and strength my son had in him. Far beyond what I could ever summon, and I am the strongest woman you will ever meet. I just wish that he would have used more of that strength and courage to fight those demons that hovered over him and would not leave him alone or help him, just a little while longer. He would have been twenty-two exactly six weeks later.

MOTHER'S REFLECTION:
Faith in the Fire

Kyle did not run from fear; he faced it and maybe that is what breaks my heart most.

He was strong. Stronger than most will ever understand. Even in his final moments, I believe he was reaching for peace, for God, for something beyond the pain.

People say fear destroys. But sometimes, it just reveals. It shows us who we are, who we trust, and what we hold onto when everything else starts to fall away.

Kyle's courage ran deeper than any wound, any failure, any setback. I will spend the rest of my life reminding the world that his strength was never the absence of pain, it was the refusal to let it have the final word.

I taught him to be brave. To trust in the Lord with all his might, and I will never stop believing that his soul found the comfort he longed for.

Because faith is not just for the living, it is for the broken, the weary, the ones who fought hardest to stay.

99

THE TRUTH WE CARRY IN SILENCE

WHEN A PARENT LOSES a child, people do not always know what to say. But there comes a time when silence no longer feels like protection. It feels like weight. I cannot carry that kind of silence anymore.

My son, Kyle, died by suicide. Those words still do not sit easily in my mouth. But they are part of our truth, and I believe the truth matters, especially when someone we love carried so much pain in secret that only a select few were aware of.

We are often told not to speak about things like this. To keep it quiet out of respect. But I have always believed that silence does not honor our loved ones, it hides them. It hides what they went through, it hides who they were, and it hides what they needed. That is not how I wanted to tell Kyle's story.

When we do not speak. When we do not talk about what really happened, others will lose pieces of them. I certainly do not want that for my beautiful son.

We lose the signs, the late-night talks, the exhaustion, the small clues that made sense only afterward. We lose the understanding of how hard they fought to stay. We bury the pain in shadows, where it only grows heavier.

I have had to sit with that silence. I sometimes had to choose, again and again, to speak or not speak through the ache. I choose to be loud!

My son was not born with mental illness; it was inflicted on him by another and then another and then another. His PTSD was completely hidden to some while others knew and chose for it to become silent to them because they were not concerned.

What it means to honor my son is telling Kyle's story, which is not about sharing every private detail. It is about showing the full picture of who he was, including the battles he faced.

He was kind. He was loyal. He had moments of laughter and strength, even on his hardest days he carried burdens that most people never saw. Yet he carried them until they became too much.

Speaking his truth, our truth, does not make him less. If anything, it makes him more, more human, more real, more deeply loved. I am writing this because someone else might need to hear it. Another mother, another father, another friend, another person who feels alone in their grief or their pain.

You are not alone.

If someone you love is struggling, I hope you will listen closer. Ask one more time and then again and then again. Stay one more minute and then another and then another. If *you* are struggling, please do not carry it quietly. You are not a burden! You matter!

This book holds pieces of Kyle's life, his joys, his fears, his love, and his losses. I wanted to tell it the only way I know how: as his mom. With a voice that sometimes shakes for my son but never stops loving him.

MOTHER'S REFLECTION:
When We Speak, We Heal

Some truths weigh heavier when carried alone. Silence, though often well-intentioned, can turn into a shroud that hides not only what we lost, but who we loved.

My son Kyle passed away by suicide. That truth is sacred. It belongs not just in whispers or behind closed doors, but in the open air, where healing can take root, and where hope can be heard.

Jesus said, "The truth will set you free." I believe God calls us to speak, not to shame, but to shine a light. Kyle's story is beyond any pain imaginable, but it is also holy. It is a story of spiritual longing, of strength unseen, of love that never left him. Speaking it does not diminish him. If anything, it restores what silence would have stolen.

There are others walking through similar storms, mothers, fathers, sons, daughters, aching to know they are not alone. This voice, this truth, is for them too.

Let this memoir be my offering: not just for Kyle, but for every soul who has wrestled with darkness and every heart longing to see the dawn.

100

THE CALL THAT
NEVER CAME

I **STILL WONDER, WAS KYLE** asking for me, his mama, in those final hours? Was he calling out for help? For his dad, or someone, anyone to intervene? I replay the what-ifs in my mind constantly.

I try to believe someone would have acted. That if a call had been made, everything could have changed. I was seven minutes away. I would have saved my son. I would have died so my son could live.

Over time, I have learned more about what happened. I have come to understand who was present, who saw signs, who could have done more. Some people simply did not act. Whether out of fear, confusion, guilt, or something else, I will never understand. I have stopped chasing the reasons. There are no excuses when it comes to saving a life.

The people who spent more time with him in that last year, the ones he lived with, cared about, or confided in, had to have seen warning signs. I was nearby. I was reachable. I was always ready. But I was not called.

Looking back, I believe others may have been afraid to act. Still others wanted peace, even if that peace came at the expense of facing reality. For years, Kyle's grandmother said what she wanted most was peace of mind. But sometimes, the pursuit of peace can look a lot like avoidance. I doubt that she ever found that peace even after death.

Kyle once told me someone close to him would post as him on social media, answering messages in his voice. It disturbed him. I noticed the differences in tone between what I knew he would write and what appeared on his accounts. It was not his writing at all. He felt erased.

He was trying to reclaim his life, talking about starting over, moving, cutting ties that drained him, choosing something better. He never told me suicide was on his mind. In fact, he told me the opposite, which was the truth.

Still, something broke.

Police were at the house. His phone was ringing. But not from the people who mattered most. His own grandma walked away from him as he was taking his last breath. *How does someone look into the eyes of their only grandchild in pain, and walk away like it is not their problem?* It takes a heartless person to abandon someone in need. Kyle could have and should have been saved.

Everyone left him. He was tormented and then deserted. He was alone, unreachable, while I was calling, texting, doing what I did every day. My baby should have NEVER been alone! No one should ever have to leave this world alone!

That is what haunts me.

In my mind, I rewrite the ending. The phone rings. I rush to him. I stop it in time. I hold him in my arms and tell him we are going to Florida as soon as possible. That it is not too late. That he is safe now.

Still, for the sake of peace in my own heart, I choose to imagine that if someone had reached out to him besides me, in those final hours, he might have answered. It may have helped; things would have ended differently.

But that call never came.

Kyle's passing was not the result of one moment, one choice, or one event. It was just so layered with grief, trauma, fear, longing, hope. My baby carried it all, far more than he needed or wanted to. He was trying to outrun it, and I was trying to catch him.

I wanted so badly to be enough.

MOTHER'S REFLECTION:
My Ledger

There are truths I will carry quietly, and truths I will speak aloud. This one? I will not bury it. They say denial protects. But it does not protect children. I saw what was happening. I was called crazy for it. But I was right. Now, I will be loud for every parent who was not heard in time.

But when I was not called, I lost the chance to save my son. I will spend the rest of my life making sure his story is told, with truth, with tenderness, and with all the love I will never stop holding.

101

KYLE'S KINDNESS AND STORIES THEY SHARED

I ASKED MANY TIMES ON Facebook, at Kyle's Angelversary, and through various avenues, for friends and family to share a memory of my son for his legacy page or send it directly so I could include it in his story. Out of everyone, including many relatives, only a few of his friends responded. It broke my heart. Kyle would have been so saddened to know that something so simple, yet meaningful, did not matter enough to most… and it was for him and him alone.

One of Kyle's longtime friends reached out to share just how incredible he was. She remembered calling him during her pregnancy, and he panicked, thinking she was in labor. He rushed to get ready like he was about to deliver the baby himself, only to find out she was just calling to chat. She was not even in labor! But even then, his excitement for her was absolutely contagious.

Later, after her son was born, she felt down at times. She told me that Kyle always had the right words, uplifting, encouraging, warm. He helped her and her husband find peace during emotionally difficult moments. He would marvel at her baby's beauty and stare with wonder every time he saw him. She said Kyle had always loved children, even in middle school, before addiction entered the picture.

"He was always amazing," she told me. "The perfect friend."

She believes if would have not been under the influence that day, he would still be here. Kyle had countless friends, he would talk to them for hours and offer guidance. This young woman reassured me that Kyle had faith, and that he spoke to her, her husband, and her mother about God. Her words comforted me: "He believed. He had faith. You will see him again where life is eternal and truly matters. Your son touched so many lives, Deanna, including mine."

Her message reminded me that Kyle's spiritual foundation held strong. All those years of church, devotionals, and scripture, the seeds I planted, had taken root. The addiction did not define him; it was a thief that stole moments, not his soul. Kyle was a beautiful human being, a loving son and friend, and a confirmed believer in Almighty God.

"With the way the world is going," she added, "it won't be long." She shared how deeply her family loved him, how Kyle loved her children, and affirmed something I had always recognized: I raised one of the sweetest souls and I did it all on my own. I taught him values that stayed with him, tucked into the quiet spaces of his heart. I am so proud of my boy.

She also told me about the last time she saw Kyle. He was glowing. He had just helped a deaf man whose car had broken down. Kyle could not communicate with him enough to help fix the car issue, so he stopped and prayed to God for the family. Minutes later, someone pulled up who could help. Kyle told the story with such joy; it was one of those moments when his faith shone.

Only God and I truly knew the depth of Kyle's faith, something he could not share with his dad who openly did not believe. Substance use did not define Kyle's character. None of our addictions or mistakes ever do. What matters is the love we hold, the service we give, and the faith inside us.

One of the most heartfelt conversations I had was with a young woman who wanted to help me retrieve a sentimental item: a jewelry box I had special made for Kyle's twenty-first birthday. It had been stolen, along with other treasured belongings, by those who claimed to love him. Theft, lies, manipulation, neglect... none of that defines love.

The box was engraved with "Happy 21st Birthday Kyle. I love you." It was tradition for me to give Kyle special gifts, for his birthdays, Easter, and Christmas. He knew I would always make sure he had those things. Only me.

This same young woman showed immense compassion for my grief. She reminded me that no one has the right to tell another how to mourn. "They didn't lose their son," she said. She and Kyle had shared many conversations about me, about our bond, about how much he loved his mama. She said Kyle regretted not fully appreciating everything I had done for him and admired my strength.

I always had my son's back. She said he conveyed to her that he wished he could give me the world. I knew how much he loved me, just as he knew how deeply I loved him. There was no doubt. Others may have tried to wedge their way in, but our love was irreplaceable.

She shared that she too had faced loss, and she and Kyle spoke about the absence of their dads. They reflected on how important it was to appreciate their moms, even through conflict, because when we (moms) are broken, we still love our babies more than anything else.

I worked hard to shield my pain from Kyle so he would never carry the weight of it. No matter what I was facing, Kyle was my priority. Always. I would never give up on him.

His friend told me that even when Kyle did not outwardly show it, I was his world. He cherished me. He knew his mom would never stop believing in him and I did not. Ever.

MOTHER'S REFLECTION:

Grief Is Not Measured in Timelines or Expectations

I still find myself longing for the rest of Kyle's story, his future chapters, his voice, his victories. But through the memories of those who truly knew him, I am reminded that love leaves an imprint deeper than sorrow. While many stayed silent, the ones who spoke helped resurrect what mattered most: Kyle's soul never stopped shining.

102

A WORLD WITHOUT COLOR

AFTER SO MANY MONTHS of living without my son, this is the best way I can describe my reality, the world is colorless and empty. The emptiness I carry is unbearable, compounded by judgment from people who assume they know me, or worse, those who never even tried. Their unsolicited opinions have never been welcomed, yet they surface, nonetheless. Even Kyle's dad, my own husband for nearly three decades, has met my sorrow with deflection and projection, refusing to acknowledge the pain or his own role in it. But I am not ashamed. I have come to understand that this reaction is textbook behavior from those who refuse to face their own instability.

I am exhausted and drained by the weight of loss, by the cruel reality of suicide, and by the unrelenting anguish of mourning my son in the worst conceivable way. The toll it has taken on me is immeasurable. I never imagined a human being could endure this much pain, emotionally, mentally, and even physically, and survive to tell the story. The waves of disbelief and gut-wrenching distress have weakened to a degree, but never fully.

People tell me to move on. They expect me to deal with his passing in a way that makes them comfortable, but I refuse to conform to their expectations. Ignoring Kyle's passing, pretending it was not the catastrophe that it was, is not healing. It is avoidance. It is callousness. My grief is my own, and I will navigate it the way I need to.

Each day, I remember what life was like with my King Kyle here, and I hold on to those memories as tightly as I can. The world without him is drained of vibrance, stripped of warmth, but in small ways, I see pieces of the color he left behind. These fragments are what keep me grounded. They are just enough to remind me that, though he is gone, his presence was real. His love was real.

Some days, I close my eyes and remember the sound of his laughter, the way his voice filled the room. Other days, I struggle to hold onto the details, afraid that time will steal them away. There is an ache in my chest that never truly fades, a hollow space where his dreams, his presence, his future should still exist. But they do not. That is something no mother should ever have to bear.

But here is the truth that no one wants to acknowledge, kids, teenagers do not turn to substance for no reason. They do not wake up one day and simply decide to throw their futures away. They are pushed. They are suffering. They are longing for relief in a world and people that have failed them.

The same is true of suicide, not every loss is the result of mental illness. Some are pushed over the edge, manipulated, conditioned to believe they would be better off gone. Some are made to feel so small, so worthless, by people that claim their love for them, that they can no longer see a reason to stay and that, more than anything, is what breaks me.

Kyle did not just leave this world. He was driven from it, piece by piece, until there was nothing left to hold onto. The world, the people around him, stole from him long before he left.

One of the greatest losses is knowing how much the world needed someone like Kyle, someone who loved unconditionally, who showed up no matter what, who embraced others without judgment. So many people will never have the privilege of knowing him. They will never experience the comfort of his kindness, the way he made people feel like they belonged. They will not even realize that something is missing from their lives, but I will.

Even now, nearly six years later, I am in disbelief that my heart still beats. The pain is staggering, and I often wonder how any parent survives something like this. Losing my son is the ultimate betrayal of my life. I would rather have suffered any physical torture than be forced to live without my son and endure this pain of his absence.

People say that suicide is a permanent solution to a temporary problem. It robs you of every possibility, every potential joy. Kyle had so much left to do, so many dreams that should have carried him forward. But insurmountable sadness clouded his mind, extinguishing those dreams before he had the chance to chase them.

What I have learned, through immeasurable pain and loss, is that grief is not something I conquer. It is something I carry. It became a part of me, it reshaped who I was, forcing me to navigate a world that is forever missing a piece of my soul.

I do not share that simply to tell my story. I share this because if one person understands, *if one parent reaches for their child and holds them closer after reading this, then Kyle's life, and his loss, has taught something profound.*

The world without Kyle has no color. No parent should have to wake up every day knowing their child is gone, taken in a way that shakes the very foundation of their existence, knowing that the world will never feel whole again. No one should have to wonder what could have been, what dreams were left unfulfilled, what love was lost to the darkness. But this is my reality. This is my truth. And if there is anything to take from it, let it be this: the pain does not fade. The emptiness does not heal. And that is why we, as parents and other loved ones, cannot look away, we cannot ignore it. We cannot afford to let it happen again to another son or daughter.

Even Jesus calmed the storm, but first, He walked into it. *So must we.* Stop being afraid to make waves. Let the truth disturb and convict because saving our children's lives is worth every storm.

MOTHER'S REFLECTION:
The Storm We Must Enter

Grief does not fade. It does not heal like a scraped knee or a broken bone. It becomes part of you, etched into your soul, reshaping every breath.

I live in a world without color. But I speak Kyle's name so others might see the hues he left behind.

Because silence does not save lives. Truth does. If we are to protect our children, we must walk into the storm, just as Jesus did, unafraid to disturb, unafraid to speak, unafraid to love loudly.

103

THE FOREVER PAIN

MY BEAUTIFUL SON PASSED from this life on earth on Friday morning, September 20th of 2019, the most agonizing time of my entire existence. His last sentence spoken to me just a day before passing, the phrase he spoke only to me, "I love ew Mom...I love ew."

He wanted to tell me what we had both said to each other countless times in our lives. Why was it such a somber voice and still a peaceful voice?

In that moment, it felt like more than just my son's voice, I sensed something deeper. Maybe it was God, reaching through the ache to speak a truth I could not yet grasp. My mind was tortured. My heart, shattered beyond recognition. And still, even there, in that darkness, I felt a love pressing in, steady and unshaken; refusing to let me go. I did not understand it then. I sensed there was a love reaching out to me in my deepest pain even then. I only knew that my God, the Holy One, held me when nothing else could.

Even though we were planning our new life far away from where we began, I still felt the last words he said to me were the last words I would ever hear from him. I wish I could describe it better, but it was a physical pain and an agonizing gut feeling that only mama would sense. I do not believe Kyle felt the same as I did, as I knew that his passing was not premeditated by him in any fashion. I fell asleep in tears as I did every night without my son. Like many others, my journey toward healing has never been about returning to "normal." Normal holds no interest for me.

Driven by my son's life and his final words, I have embarked on a quest for truth, a truth I instinctively knew I could not rest without finding. This journey has demanded that I examine every corner of my soul, leaving nothing untouched. It has been an arduous and painful process, made even harder by the silence of those who were closest to him: the family, the police involved, and others. Their silence echoes guilt. I still ask myself, "Is this reality? Surely not. I hope not." Unfortunately, it is to this day. Especially when my family, my in-laws, my ex-husband, and many others have shut down and will not speak to me about what happened. I cannot get answers, nor do I believe that any answers they might give would be authentic or truthful.

They say they are grieving, but it feels more like a self-focused sorrow, centered on their own pain, not on Kyle's. Sometimes, it feels like their anger is aimed at me, as if causing more pain to his mother could somehow ease their own. I cannot help but wonder if guilt and shame are hiding beneath the surface, guilt for not listening, for dismissing the signs, for not taking his pain seriously. I sure hope so. I do not know if they feel any remorse. I hope, at the very least, they reflect on what they missed. What they might and could have done differently.

A person's brokenness can open a door to end their pain that they did not know remained. I was given that choice and did not take it. Even if my grief unlocked the gates of Heaven, I would never have chosen it. Not like this.

But my baby was not in his right mind at the time, not even aware of the substance that was shoved in him. If he was, he surely would not have done what he did, knowing what we both had planned together. He would never have left his mama. I understand this was a split-second impulse decision made in the moment, not a desperate last resort to escape them, the influences, because nothing else had worked.

That is the thing, maybe he felt it was not a choice? It was handed down to him. I do not care what anyone tries to tell me; it may have been inevitable. My son's pain and passing seemed to come out of no-where so quickly, yet so subtle, and then it leveled everything, destroy-ing the solid foundation I tried so carefully to manage throughout his life. In one instant he was gone.

There had been no choice on his part, at least he felt as if he had no choice other than to get away from the one that hovered over him, the one that left him and broke his family, and the demon that dwelled inside his grandma's house that he said felt more like a dungeon. The agony and the substance that was pushed on him and hidden from him took over. His judgment was clouded. Even knowing that he could have come to Mama or called me, he could not think past the substance in his body and the pain in his heart.

Kyle has now broken the cycle in the Wiley family.

I want to be crystal clear; I also hold myself accountable for the loss of my son. I have done my best to face this with courage and maturity, to take responsibility where I can and while I am not in the same class as others, I have also seen them retreat into silence, into blame, into fear. And while I cannot speak for their hearts, I know I have chosen a different path.

Reflecting, there were many moments, especially involving some-one close to him, that shook me to my core and were huge warning signs of what was to come. Those moments were a clear indicator that my son's future was tragically limited. I feel that my son did not have much of a chance to live a normal, long life after that. I will carry the exhausting weight of blame every single day for the rest of my life.

Although I still carry love for the man I once married, I now see how deeply I misunderstood who he truly was. Over time, I was drawn into a version of life he painted for us, one I believed in with all my whole heart. I placed my trust in him completely, believing he would protect us, provide for us, and love us unconditionally. For a while, we held together, even through the unraveling. But I could not see the storm that was coming, the unraveling that would eventually touch every part of our family, including our beautiful little miracle. Kyle trusted him too, for as long as he could. Looking back, part of me wishes I had seen it all more clearly. But if I had, maybe I would not have had Kyle and that is something I will never, ever regret.

At one point, my husband told me we were brought together for one reason only, to have Kyle. It was through my mother-in-law's or another family members' warped thinking that she said this, and he believed it. But I cannot accept that. I do not believe God orchestrates relationships just to deliver a child into the world and then abandon the rest. That kind of thinking feels hollow, even callous.

Kyle was not the product of a broken union; my son was the miracle that rose from it. A light amid turbulence. A gift I would never trade, no matter what pain followed. His life had purpose far beyond the circumstances of his birth and I believe, with everything in me, that God's hand was on him from the very beginning.

I make sure every morning before my feet hit the floor that I pray to God, and I ask for forgiveness from Him for my blindness and for my anger toward others and their part in my son's passing. Whether they choose to acknowledge it or not is irrelevant. Also forgiving those that hurt my beautiful boy repeatedly is what I need and want to do to be able to carry on for Kyle and finish what I started.

I know I do not take care of myself as well as I used to. People around me have noticed and been outspoken about it. That is quite all right. I lost my baby boy. Sometimes I am not sure how to take care of myself anymore. If I could not save my son, how could I possibly save myself? All I can do is attempt one day to do for myself again what I would and once did for my child. I will try one day to take better care of myself as much as possible, knowing that my son's love for me and the love I will always have for him will ascend through this infinite journey. Realizing I do have a choice.

I can stay stuck in the pain as a victim, or I can choose to live in the truth of today. I have chosen to live, allowing the world to become an open vault of possibilities, despite the deep sadness I feel along the way. I realize that I would not decide to explore these paths had I not been in such profound pain, especially with the thoughts of my son guiding me every step of this horrific journey.

I have discovered that this world, and certain people who I once considered dependable, have proven themselves deceptive, making promise after promise that they have refused to keep. I have not yet found that there is a life out there after Kyle, that I never dreamed of possible, perhaps because I have been trapped in a nightmare. The worst possible nightmare of my life. One nightmare and reality that I do not ever wish on anyone.

I have been told throughout my life as a Christian that heaven was always "within" me, and not just some distant dream, I have always believed this since my grandma shared it with me when I was a little girl. There are also many people that do not believe it. I also conveyed to my son on a regular basis that God was within him, but he seemed to have a tough time believing it in his later years when people around him were trying to alter his decisions and pull him away from God and mom. I know in my future is Heaven, where I will be reunited with my son and find release from such pain. I will wait upon God, and I do know regardless, that eternity lasts forever. I also know my son will be there waiting for me with arms wide open when it is my time.

I have feverishly tried many times to rewrite the last chapter of my son's life without my emotion, my pain and anger because this book is not about me. I want it to be about my beloved son and his life and memory. It is so excruciatingly difficult. I have done my best. I do not want the ones that are truly responsible for his pain and passing to think for a second that I am not hurting or angry that they have gotten away with such callous devastating acts toward my son. Believe me when I tell you Almighty God's words stand true to this day. We all reap good and bad. Even though I forgive the ones that hurt him every day, I need to express what losing my boy has done. Please forgive me for being quite forward in a few instances.

I am broken beyond understanding, and within this brokenness, the cracks only deepen. Yet, if I allow this brokenness to guide me and step into the great unknown, perhaps I will uncover what I have always been searching for, even before Kyle transitioned into the spirit world. I feel a profound love between us, a love that transcends words and was reflected in his final words to me: "I love ew, Mom." Through my brokenness, I find myself led to the greatest love imaginable.

May God's abundant blessings and peace be with all who are reading my son's story. May you discover moments of silence, a bit of self-reflection, and maybe even redemption through the life of my son Kyle as he journeyed to his eternal Heavenly home.

THE RECKONING:

A MESSAGE FOR EVERY ENABLER

THIS MESSAGE IS NOT just about Kyle; it is about every child who has been handed pain disguised as a *"good time."* To those who hand out substances like they are harmless. To those who whisper, *"It's just for fun,"* knowing full well the pain it masks. To those who watch a child spiral and say, *"It's not my place."* To those who turn away, stay quiet, or call it freedom instead of destruction, this is for you.

You saw them chasing something, acceptance, relief, or escape. You saw it and fed it. You told yourselves *"They will be fine, they grow out of it, or it wasn't your fault."* But every high you offered came at a cost you did not have to pay. They did.

Kyle paid.

You enabled them when they needed guidance. You smiled at them when they needed boundaries. You handed them a mask when what they really needed was safety. Maybe you were hurting, too. Maybe no one taught you better. But now you know and now, silence becomes complicity.

The damage you helped cause does not end with them. It ripples through grieving families, through the friends who watched and did not speak up, through systems too slow to intervene.

This is your reckoning, not one of vengeance, but of truth.

If you want redemption, start with honesty. If you want healing, begin with responsibility. If you claim to care, then care enough to confront the legacy you have left behind.

Kyle's story is not just his. It belongs to every person who stood at a crossroads and made the wrong turn. It belongs to every enabler who still has a chance to turn around. But will you?

WAKE-UP CALL TO ALL PARENTS

I WANTED TO WRITE ABOUT my beautiful boy but also wanted something that does not just speak to parents. I want this story to shake them. I want these words to pierce through the distractions, the indifference, and force them to stop and see the consequences of their choices.

I want words that make it impossible to dismiss the reality their children live in, the pain they may cause without realizing, and the futures they shape without thought or care. I want this message to carry the direct weight of truth that all parents need to face without excuses.

Your child is watching. Always watching. Every late night, every missed hug, every broken promise...they do not forget. The lessons you do not teach, the love you do not give, the pain you choose to ignore, it stays with them. It becomes the voice in their head, the weight in their chest, the decisions they make when you are no longer there to guide them.

Neglect does not have to be loud. It does not have to look like bruises or screams. Sometimes, it is silence. Sometimes, it is absence. Sometimes, it is being so consumed by your own self-centered wants that you fail to see your child slipping until it is too late.

You cannot rewind time. You cannot take back the nights they cried alone and needed you. You cannot erase the moment they realized you would not come to help them.

Every choice you make builds the person they become. If you refuse to acknowledge them, they will spend a lifetime searching for someone who will and may fall into bad company along the way. If you betray their trust, they will never believe in love the same way again. If you abandon them, physically, emotionally, spiritually, financially, they will carry that wound in ways you cannot imagine.

You do not get to be careless with the life you brought into this world. You have no right to do that! Parenting is not a convenience. It is a responsibility and a privilege that demands presence, it demands sacrifice, and it demands unwavering protection.

Show up. Be vigilant. Stop waiting for "later," because later is too late.

Kyle was not a cautionary tale, he was a boy with a heartbeat, laughter, purpose. *What will it take for us, as parents, as people, to stop looking away?*

Your child is watching. What will they remember?
Everything!

A LETTER FROM KYLE
(AND HIS MOM, TOO)

To EVERY KID, TEENAGER, young adult who feels invisible, overwhelmed, or alone.

Hey you,

I don't know what you've been through. I don't know how deep it hurts. But if you're reading this, it means you're still here, and that matters more than you realize.

There were days I smiled when I didn't want to. Nights I stayed up replaying things I wish I could undo. I know how it feels to be surrounded by people and still feel like nobody sees you. That emptiness? That ache? You're not the only one who feels it.

I tried hard to be strong, for my friends, for my family, for myself. But sometimes even strength feels like a mask, doesn't it? Sometimes you just want someone to look at you and say, "You don't have to pretend."

So let me be that person.

You are not broken. You are not weak. You are not too much or not enough.

You are needed.

You are wanted.

You are loved.

If you're fighting through something dark, reach out. If you're tired of carrying the weight, share it. You don't have to do this alone.

I wish I could sit beside you right now and say it all in person. But maybe this letter is close enough.

I let pain pile up. I let people tell me who I was. I went quiet because I thought maybe my voice didn't matter. But it did and yours does, too.

You're not weak for feeling broken. You're not wrong for being overwhelmed. You're not lost just because you're still figuring it all out.

And if you've ever thought about giving up, I'm here to say: *Please don't.* Your life isn't over, it's still unfolding. There are people out there waiting to love you the way you deserve. Safe people. Real people who care. Not the fake ones. Sometimes, they show up in the most unexpected ways.

I wish I could've seen that earlier. I wish I could've held on a little longer. But maybe my story will help you hold on now.

And for my mom... she still talks to me every morning and every night and in between. She still sits with me every day.

My mom is still fighting for me, every single day. She still believes in me, even now. She believes in you, too.

She's speaking out so that people like you won't be forgotten. So that you know, somebody cares. Somebody believes in you. Even if it's just one voice.

So, hear both of us when we say this. You are seriously **worth loving.** You are **stronger than your worst moment**. You are **not alone**, even when it feels that way. You are **needed**, right here, right now.

All of you have a unique purpose; that is why God sent you here. *So, stay and find that purpose and fulfill that purpose, okay?* Don't be afraid to share your emotions with someone, anyone.

So go ahead and keep trying. Keep breathing. Keep reaching for the light.

Stay. Please stay.

You're still here. That means something.

Your story isn't over. Your healing can begin. Your light, even dimmed, still shines.

With love that never fades,
Kyle (and his mom, who loves you like she loved me)

EPILOGUE

As YOU TURN THE final pages of this journey, take a moment to reflect on the beautiful spirit that was, and still is, my son. Though his time with us was tragically cut short, his legacy lives on in the hearts of all who knew him, and in the lessons he imparted through his life.

Kyle was a beacon of love and empathy in a world that can often feel cold and unforgiving. Despite the turmoil he endured, from partnerships that exploited his generosity to a childhood shaped by manipulations from weak men who should have been positive role models, Kyle never lost sight of the goodness in others. Even when hurt, his capacity to care was a testament to his profound ability to love. He taught us that love is not merely an emotion but a choice, one that can be given freely, without expectation.

Kyle longed, as many children do, for a world where parents could set aside their differences and prioritize their children's well-being. He dreamed of two civil-minded and mature parents modeling a loving, God-centered environment. It is a heartbreaking truth that many children, like Kyle, are left to navigate their lives in the shadow of adult conflicts. Parents must remember that their selfish desires should never outweigh the needs of their children. By working together, they can create a future filled with hope, love, and stability.

To fathers everywhere, I know my son would plead with you to embrace the vital role you have been given, to protect, provide, guide, and love your children with integrity. Too many mothers are left raising children alone when there's no good reason for it. Kyle would urge dads to "man up" and realize that being present for your child is the greatest experience life can offer. It is a sacred blessing and responsibility, shaping the next generation and creating lasting memories you will never regret.

Despite the immense turmoil and hardships his dad brought into his life, beneath the weight of grief that could not be lifted, one truth remained unchanged: the love he had for his dad was never lost and will endure for eternity.

In his short life, Kyle showed us the importance of kindness, compassion, and understanding. He believed deeply in the power of community and the necessity of supporting one another, especially in times of struggle. Kyle would want us all to remember that even the smallest acts of kindness create ripples that inspire others. He would urge us to be kinder, to reach out to those in need, and to never give up on loved ones, even when they falter.

As a God-loving believer, Kyle had faith in a brighter tomorrow, a tomorrow he now embraces in the eternal peace of Heaven. He faced what lay ahead without fear, finding solace in God's love and the promise of our reunion. To honor his memory, let us strive to live by the values he cherished: serving without seeking reward, loving without condition, and supporting one another in life's journey.

Though Kyle is no longer with us in body, his loving spirit endures. He showed us that every life is precious, and every life can make a difference. Let us carry his message forward by sharing the same kindness he gave so freely. Together, we can create a world that reflects the beauty of Kyle's heart, a world where love triumphs over adversity and every person is valued.

In loving memory of my son, Kyle Alan Wiley, may we always uphold the love and empathy he lived by. Kyle, you are my brightest shining star in the heavens. Until we are together again, I will miss you profoundly and never allow your memory to fade.

I love you, Poo Doo.

Dear Almighty God,

God of light and mercy, I lift every soul reading these pages, especially the weary, the grieving, the afraid. Hold the hearts of parents who ache to understand. Who battle confusion, denial, and the weight of questions they do not know how to ask. Give them courage to see, strength to stay, and tenderness to speak truth even when it hurts.

For every child who feels unseen: Let them feel Your presence in their quiet moments, Your love in the spaces where others have failed to show up. Wrap Your arms around those spiraling in silence, and whisper to them that they matter, that they are not alone.

For Kyle...May his spirit rest in peace and power. May his love ripple through generations, and may his story awaken a compassion fierce enough to heal. Let his light guide us toward honesty, toward healing, toward choosing love when the world offers less.

In Your Son Jesus's Name,

Amen.

THE DISTINCTION
THAT NEEDS
TO BE MADE

SINCE MY SONS PASSING, I have encountered many assumptions, some spoken gently, others not. One of the most persistent was the claim that my son suffered from depression. It is a term used easily, and often without full understanding. But depression, as defined clinically, is a diagnosable mental health condition, a persistent internal state of hopelessness, deep sadness, and emotional detachment.

What I lived through was not that. What my son endured was not that.

Tell me, what does a mother feel after such a loss? Depression, just a label without context? Oppression, the crushing weight of everything that led him there? Or something heavier than both, forged from love, betrayal, and a fight no one else saw?

What we faced was oppression, a prolonged experience of hardship caused by several external factors, especially abandonment, deceit, emotional isolation, and physical abuse. These were not isolated incidents. They came from those whose actions eroded trust and demanded submission yet violated both; leaving us emotionally betrayed.

Legally and linguistically, oppression refers to unjust treatment, the denial of access to resources, or the infliction of psychological distress through manipulation or control. It is not a diagnosis. It is a condition imposed from the outside. The PTSD he suffered resulted from the prolonged, systematic, and physically traumatic oppression.

There came a time when support vanished completely; shelter, stability, and financial means all disappeared. What remained was a condition often described as constructive abandonment: the withdrawal of care and responsibility that leaves the harmed party emotionally and materially devastated. That is what we both lived through, regardless of what others choose to believe.

I persevered. Somehow. Step by step. I lived under enormous pressure, but I did not completely collapse. I knew I needed to be as strong as possible for Kyle alone. My son, however, was younger, less shielded from the psychological fallout of such betrayal. He was drawn into despair, into substance use, *not* because he was mentally ill, but because the environment around him became untenable. This was not clinical depression in a vacuum. It was the result of emotional duress, coercive conditions, and isolation, terms acknowledged in both psychological and legal frameworks.

To reduce what happened to him to mere illness would strip away the context, and context is everything. His pain was not born of disorder nor mine; it was born of abandonment, betrayal, and isolation. Even in his darkest moments, he showed courage, love, and resilience because that is who my son really was. Kyle embodied authentic, unconditional love because love with condition is not defined love at all.

"If you love until it hurts, there can be no more hurt, only more love."

Mother Teresa

This letter is my act of restoration, of redefining the narrative and diminishing the false narratives of other's perceptions. *Not* to assign blame. *Not* because I believe those who caused harm acted with dignity or accountability. *Not* because I care to protect their identity. But because I am choosing to speak truth legally, knowing full well that those responsible recognize themselves without being named. Their actions speak for themselves.

I will also say this with every ounce of conviction: the stigma must end! The assumption that every person who passes over by suicide is mentally ill can be misleading and harmful. There are individuals, like my son, whose lives are lost not to internal disease, but to external devastation. Until someone has taken the time to truly understand this distinction, until they have educated themselves beyond oversimplified labels, they should not speak with authority on anyone else's pain.

In my experience, judgment without compassion does not serve justice, it deepens cruelty. Pride may blind us to others' pain, and ridicule has no place in the presence of grief.

My son was not just broken. He was burdened even though we carried that weight together, the best we could with as much love as we could.

This memoir reflects the author's personal experiences and interpretations. It is not intended to diagnose, accuse, or defame any individual or entity. but to advocate for deeper understanding and compassion in the face of grief.

ABOUT THE AUTHOR

Deanna Wiley is a devoted mother, memoirist, and advocate whose work centers on love, loss, and truth. Her son's life is the soul of this biography, a deeply personal tribute shaped by memory, reflection, and the enduring bond between them.

With emotional clarity and unwavering honesty, Deanna brings a reflective voice to themes of growth, vulnerability, and transformation. This work preserves Kyle's legacy, illuminating not only who he was but the impact he continues to have.

Deanna's life has always revolved around her son and always will. His presence guides her writing, fuels her advocacy, and lives on through every page she pens.

She is currently developing a memoir about surviving emotional and psychological abuse, along with a poetry collection and a series of children's books dedicated to Kyle's memory. Her hope is that these works offer connection, healing, and advocacy through a grieving mother's compassionate lens.

Her writing is not about being a professional. It is about being a mother who refuses to let her son's story be forgotten. Her voice is raw, real, and necessary.

She continues to explore ways to share her work with communities seeking strength, healing, and understanding and plans to donate book proceeds to suicide awareness and prevention.

Author's Cover Reflection

This sculpture on the cover, it is not just art. It is a moment between me and my son, Kyle, preserved in stone. Cast on Valentine's Day, 2000, it features his young three-year young hand tucked inside mine. My hand does not simply hold his; it shelters it. Protects it. And even now, it cradles his memory with the same fierce tenderness.

When I look at it, I see love that never needed words yet speaks a thousand. It tells an eternal truth; of unwavering presence, sacred connection, and the kind of bond that transcends time. The rough stone base grounds it in reality, while the smooth texture of our cast hands, binds us beyond time.

The brass plaque reads "Kyle & Mommy Valentine's 2000", a timestamp of our affection. This image is more than a keepsake. It is a tactile echo of who we were together, a promise I still carry. I will never let go, even when life tries to separate flesh and spirit.

For me, as his mother and the author of this memoir, this sculpture represents everything you have read. The fierce protectiveness. The quiet grief. The love that still lives. The story within these pages is not just about loss, it is about legacy. Kyle's and mine.

If I am quiet, still listen. If I am gone, still speak.